PRAISE FOR

The AIRMEN and the HEADHUNTERS

"Sixty years later, World War II is still giving up its secrets. *The Airmen and the Headhunters* recovers a forgotten tale from the far Pacific that should interest anyone who cares about the gallantry of our aviators who flew into harm's way."
—James D. Hornfischer, author of *Ship of Ghosts: The Story of the USS* Houston, *FDR's Legendary Lost Cruiser, and the Epic Saga of Her Survivors*

"Few writers could have tracked down this captivating story. [Heimann] paints a vivid picture of the indigenous people who comfortably inhabited the dense jungle and carried on a flourishing trade with the coast . . . A fascinating anthropology lesson, delivered with the bonus of a dramatic adventure and a happy ending."
—*Kirkus Reviews*

The AIRMEN and the HEADHUNTERS

Also by JUDITH M. HEIMANN

The Most Offending Soul Alive:
Tom Harrisson and His Remarkable Life

JUDITH M. HEIMANN

The AIRMEN and the HEADHUNTERS

A True Story of Lost Soldiers,
Heroic Tribesmen
and the Unlikeliest Rescue
of World War II

A HARVEST BOOK
HARCOURT, INC.
Orlando   Austin   New York   San Diego   London

Requests for permission to make copies of any part of the work should be
submitted online at www.harcourt.com/contact or mailed to the following address:
Permissions Department, Houghton Mifflin Harcourt Publishing Company,
6277 Sea Harbor Drive, Orlando, Florida 32887-6777.

www.HarcourtBooks.com

Maps by Helen Phillips

The Library of Congress has cataloged the hardcover edition as follows:
Heimann, Judith M.
The airmen and the headhunters: a true story of lost soldiers,
heroic tribesmen and the unlikeliest rescue of World War II/
Judith M. Heimann.—1st ed.
p.   cm.
Includes index.
1. World War, 1939–1945—Search and rescue operations—Borneo.
2. World War, 1939–1945—Aerial operations, American.   3. United States.
Army Air Forces. Bomb Group, 5th Squadron, 23rd—History.
4. Airmen—United States—Biography.   5. Dayak (Indonesian people)
I. Title.
D810.S45B65   2007
940.54'25983—dc22   2007009587
ISBN 978-0-15-101434-7
ISBN 978-0-15-603325-1 (pbk.)

Text set in Bodoni MT
Designed by Linda Lockowitz

Printed in the United States of America

First Harvest edition 2008
A C E G I K J H F D B

To my son Paul, a pilot

CONTENTS

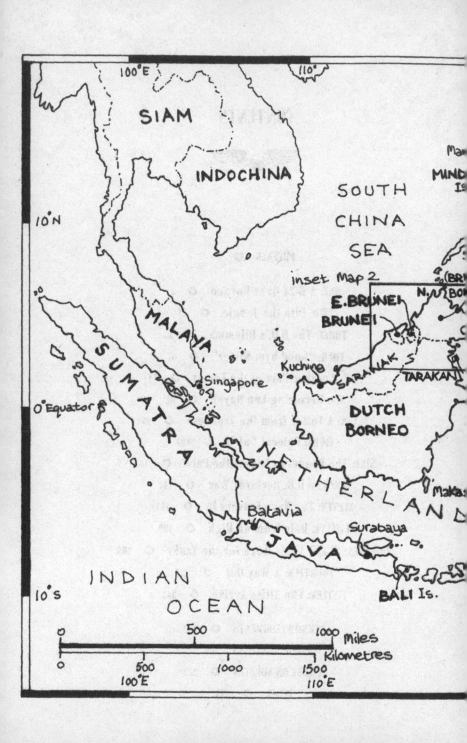

Insular Southeast Asia and Surroundings
1944 - 1945

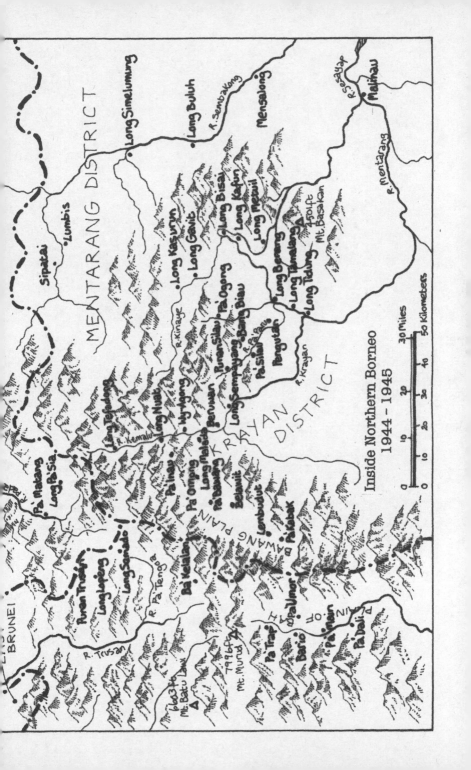

Inside Northern Borneo
1944 – 1945

PREFACE

We like to think of war stories from the twentieth century and earlier as straightforward accounts of derring-do, with a familiar cast of heroes and villains. There is even a subcategory of stories about how our brave soldiers managed—or died trying—to make their way home from behind enemy lines. But the circumstances of war can be more complicated. This story happened during World War II—which was truly a *world* war, drawing into its orbit even such normally isolated people as the headhunting Dayaks (as the tribespeople of Borneo's interior were then called), people whose mountainous tropical jungles had yet to be mapped.

I first traveled to Borneo more than twenty years after the events described here and spent two years there as the wife of an American diplomat. Already speaking Indonesian/Malay, and with privileged access through my husband's work, I was able to visit much of northern Borneo and make a number of local friends—Dayak, Chinese and Malay. I have kept some of those friendships ever since and have also drawn upon scholarly friends and publications to feed my enduring interest in all things Bornean.

This morsel of Borneo's World War II history has never before been told in its entirety. No single person knew more than a fragment or two of it. I came across snatches of the story of American airmen stranded in headhunter country in the last year of the war while I was researching another book about an Englishman, Tom Harrisson, who also figures in this book. But it was only when I sat in the Australia War Memorial Library in Canberra in 1992 and held in my hand a letter to Major Harrisson written in rounded Palmer Method cursive by a certain Philip Corrin, 2nd Lt., U.S. Army Air Forces (USAAF), that I knew there was a story there that *had* to be searched out and told.

I tried to fit it into my book about Harrisson, but it kept growing bigger as I learned more. I eventually decided to give it a book of its own. It took me ten years and three continents to collect the facts presented here and fit them together.

My narrative draws on what various direct participants said or wrote in 1944–1945 and later. I interviewed the airmen and/or their families repeatedly and collected documents and pictures from them. An Indonesian woman who was connected to the events by childhood memories and family ties and I separately interviewed more than a dozen Dayaks who had either taken part in these events or were the spouses or children of those who had. My account necessarily has gaps. Some informants were more forthcoming than others, and some people I would have wanted to interview were already dead. So I made some educated guesses about what people at the time may have thought and the gestures they may have made, but when the narrative quotes someone, there is solid evidence that the person said or wrote it.

Probably the most crucial written account used in this book is an unpublished manuscript dictated in 1981 by a man who was neither an American airman nor a Dayak headhunter, a man with a difficult name—Makahanap—and a complicated character. But that is getting ahead of the story. . . .

CHAPTER ONE

A B-24 Over Borneo

About twelve thirty midday on November 16, 1944, District Officer William Makahanap looked up from his draft report on the expected rice production in his East Borneo district of Mentarang and realized that for the past few minutes he had been hearing a whining noise. The overhead fan in his old office back in the Celebes used to sound like that, but here in the little settlement of Long Berang there was no electricity to run a fan. The whine could have been from mosquitoes, but it was the wrong time of day for their assault. Such a loud noise was unusual in the quiet midday period, when able-bodied Dayaks (the general term for the various tribes of inland Borneo) were away in the rice fields or the jungle, and nearly everybody else was dozing. Even the schoolchildren, curled up on mats in the schoolroom down the road, would be taking a nap while the day was hottest.

The whine grew louder and Makahanap finally recognized what it was: the engines of a big airplane. Then, above the engine noise, he heard people yelling out in the fields. What could be disturbing the Dayaks? He stepped outside and heard them shouting that "the big thing in the sky" was "breaking apart" and "going to fall to the ground."

Standing on his office steps, he squinted up into the shimmering sky above the jungle at the edge of the little settlement.

He could see that the plane, flashing in and out of the cloud cover, had four engines and big wings, but he did not know enough about aircraft to recognize a B-24. Nor could he tell whose plane it was, Allied or Japanese. What he did realize was that the Dayaks were right. It was about to break apart and fall out of the sky.

Standing there on his front step, blinking at the bright sky, Makahanap's first reaction was probably annoyance at being interrupted. But his next would have been anxiety. In his experience of the past three years, the arrival of something new was rarely a blessing for himself, his family or his district.

He could see, though, that the Dayaks were filled with wonder. None of them had ever seen anything like this thing in the sky. He could no longer see or hear it. Had it gone down somewhere behind the mountains to the northeast? What had happened to it? Where was it now? Above all, was it Japanese or Allied?

November 16, 1944, had begun as a routine Thursday for pilot 2nd Lt. Tom Coberly, USAAF, and the ten men of the crew of his B-24 (a four-engine bomber also known as a "Liberator"). They had been awakened shortly after two in the morning and given breakfast: a choice of hot or cold cereal, along with powdered eggs scrambled and Spam fried and liberally doused with tomato ketchup. They washed it down with tall glasses of milk and orange juice and enough coffee to wake them up.

It was the coolest, best time of day at their air base on Morotai, a small island of the Moluccas in the Netherlands East Indies. Just south of the Philippines and hundreds of miles due east of Borneo, Morotai was built on a foundation of coral and was relatively bare. Much of its scrub plant life had been cleared away to make the coconut plantation that was now an airfield. There was nothing to do there but wait to fly out.

Lieutenant Coberly's crew, simply called Coberly's, had been on Morotai less than a month. Their Twenty-third Squadron belonged to the Bomber Barons, the Fifth Bomb Group that was an arm of the tiny Thirteenth Air Force (sometimes called the Jungle Air Force) of the USAAF whose missions were to retake the Japanese-occupied Philippine Islands and cut off Japan's Pacific oil supplies.

In response to the prewar U.S.-led oil embargo against Japan after the latter took Indochina, the Japanese military had launched a brilliant offensive in 1941–1942, starting with the December raid on Pearl Harbor that had destroyed an unprepared American sea-and-air armada. Next, Japan's troops had taken over the American and European holdings in the Pacific, virtually without a struggle, while America devoted most of its energies to beating back Hitler's armies in Europe and North Africa. Japan hoped its new empire—which it called the Greater East Asia Co-Prosperity Sphere—would make it self-sufficient in the oil, tin and rubber needed for its growing industrial economy. But the effort to secure and run such a far-flung empire was making Japan the victim of its own success.

Its forces were spread so thinly across an area that ran from China to the South Seas that it risked losing all or part of its new colonies if the natives rebelled or the Allies invaded. Lacking the manpower to match its territorial ambitions, Japan relied in part on the fear inspired by the harshness of its occupation to keep the subject peoples in line.

Japan really needed Borneo's oil: In 1943 and 1944, it counted on Borneo for 40 percent of its fuel oil and 25 to 30 percent of its crude and heavy oils. By 1944, cutting off these

Japanese oil supplies had become a major goal of the Thirteenth Air Force's bomber arm.

Liberator squadrons of the Bomber Barons had had increasing success bombing Japanese shipping, including the ships bringing oil home from Borneo. The Bomber Barons were not just attacking transport vessels; in October 1944, some squadrons had taken part in the massive naval battle of Leyte Gulf, in which the Japanese navy had lost close to a hundred ships, including three battleships, four carriers, six heavy and four light cruisers and eleven destroyers.

With this naval victory, the Allies began to feel that a corner had been turned. From now on, the Allies reasoned, not only would the Japanese have more trouble protecting their shipping, but they would be unable to prevent the tropical islands from being liberated by the Allies and serving as stepping stones for the planned invasion of Japan itself. Moreover, the Imperial Navy now lacked enough carrier platforms for the fighter planes needed to protect the Japanese homeland from air attack.

Today, Coberly's squadron had been scheduled to attack a Japanese-held airfield in the central Philippines. But the previous night, after supper and a briefing on the morning's raid, the men were watching an outdoor movie when they were summoned back to the briefing tent. Their mission had changed.

They were now told to prepare for an attack against a Japanese heavy cruiser. There might also be an aircraft carrier, which had been seen "lazing along like a fat duck in Brunei Bay." Their orders were to hit the largest ship. Coberly's plane was quickly reloaded with weapons appropriate to its new mission: five one-thousand-pound, armor-piercing bombs.

Before the predawn breakfast that Thursday, flight engineer/gunner Cpl. Jim Knoch and armor gunner Cpl. John Nelson decided to launder their khaki uniforms using a new technique. They tied their dirty clothes to a long rope and threw them into the dark surf at the edge of the airfield, so that the ebb and flow of the waves would scrub them clean by the time they returned from their mission. Like all such busy work before a combat flight, this helped the men avoid thinking about what was to come. Some men would play a little mind game, telling themselves, "Don't worry, you're dead already; you died last week," to steel themselves for what might happen this time.

The original crew of Coberly's had been together since June 1944, when these airmen were assigned to phase training at March Field, near Riverside, California, not far from Los Angeles. Perhaps the most striking thing about Coberly's was their youth. Tom Coberly himself, at twenty-two, was the eldest on board.

Nineteen-year-old Cpl. Jim Knoch was the leader of the plane's seven enlisted men, because of his position as flight engineer. Jim was tall, slim but powerfully built, with dark eyes, a permanent tan and dark blond curly hair. Though he liked to laugh and could play the clown, he had an imposing presence. He had been raised in Sacramento, the son of a mechanic with the Otis Elevator Company. His father hated bureaucracy and did not like being told what to do or how to do it. An only child, Jim had inherited his father's skills and prejudices. At eighteen, he had become a crew chief, directing the grown men at McClellan Air Force Base outside Sacramento who were building the B-24, and he knew the plane intimately. Though he was one of only two in the crew from a blue-collar family, he had the respect of everyone in Coberly's for his skill as an engineer and for his spunk.

Jim led Coberly's into practical jokes and minor acts of rebellion against authority. He had a mischievous sense of humor and did not mind flouting the rules. He had a natural gift for making things work and liked not only to repair but to prevent mechanical problems. Crewmates remembered one terrifying occasion when they had been on a training flight in a B-24 about twelve thousand feet above downtown Los Angeles. Jim was practicing pumping fuel from the bomb-bay tanks to the main-wing tanks when, without warning, all four engines quit. The plane sank like a stone to about three thousand feet before the pilot managed to get the engines restarted. The others would never forget how Jim had calmly continued the refueling until it was done.

John Nelson, with whom Jim Knoch threw his dirty uniform into the surf at the end of a rope, was at age eighteen the youngest man in the crew, but no less experienced than most of the others. Bright enough to finish high school at age seventeen, John had immediately left his small town in Idaho to join the Army Air Forces' cadet program.

Most of Coberly's enlisted men had the IQ and other qualifications to have become officers had they not been forced to enlist or be drafted after March 1943, when the various armed services, urgently needing replacement enlisted men, had closed down all the college-based officer-candidate programs. But they still wanted to fly. John, a woodsman who knew about guns, was invited to stay back to teach at gunnery school but he "decided that was not for me and went on my way to combat" as an aerial gunner. "Wide-eyed wonders," their seasoned, skeptical and somewhat envious sergeants at basic training camp called such enlisted men.

Air crews, like other combat units, typically forged strong ties of comradeship, and this was particularly true for Coberly's. All four officers—Tom Coberly, Jerry Rosenthal, Fred Brennan and Phil Corrin—came from California. So did two of the enlisted men, Jim Knoch and his boon companion, the laconic but highly competent radio operator Dan Illerich.

These West Coasters set the social style for the rest—clean-cut, quiet spoken and modest. The only way most of the crew learned that pilot Tom Coberly's father owned the biggest Ford dealership in Los Angeles was when he told them that was why he had the gas coupons that allowed him to drive his car into town when he and the crew had passes to leave the base. Copilot Jerry Rosenthal did not boast of the movie stars who figured among his Hollywood lawyer father's clients. You would not have guessed that bombardier Phil Corrin was the son of the vice president for advertising of Los Angeles's big department-store chain Bullock's. Navigator Fred Brennan's father was a movie screenwriter with a big current hit, *A Guy Named Joe,* but the crew only learned that after months together when someone asked him what his father did for a living.

Basically, they were all just kids. Their voices had changed, but most of them did not need to shave more than once a week. Only one of the original eleven was married, ring gunner/assistant radio operator Technical Sgt. Clarence T. Capin (known as Tom). Capin was a six-foot-five-inch redhead, a serious-minded, ambitious young man, the only child of a poor family in Fort Wayne, Indiana. He had met his wife, Betty, when she had been a student at a college where Capin was leading an aviation ROTC group marching around the campus. He spotted the attractive coed and led his column of men right into her path, forcing her off the pavement. They married shortly before he went abroad and, at his request, she moved in with his parents, so that he could visualize where she was and what she was doing while he was far away. Of the rest of the original crew, only Jim Knoch had a regular girlfriend.

The sudden, seemingly unprovoked attack on Pearl Harbor had instilled in these young men not only a patriotic desire to defend their country but an intense, visceral hatred of the Japanese. Radio operator Dan Illerich, who had Japanese American high school classmates and happy memories of buying strawberries from the Japanese farmers of the San Joaquin Valley, made a clear distinction between the Japanese he knew and the horrifying enemy he remembered from a piece in *Life* magazine on the Rape of Nanking of December 1937, which showed Japanese soldiers using Chinese tied to posts for bayonet practice.

After Coberly's completed stateside training, they were flown in a C-54 transport plane from Hamilton Field via Hawaii and Guadalcanal to Nadzab, New Guinea, where they arrived in early October 1944. They stayed more than a week at Nadzab, the air force replacement center for the South Pacific, and spent three days in the jungle with seasoned Australian troops to learn survival skills. While based at Nadzab, they flew one combat mission, dropping bombs on the runways of a Japanese-held airstrip at Wewak, New Guinea.

Their next move was to Neumfoor, a small island off New Guinea, where they joined the Twenty-third Squadron of the Bomber Barons on October 13. The men of the Bomber Barons, like army airmen elsewhere, loved the B-24. A Liberator, though it waddled on the ground, was a wonderfully adaptable flying machine for its time. It had been deployed in more operational theaters and for a considerably longer period than any other World War II bomber. The B-24 had been modified often to correct flaws and enhance its versatility; the Twenty-third Squadron had the J version. It could carry a bomb load of eighty-eight hundred pounds, but it was also effective as a spy plane or as a transport for paratroopers and their supplies. Its maximum speed was roughly three hundred miles per hour, with a cruising speed of two hundred miles per hour or better. Some models could fly higher than twenty-eight thousand feet.

If stripped of its excess weight, such as armor plate and ball turrets, the Liberator gave the term "long-range bomber" new meaning. With a range of nearly three thousand miles, it was ideal for use in the vast Pacific theater. Its most distinctive features were its beautiful, long, slender wings, with a span of 110 feet and a wing area of more than a thousand square feet.

As newcomers, the crew spent the first few days watching B-24s, loaded to the limit with fuel and bombs, try to get off the runway. They knew that the B-24 was huge in comparison with other planes then flying. It could take the biggest bomb load of any plane, but it was very hard to maneuver on land. It was slow to respond and hard to steer, making takeoff an especially tense moment. A fully loaded B-24 couldn't get into the air without full power or a long runway. John Nelson saw what happened when two of these planes did not make it and grimly concluded that "raw gasoline and sea water are a lethal combination."

Their only accident occurred during the week on Neumfoor. Charlie Burnette, their perennially airsick tail gunner who liked to make things in his free time, had a trench knife slip from the sheet metal he was trying to cut and lodge itself deep in his thigh. S.Sgt. Francis Harrington, a married New Englander in his thirties, was looking for a combat crew to join, and replaced Charlie as tail gunner.

Coberly's flew several missions out of Neumfoor. On one flight, en route to support the Allied invasion of the Philippines, the crew saw the entire U.S. Pacific fleet below them— probably heading toward the Battle of Leyte Gulf. It was a thrilling sight. Here was tangible proof that they were not merely attached to one of a few bomber squadrons out in the middle of the nearly empty Pacific, but were a cog in what was probably by now the single greatest military machine the world had ever seen.

The men got their first real taste of air combat when the squadron was attacked by Japanese fighters. Young John Nelson was handling the tail gun that day and could see his opposite number in the enemy plane firing directly at him in the tail turret. "We were both firing away. I thought I felt his bullets slamming right into my guts. I know he missed me but I don't know how he fared."

But these were still early days for Coberly's. They had only flown seven of the thirty-five combat missions they had to complete to get home. They were fresh, fit, confident and eager to show what they were made of.

After breakfast on November 16, the eleven airmen were handed their flight lunch of cold turkey sandwiches and were driven to the airfield. The plane they were assigned, however, had a problem with one of its turbochargers. Jim Knoch had found that the number-two engine was capable of only 1,800 rpm; they needed 2,400 rpm for takeoff. Mechanics were called but they could not fix the problem. The airmen climbed out, convinced that there would be no combat mission for them that day. After boarding a truck to take them back to their tent, they opened up their flight lunches. The turkey sandwiches no longer seemed like such a treat.

The men felt let down. They were already awake, and would not get their leave in Australia until they had flown one more mission. Copilot 2nd Lt. Jerry Rosenthal was especially disappointed at the cancellation because he hoped that his growing cockpit experience would help him overcome his lack of formal pilot training so that he could captain his own Liberator, after this flight or the next one. Rather than abandon this mission, he and a friend, an operations officer from the Thirty-first, cruised around the airfield in a jeep until they found a B-24 from the friend's squadron that was ready to go but did not have a crew. Then they collected the rest of Coberly's.

Tom Coberly, brought to plane-side, took a quick look and said, "OK, we'll go with this airplane." This B-24, unlike the one they had left for repairs, was hot off an assembly line back in the States and so new that it did not have a name painted on it yet. The crew decided they would call it *Lucky Strike*.

Before boarding, bombardier Phil Corrin, the most junior officer, showed the other crew members his silk map of the island of Borneo, the biggest landmass between Morotai and Brunei Bay. Due south of the Philippines, Borneo was big but evidently not well mapped. Phil's 20-by-36-inch piece of silk showed the equator cutting through the island, but most of Borneo's interior was whited out, indicating that it was unexplored. Before a mission, airmen were usually given escape instructions in case they wound up on the ground. This time, they were told that they could expect a submarine or maybe a seaplane to pick them up near Kudat, on Borneo's northern tip, if they dropped over water or near the coast. There were no escape instructions to follow should they end up inside Borneo. The absence of such guidance did not strike Phil or the others as important; they did not expect to need it.

Soon the B-24 was stocked for its new mission, and the men were at their usual takeoff stations. In the nose were gunner Cpl. Eddy Haviland, a quiet and studious eighteen-year-old Easterner, and twenty-one-year-old bombardier 2nd Lt. Phil Corrin. In the cockpit were pilot 2nd Lt. Tom Coberly and copilot 2nd Lt. Jerry Rosenthal. Standing between them was Cpl. Jim Knoch, the flight engineer. Behind a bulkhead and seated at a table on the left was navigator 2nd Lt. Fred Brennan. At a table to his right was radio operator Cpl. Dan Illerich. Above Dan's head was access to the top turret, where his other job was to fire the turret gun. Behind the flight deck was the bomb bay, with its access to a small upper deck where the flight engineer occasionally had to go to handle fueling or electrical problems. This plane had two .50-caliber ring guns mounted into the floor in the plane's waist in the spot where the usual B-24 would have had a ball turret. Gunners Tom Capin, on the left, and John Nelson, on the right, manned these guns. Aerial photographer Sgt. Elmer Philipps was crouched near the floor hatch that could be opened to use for cameras or for parachute drops. On board just for this flight, Philipps had asked Tom Coberly if he could have one more chance to see the world from the air before returning stateside; he was ready to take over a waist gun if necessary. S.Sgt. Francis "Franny" Harrington was in the tail turret, manning the tail gun.

As they taxied out for takeoff, the crew discovered a new problem. The parachute packs they had brought with them from the Twenty-third Squadron were incompatible with the harnesses for this plane. By the time the crewmen had grabbed chutes with the right kind of fasteners from another grounded plane, theirs was the last Liberator in the Fifth Bomb Group to take off.

The Twenty-third Squadron would be leading the attack, as usual. It was one of four Bomber Baron squadrons of B-24s, with six or seven planes per squadron. Farther back in the formation would be four B-24 squadrons of the 307th Bomb Group, known as the Long Rangers. Being in squadron formation was a scary experience—flying wingtip to wingtip with other planes while going faster than the men had ever experienced on land. But they got a thrill out of being one of fifty-four four-engine Liberators all in the air at once. The Bomber Barons liked to fly as close together as possible. Experience had taught them that not only did staying close increase the impact of their bombs, but it also made it difficult for Japanese fighter planes to get inside the formation. To help them deal with fighter attacks, the formation had some P-38s assigned to provide top cover. Some days the P-38s did not get there or could not keep up with the Liberator's greater range, but today they were where they should be.

Having started late, Tom Coberly needed to put on some speed to reach his usual place as wingman on the right-hand side of the squadron's lead plane, in the first three-plane element. Strikingly handsome, Coberly was admired by his crewmates for his skill as a pilot. He really knew how to fly the Liberator, and his crew felt safe with him at the controls. During training, Coberly had become ill and had been hospitalized for nearly a week. His crew had been offered the choice of dropping back one six-week period in their training to wait for him or getting another pilot from the replacement pool. They all chose to stick with Coberly.

It was a clear day with flawless visibility as *Lucky Strike* sped past the rest of the squadron toward the front. The men on the flight deck could see that they were burning more fuel than usual in order to catch up with the lead plane, but attacking a cruiser or a lone carrier should not require a lot of fuel. But then, as Coberly headed toward his usual place in the formation, he found another B-24 already there and had to quickly maneuver from the right to the left side of the squadron leader without touching the planes just behind him. It would be a bit awkward, at first, going into combat from an unaccustomed place in the squadron, but they were now in formation and heading toward Brunei Bay.

As they began to fly west toward Borneo, Phil Corrin shared the general belief that this mission would be a routine flight. A heavy cruiser or a flattop in Brunei Bay ought to be an easier target than a duck in a rain barrel.

But instead, when they were more than twenty miles from the target area, they could see in the bay three enemy battleships, three heavy cruisers, four light cruisers, five destroyers and more auxiliary ships than they could count. It looked to Phil Corrin in the nose and John Nelson in the waist as if the entire Japanese imperial fleet was down there—and much of it was. What they saw was all that remained of the fleet that had retired discreetly after the October battle of Leyte Gulf to the relative safety of Brunei Bay, where it now floated dead in the water.

Despite the target's being much bigger and more dangerous than expected, all the planes on this combat mission followed the lead plane and continued as if they were still attacking a lone cruiser or carrier. They prepared to go in over Brunei Bay low, at only ten thousand feet, straight and level, taking no evasive action. This was perhaps because of the lack of experience of the Twenty-third Squadron's new commander, Major Saalfield, who had been put in the lead plane when the squadron's previous leader, Major Musgrove, had been grounded. This was only Saalfield's third or fourth combat mission. He may have been too amazed to report what he saw back to base and get instructions on what to do now.

Phil Corrin in the nose turret and Dan Illerich sitting in the flight deck each watched with growing alarm as Major Saalfield led the squadron straight into harm's way. Phil and Dan felt sure Major Musgrove would not have done that. They could not understand why Saalfield was continuing on this low, straight and level course. It made the squadron an easy target for enemy guns. Dan thought that if Musgrove had been in charge, he would probably have called for the navy to come to their aid and divided the squadron to control both sides of Labuan Island, sealing the Japanese fleet inside the bay.

Phil, eyeing the crowded bay and remembering the briefing the night before, must have wondered why Saalfield did not radio back to tell the base he was taking the formation to its number-three target, the oil field at Tarakan Island, just off

Borneo's east coast. (Alternative target two was Labuan Island, which would be too dangerous.)

Antiaircraft shells started bursting near their Liberator when they were still fourteen miles away from the target. Now, as they neared Brunei Bay, the men of Coberly's could hear big Japanese navy guns firing salvos at the squadron. Between the antiaircraft guns on the ships and a few Japanese fighter planes that had flown close in toward the squadron at the same time, flak started coming at the squadron in a pattern so thick, it looked as if the crew could walk on it.

Adm. Matome Ugaki, who had just been relieved of command of a disbanded battleship division, was traveling as a passenger on the Leyte-damaged, homeward-bound battleship *Yamato*. Still slightly hungover from the previous evening's farewell celebrations in his honor, he looked up at about 11 A.M. to see "forty B-24s and fifteen P-38s" coming in to attack the fleet. "Our main batteries gave them ten salvos at more than twenty thousand meters," he observed, while "our damage [was] almost nil."

Within the next three minutes, shells hit Saalfield's lead plane, Coberly's and Lieutenant Norris's plane in the second element of the squadron.

John Nelson saw "one shell burst right over me and knock the waist window loose, which then dropped on my head." Luckily, John had his flak helmet on and was not hurt, but the right waist window jammed down, and he could no longer see anything that was going on with the rest of the formation or with the Japanese fleet below. Tom Capin and Elmer Philipps may have seen the damage done to Major Saalfield's lead plane and Lieutenant Norris's, but they could not see what was going on in their own plane.

What the men in the waist could not see, they could feel and hear. At about 11:30 A.M., when Coberly was still several miles from the bay, their plane gave a sudden sharp lurch and they heard pieces of shrapnel hitting their hull. It sounded like the aircraft was being ripped to shreds.

The men on the flight deck, having just seen Saalfield's plane take a hit and peel off, sat helplessly while the front of their own plane was hit by a big naval shell.

Dan came back down from manning the top turret gun to assess the damage. "Tom's hurt; they got Tom," he called out through the intercom. He could see that the pilot's leg had been shattered; blood was coming out of the wound in ropes. Then he saw that shrapnel from the same shell had hit the back of navigator Fred Brennan's head and blown off his face, killing him instantly. Copilot Jerry Rosenthal had a big wound on the left side of his head. His left ear was gone. Nonetheless, Dan saw that Jerry was managing to exert the strength needed to hold on to the yoke and keep some control over the plane's movements, even though the rudder control had been shot away. Under protective cover from four P-38s, Jerry quickly cut the B-24 out of what remained of the formation and veered east, trying to head back to Morotai.

The same antiaircraft shell that had done such harm to the flight deck had also shattered the nose turret, and some of the Plexiglas had blown into nose gunner Eddy Haviland's eye. Phil Corrin, the only officer unhurt, felt cold air and oil spray coming at him as he helped the partially blinded young corporal to the flight deck. He gave Eddy what first aid he could and then returned with him to the nose.

Back in the waist, aerial photographer Elmer Philipps was manning a ring gun while John Nelson sorted himself out. This mission was not turning out to be the busman's holiday Philipps had hoped for. Jim Knoch, who had been checking out damage to the plane in the waist, went forward to see what was happening there.

When Jim reached the flight deck, he found what must have looked like a slaughterhouse. One glance at navigator Fred Brennan's head told him there was nothing to be done for him, but Tom Coberly, weak from loss of blood, was asking to get out of the pilot's seat. Jim, with Dan's help, moved the pilot onto the deck floor and gave him two shots of morphine. While Dan tried to get the radio to work, Jim moved with brisk deliberation to put on his own chute pack and sit in Coberly's seat, where he helped Jerry hold on to the yoke until the plane was more stable. In moments of crisis such as this, Jim was, in Dan's words, "all action, no noise."

Sitting in the pilot's seat, Jim saw that the number-one engine was smoking and, judging from the fuel gauge, there seemed to be a hole in the number-two fuel tank. Jerry gave him a thumbs-up to signal he could now control the plane by himself, so Jim climbed up the bomb bay to the fuel tanks above and carefully transferred some of the hoses to salvage as much fuel as possible. Unlike that day a few months earlier over downtown Los Angeles, this time the problem wasn't stalled engines.

Jim then came back down to jettison the bombs to reduce the load so that the fuel would last longer and the bombs would not explode on board if the plane crashed or was hit again. He collected his chute harness, which had been hung up on the now-empty bomb rack. With the bombs gone, he could see through a hole the size of a barrelhead on the left side of the bomb bay: part of the electrical system and almost the entire hydraulic system were gone. Standing on the slippery catwalk, still without his harness on, he took the time to manually crank open the bomb-bay passage door and the bomb-bay doors.

Dan was still trying to alert their base to the plane's critical damage. He could not get his radio to receive or send.

Jim came back to the flight deck and Jerry again gave him the thumbs-up sign. It was only then that Jim noticed the co-pilot's ear was gone. Leaving Jerry at the controls, he sped back toward the waist again, suddenly remembering that Tom Capin had received some training in how to fly a B-24. Pausing on his way just long enough to secure his chute to the harness, Jim had nearly reached the waist (where he found a hole on the left the size of a door) when he sensed that the plane was about to go into a spin.

Phil, having scrabbled out to the flight deck to get para-chutes for himself and Eddy, was now back in the nose and both men were chuted up. Phil looked down and saw that they were still over the jungles of northern Borneo, the most desolate-looking mountain scenery he had ever seen.

Jerry called over the intercom: "This is it, guys. I'm going. Hit the silk!"

CHAPTER TWO

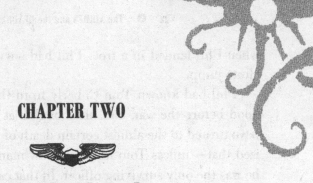

Into the Jungle

John Nelson and Franny Harrington were the first men out of the plane. Elmer Philipps had been chuted up and was standing at the open camera hatch, but John had sensed the photographer's hesitation, so he had moved Philipps out of the way and jumped. After Franny leaped out, Philipps followed.

Jim Knoch, having gone back to the waist to fetch Tom Capin, was just in time to see all six-feet-five inches of the red-headed gunner disappear down the camera hatch. Jim rushed back to the flight deck to get the sedated Tom Coberly chuted and harnessed. Dan Illerich had already slipped out the front end of the bomb bay, thanking God that Jim had opened the bay doors before centrifugal force would have made the task impossible. Next went Coberly, then Jim. Up front in the nose wheel hatch, Phil Corrin helped the half-blind Eddy Haviland out and then jumped himself. Jerry Rosenthal, the dying co-pilot, remained on board with the dead navigator.

Phil Corrin jumped from the nose when the plane was already below one thousand feet. Once out of the plane, he quickly yanked the rip cord and said a brief prayer. As if in answer, the chute blasted open. The beautiful, big white flower had barely blossomed above the broccoli green jungle canopy when Phil landed in a tree. Phil had survived his first parachute jump.

Phil had known Tom Coberly from their California boyhood before the war, and his thoughts at this moment must have turned to the almost certain death of his friend. He realized that—unless Tom had somehow managed to make it—he was the only surviving officer. In that case, his primary job was to figure out how to stay alive and take care of what were now his men.

Dan Illerich landed some seventy-five feet away from Phil. His G.I. Elgin watch showed the time as 12:35. He reread the dial. It was hard to believe that only an hour and five minutes had elapsed since that big Japanese naval shell hit the front of their B-24.

He heard Phil call out to him.

He yelled back, "I'm okay. Are you?"

Shouting to each other through the undergrowth, they finally met. Never had two men shaken hands so fervently. Phil didn't have a scratch on him; neither did Dan. As far as they could tell, nobody else from Coberly's was nearby, so the two of them decided to find the wreckage of the plane.

They set off through the Borneo jungle. Under the dark trees—between fifty and a hundred feet high—they found the underbrush relatively sparse, making progress easier. They soon learned to avoid the more open areas, where the foliage was a lighter green because the underbrush there was almost impenetrable.

To their surprise, even in the darker jungle, nowhere was it really dark. Sunlight pierced the overhead canopy in many places, dappling the jungle floor. There were vines everywhere that twisted, turned and tangled into fantastic shapes hanging from the trees. These could sometimes be used for handholds when the ground rose or fell steeply, though the airmen found the vines were often covered with biting ants. In places, the fronds of young palm trees caught at their clothes and rasped the bare skin of their faces and hands. On the lookout for snakes, which the vines eerily resembled, the airmen saw none. They did not see any recognizable flowers, birds or other animals, though they were surrounded by a blanket of shrill noise produced by a chorus of countless insects and birds. If the men listened hard, they could make out the sound of water coursing downhill, presumably from hidden rivers or streams.

As they walked, they realized they had landed in an area of steep slopes. The airmen could tell from the relatively moderate temperature—no more than 90 degrees Fahrenheit even at midday—that they must be a few thousand feet up. The uneven jungle floor was broken into narrow ridges and knife-edge crests that made it hard to stride ahead. An enveloping dampness added to the difficulty of making their way. Their boots slipped on the wet leaves underfoot. The dark jungle with its giant trees showed no sign of having been touched by man. The utterly unfamiliar landscape seemed unwelcoming.

Though they had seen their plane dive behind a mountain not more than a mile or so from where they had landed, it took the men hours of plodding through the jungle to reach it. Flames and smoke from the still-burning fuselage served as a beacon. But as they moved closer, there came the unmistakable popping of gunfire. It sounded to Phil as if the whole Japanese army was shooting at them. Anything was possible; they had no idea how near the enemy might be. The two men instinctively hit the dirt until the shooting gradually subsided. Only then did they realize that the sounds had been their own plane's ammunition exploding, touched off by the fire.

Approaching, they saw that their brand-new Liberator was now a total wreck. The tail section was gone, and Phil and Dan could see that the charred remains of Fred and Jerry were still too hot to move. All they found worth salvaging were two jungle survival kits and an inflatable life raft. Phil also found a pair of leather gloves.

Phil and Dan opened up the jungle kits, the only emergency supplies the AAF had provided. Inside the ten-pound tan canvas sacks that had been used on board as seat cushions, they found a red paperback booklet titled *Survival: Jungle-Desert-Arctic-Ocean Emergencies.* Though the first chapter was devoted to the jungle, a glance at the text and the black-and-white drawings showed little information that looked relevant or useful. It announced, for example, that "natural food is plentiful in most jungles if you know where to look for it." Beside the booklet were a few dollars and gold coins, a glossary of useful terms in English/Dutch/Malay, a few promissory notes to give to those who helped an airman and a printed card with phrases in Malay and Dutch that a downed airman could use to ask directions.

There was also a small sheaf of official government letters—*blood chits,* the airmen had been told to call them. The blood chits had texts in English, Dutch and Malay that told why Allied forces were in the area of the South China Sea. The chits stated that the airman holding this paper is a friend, his plane has crashed, he does not speak your language and he needs food and maybe medical attention. The chit went on to ask that the airman be hidden and promised that President Roosevelt, King George or Queen Wilhelmina would reward those who helped him.

The survival kits held other items that someone in the War Department must have thought might be useful: a folding machete (perhaps the clumsiest knife ever made), a stone to sharpen it with, a two-ounce container of Sta-Away brand antimosquito lotion, a pocketknife, a packet of six fishhooks and ten yards of fishing line, a few water-purifying tablets, a few high-nutrition chocolate bars called D rations, a red signal flare, a pocket compass, a few packets of dry crackers, little metal cans of cheese, a packet of Wrigley's chewing gum, four Chesterfield cigarettes and twenty rounds of .45-caliber ammunition.

Each of the survival packs also had a small first-aid kit with bandages, sulfa powder, Band-Aids, a tourniquet, U.S. Army dressings, a box of iodine swabs, a tube of tannic ointment for burns and aromatic spirits of ammonia. The airmen thought that if this was all they had to survive on, their prospects weren't very bright.

Phil and Dan examined the one-man inflatable life raft. With its orange top and bright blue underside, the raft was an ungainly five feet long and weighed fifteen pounds when not inflated. Phil decided to bring it along in case they could find some use for it. They each were carrying a small G.I. New Testament in a protective metal cover and Phil still had his silk map, although they thought they were now south of the area it covered. He put the map back in his pocket along with the pair of leather gloves he had found in the plane.

They had the clothes they were wearing and their side-arms, G.I. Colt .45-caliber automatic pistols. Dan also had his own .32-caliber semiautomatic. The big white silk parachutes completed the inventory of their possessions.

Seeing what they had to survive on made them wish they had taken more seriously the guidance from the Australian soldiers who had spent three days giving them pointers on how to live in the jungle. The Australians had told them to be prompt in putting distance between themselves and the wreck, in case the enemy had spotted it. The Aussies had instructed them to follow streams downhill to a river and then go downriver to the sea, if they were ever lost in a tropical rain forest. Back then, sitting in the comfort of a beery bivouac in

New Guinea, such a predicament had seemed almost laughably unlikely.

Phil and Dan now doggedly obeyed the Aussies' advice. When they came across a rivulet, they followed it downstream until it gradually broadened into a larger stream. Nearly four hours had passed since they had jumped.

Hot and wet—partly from their exertions and partly from the air so close they felt they could have parted it with their hands—they sat down in the brush, a few yards from a muddy bank. Their leg muscles ached. (Phil had chronic shin splints, inflammations that resulted from the pounding he had given his legs as an athlete in high school and college.) Massaging their limbs, the men debated whether to continue downriver or to pitch camp for the night. Their chief concern was to find drinking water. They had not known to look for water in the cups of the many pitcher plant blossoms or inside the liana vines all around them. They had a muddy stream beside them and could hear the sounds of flowing water above and around them, but how safe would it be to drink?

They were too tired and overcome with the strangeness of their situation to devote much thought to worrying about snakes or other jungle wildlife, but they were very anxious about what kind of people they might come across. Almost all they knew about Borneo's natives could be summed up by the Barnum & Bailey sideshow "The Wild Man of Borneo." Dan was a great reader but he had not read any books about this part of the world, although he had seen pictures of tropical jungles in his dad's copies of *National Geographic*. The crew had seen few natives in New Guinea, and the Aussies they met there had had little good to say about any of the Pacific Islanders.

Now the airmen needed to know exactly how wild were these men of Borneo, whom the Aussies had called Dayaks.

Were they cannibals or headhunters, as some of the Aussies had said? Were they real men you could deal with? Or were they almost another species, like the pygmy that had once been on display at the Bronx Zoo?

The airmen were even more worried about how near the Japanese could be. They spared a moment of gratitude to Jerry who had brought them so far from the enemy-infested coast, but the Japanese might have outposts inside Borneo, too. If so, how near here? Or maybe the natives near here were cooperating with them. Phil and Dan had heard that after Pearl Harbor the Japanese army had been able to walk into Southeast Asia and take charge because the native people had welcomed them as liberators from their colonial oppressors. Was that true for Borneo? The two airmen knew they were likely to find out soon.

After sitting awhile and delicately picking off the bloated leeches that had left bloody trails on his legs and ankles, Phil peered closely at the vegetation across the river and made out the outlines of a small lean-to. He pointed it out silently to Dan, and they quietly waded across the waist-deep cloudy water to explore it. Inside, they saw what looked like the hulls of dugout canoes propped up against the bamboo walls. Phil made a mental note to remember these longboats, since he and Dan and the rest of the crew—if they were still alive—might need them for their escape. Then Phil noticed a stalk of green bananas on the hut's dirt floor. Someone had been there recently—and would be coming back.

Phil and Dan tried to draw courage from the fact that this hut seemed to be native built, not Japanese. They did not know that Major Saalfield's plane had crash-landed farther west in northern Borneo and that the surviving crew members had all been killed by the Japanese—but such news would not have surprised them. Their survival briefings had included warnings that the Japanese military regarded surrendered soldiers as less than human and that they routinely killed downed Allied airmen.

Phil and Dan came out of the windowless hut so that they could keep an eye on their surroundings. They sat quietly for an hour or so under a tree near the bank of the stream, more fearful than watchful, until a black head popped up above a clump of bushes some twenty yards across the water. Thank God, it did not look Japanese.

Phil stood up and said, "Hi there!" in a tone that he felt sure Dale Carnegie would have approved. The head disappeared, but in a few minutes a dozen or more armed men appeared in its place. These must be the Dayaks. They all had tan skin; each wore a loincloth, had a machete in a holster slung around the hips and carried a long pole with a menacing spear at the end. Their lips were stained black, making them look like the savage Moros of the Philippines, about whom the Yanks had been warned by old Philippine hands.

"Grin," Phil said to Dan.

Both airmen grinned like models in a toothpaste ad. The men in loincloths grinned back, exposing black teeth. Their straight black hair was bowl cut in front and some had it tied in a knot in back while others wore a pigtail. Curved animal teeth adorned their upper earlobes, and some of the Dayaks had brass rings in their lower lobes. Most of them wore a series of tight-fitting wicker armbands at the elbow, wrist and just below the knee. A couple of the men wore sleeveless and collarless beaten-bark vests open in front, exposing well-muscled, hairless chests. They were not as tall as the airmen but they were well built, with powerful thighs and legs. They bowed as one man.

The airmen were all thumbs, trying to get rid of their

sidearms. "We're Americans," Phil kept repeating. "We're your friends."

As soon as Dan and Phil dropped their gun holsters, the Dayaks waded across, dropping their machetelike swords on the bank of the stream. Next, they took their poles (actually blowpipes) and stuck them into the mud. They held out their empty hands to shake hands with Phil and Dan.

One of the tribesmen looked down at the gun holsters on the ground and, to Dan and Phil's amazement, shouted out, "U.S., U.S.," and started dancing about. Then he beckoned to Dan and Phil to follow him, and the whole party, including a dozen scarred, ginger-haired curs, moved off together. After a short walk in the mud through thick brush, they arrived at a hamlet, where nearly a hundred Dayaks swarmed around the airmen. For what seemed like an age, Phil and Dan stood while a crowd of gesticulating natives of both sexes and all ages gathered around them and gabbled away in a language incomprehensible to the airmen.

Some of the women (not the youngest or prettiest, Phil and Dan observed regretfully) were naked to the waist. Most of the other women wore woven-reed bibs tied at the neck that loosely covered their breasts. The women's earlobes stretched down to their shoulders, distended by the weight of brass rings. The women, too, were well built, with very few noticeably overweight or too thin. The girls' round faces were open and fine featured, although their smiles revealed that the insides of their mouths were black and many were missing both front teeth.

Phil and Dan had been standing in the late-afternoon light for some time when a middle-aged man who seemed to have some authority approached. He motioned the airmen to follow him into a tall thatched hut about forty feet long that rested on stilts some six feet high. The two Americans awkwardly found their footing on a fourteen-foot notched log that served as a ladder to a raised bamboo veranda. Pigs and chickens protested from their smelly quarters below while the dozen twisted-tail dogs that had accompanied the party now swirled around them, barking excitedly.

Phil and Dan followed their guides through a gap in the long wall that separated the veranda from the indoors. The light inside was dim and the air smoky. The last of the sunlight coming through glassless windows and glancing off the interior longhouse walls and floor gleamed a dull gold. The floors were made of long wooden planks, and the bamboo walls were covered in mats made from woven reeds. There were no interior walls to parcel out the space. Instead, a series of cooking fires was scattered on the floor, with tall shelves behind them to hold firewood. Thin straw mats woven in complicated figurative patterns were spread out in front of most hearths. From within, the longhouse seemed bigger and more solidly constructed than it had first appeared. The underside of the high-pitched roof was neatly stitched together from palm fronds.

Phil and Dan were looking up at the ceiling in admiration when suddenly they froze. They saw what were clearly human skulls on wicker shelves high up under the rafters. The heads looked old and dusty, almost skeletal, but there were bits of what appeared to be fresh food in front of their shriveled jaws. It seemed to the airmen that the warning from the Australians back in New Guinea that the interior of Borneo belonged to headhunters must be true. And they had landed in the midst of them.

Not wanting to raise the subject with their hosts, they looked down and saw their escort motioning for them to sit on reed mats in the center of the floor. The group who had led them to the longhouse arrayed themselves around Phil and Dan, legs crossed or squatting with their arms resting on their knees, their bare buttocks hanging an inch off the floor. They stared at the airmen without expression. Their faces had a curious blankness, which Phil and Dan came slowly to realize was caused by the total absence of eyelashes and eyebrows. A few of the bolder ones came up and touched the fuzzy hair on the airmen's arms, so different from their own smooth bodies. As the silence lengthened, it was clearly the Americans' turn to do something.

Phil and Dan opened up their backpacks and handed every article to the chief: the jungle survival books, the blood chits, the Bibles, the folding machetes (which, when unfolded, provoked a laugh), the one-man inflatable life raft, the compasses, the chocolate bars, the crackers and cheese in their wrappings, the first-aid kit, the guns and the parachutes. The chief inspected each item without comment or change of expression and passed the article on to the others, who eventually passed it back to the airmen. The men sitting around them seemed to be scowling at Phil and Dan.

With their jungle packs empty, Phil hesitated. Then he pulled out of his pocket the last item salvaged from the plane wreck, the leather gloves, and handed them to the chief. The chief threw the gloves back to Phil, who slipped his hand into one of them. The chief's men bolted to their feet and reached for their machetes. Phil quickly put his other hand in the remaining glove and wiggled his fingers. The chief cackled, the others laughed and Phil continued to wiggle his fingers wildly.

The atmosphere was suddenly less strained. Two women appeared, wearing long, dark skirts made of vegetable fiber, their long, brass-weighted earlobes swinging against their nipples, their hands and feet tattooed in elaborate black swirls. They brought Dan and Phil big portions of cooked white rice in leaf packets along with unfamiliar cooked greens in blue-and-white Chinese bowls. Later, when the airmen looked around in the light of the resin torches that illuminated the interior of the longhouse they could see ancient-looking Oriental ceramics—huge, high-shouldered, dark brown jars and brilliant blue-and-white plates. For now, Phil and Dan did not think to wonder how or why these treasures were there.

The chief rubbed his stomach to invite his guests to eat. It was now dark outside and surprisingly chilly—further confirmation they were in the uplands. Three of the chief's men built a fire in the hearth in front of the airmen. Ignoring their survival pamphlet instructions—"Don't stay in native houses and don't eat native food"—the airmen began to eat. Using the thumb and three fingers of the right hand, the way they saw the others do, they got down as much as they could manage of the huge pile of plain, unsalted white rice. They tried the stringy, dark green vegetables alongside and found them bitter. But they eagerly accepted some roasted ears of corn. When they had finished, not knowing what else to do, they put the cobs on the mat beside their Chinese bowls. Their hosts snatched up the discarded cobs and tossed them off the veranda to the noisy pigs and chickens down in the mud below. Phil and Dan put their hands on their bellies to show they were done with the food in front of them. Their hosts gave them green bananas that tasted surprisingly ripe and sweet.

After dinner one of the tribesmen came crouching up to the airmen and offered them dried tobacco tied up neatly in a big green leaf. Phil and Dan sensed that this creeping while squatting on one's haunches was a friendly gesture. The man took out a match from a tiny matchbox. He had started to light the tobacco when Dan and Phil both noticed that the cover of the matchbox was decorated with the emblem of the rising sun, the dreaded Japanese imperial symbol.

The airmen recoiled instinctively. Then they tried to hide their feelings but they could see they were fooling no one. The man lighting Dan's cigar made a gesture as if to throw the box away, which the airmen took as reassurance that these head-hunters—if that was what they were—were on the Allied side. Still, the airmen continued to wonder anxiously how and when the man had come by that matchbox.

After the women had cleared the food away, one of the men took Dan and Phil out on the veranda and showed them how to relieve themselves over the edge while keeping their genitals modestly covered. Upon their return inside, the long-house chief pantomimed sleep by closing his eyes and pointing to the floor by the fire. Although Phil was reluctant to sleep with twenty pairs of lashless eyes on him, he spread out his parachute, lay down on it and closed his eyes. Dan did the same, and the young men, having agreed to stay awake by turns for two-hour stretches, were both soon fast asleep.

CHAPTER THREE

The D.O.'s Dilemma

If Makahanap had looked up from his still incomplete report on the Mentarang District's rice production, he might have seen four Lun Dayeh tribesmen standing in the doorway of his office waiting to be noticed. (The Lun Dayeh do not break in on another person's thoughts or dreams abruptly, for fear of making the inner spirit ill.)

Eventually, Makahanap saw Yakal and his brother, Busar, and two other young men he did not know, who must have made the trip with Busar from Long Gavit. For Yakal to be at the D.O.'s door was no surprise. Yakal was staying in Long Berang while Makahanap helped him study to be the first Lun Dayeh pastor of the Kemah Injil, an evangelical Protestant church.

Although Busar was Yakal's best friend, as was often the case among Lun Dayeh siblings, the D.O. wondered why Busar came ten hours downriver by longboat during the hunting season on the Kinaye River, just before the heaviest monsoon rains began. Moreover, the men's wives would need help at home with the children and the old folks, because this was when the women were busy weeding the rice fields. Furthermore, enough rain had already fallen that the river's downward current was growing stronger every day. It would take Busar and his two companions—who, he now remembered, lived at Long Kasurun, the next village upriver from Busar's longhouse—at least thirty hours paddling against the flow to get back home.

Makahanap greeted the group courteously, with the usual question: "You have come?"

"We have come, we are three," replied Busar, rushing through the exchange of questions and answers that are the standard greeting among the Lun Dayeh. Busar's hasty replies alerted Makahanap that his visitor was anxious to move on to his urgent news, so the D.O. smiled an invitation for Busar to begin.

Yesterday midday, Busar exclaimed, he and his neighbors Tawan Libat and Sugiang Baru had been out hunting together when they saw a huge object fall from the sky near Long Kasurun. When the big thing hit the ground, it burst into flames and made a lot of strange noises, louder than anything he had ever heard, louder than when a great tree falls. (He shivered. The sound of a tree falling on the mountainside when you are engaged felling a tree elsewhere is a terrible omen among the Lun Dayeh, even for those who are Christians, like Busar.) Busar and his friends had gradually come to realize that this burning metal thing must be an airplane, like those they had seen in the missionaries' magazines. But it was so much bigger than it had looked up in the sky. Imagine! It was as big as a longhouse. Up above, it had not seemed big enough to hold even one man. Busar's friends spoke up, confirming his story.

Makahanap nodded. There being no roads in Borneo's interior, few Dayaks would have seen a wheeled or motored vehicle before, much less a flying one. Certainly the Lun Dayeh had no need for wheels or engines. They plowed their steep fields with a hoe dragged by water buffalo or by several men, and the women planted the rice seed in holes in the mud made by the men with pointed sticks. They traveled barefoot and single file up and down jungle slopes, going from the head-waters of one river system to another, the muddy banks serv-ing as natural paths. In those few places upriver where the streams were navigable, they paddled a dugout canoe (*perahu*). Where rocks and rapids made boating impossible, they would pick up the light craft with its heavy contents—maybe a buf-falo calf or jungle products for market—and carry it on their shoulders.

Busar waited for the district officer's response to his story, but Makahanap wanted to get a sense of how the plane crash had struck these Lun Dayeh without giving a hint of his own feelings. He merely stood there, looking interested. So Busar continued. He said that he, his little son, these companions and a dozen or so others who had been hunting with them had seen white, mushroomlike shapes coming down from the sky at roughly the same time as the plane was falling. As the shapes came nearer to earth, he and his friends could see that they were not mushrooms but men, hanging from ropes under white, cloudlike cloth tents. Two of the men had floated to earth behind nearby hills and could no longer be seen. Even-tually Busar and his friends saw them again across the Kinaye River. Two foreigners with guns. Soldiers.

This *did* get a reaction from the D.O., who interrupted to ask Busar to describe these soldiers exactly. Busar told Maka-hanap that he and his friends could tell from their skin color and faces that the soldiers were white men, not Japanese. But they did not seem to be Dutch; their bodies were not that bulky. Busar said he and his friends had stayed and watched them for some time.

Makahanap smiled. It amazed him how these men who were often so noisy and boisterous in the evening gaiety of their longhouses could, when out hunting, stay perfectly still for hours, even when a parade of fire ants walked across them.

If the Lun Dayeh did not want to be seen, no stranger would know they were there.

Busar went on. He and his friends had stood up and showed themselves from across the river. There had been a tense moment, he said, while they waited to see what the strangers would do. But finally, when Busar and the others had walked across through the water and thrown their machetes on the ground, they all had shaken hands and laughed.

It was then that Busar had spotted a U.S. insignia on the gun holsters that were lying on the ground. It told him that these men must be Americans, from the same country as Brother John Willfinger.

Makahanap nodded again. Brother John Willfinger of the Kemah Injil Church had been among the first to bring the good news about Jesus to the longhouses of the Krayan and Mentarang districts, before *masa Jepun,* "the Japanese time."

The district officer now had an idea of the Dayaks' initial reaction to the arrival of the American airmen. He also sensed that Busar was about to change the subject. The D.O. had learned over the years that the Lun Dayeh greatly valued the spoken word, and they would tell and listen to stories that could go on for days. No Lun Dayeh story was ever meant to be told in a straightforward fashion, any more than a Lun Dayeh jungle trail could be made straight; there always had to be deviations and complications. But the D.O. was not to be distracted. He looked straight at Busar. "And then?"

Busar, seemingly gratified that his listener was still eager to hear more, told how he and his friends had brought the Americans to Long Kasurun, where the village headman, though not a Christian, had welcomed the soldiers and tried to feed them rice. But the Americans did not know how to eat rice. Busar and his Long Kasurun friends gave animated accounts with comic gestures of how the strangers picked at the food. They told of everything their hosts had given the strangers to eat, all in vain, except for some corn. "So in the end we gave them bananas—and they ate them," said Busar, his recital at an end.

Makahanap remained silent for a bit. When he spoke, it was quietly, soft speech being the way Lun Dayeh signal that what they are saying is important. Almost whispering, he said as emphatically as he could that Busar, Yakal and their companions must keep this story to themselves. Only *Ama* (Papa) and Mama Makahanap and a few others were to know. Busar and the others promised the D.O. they would not tell.

After the young men had left, the D.O. stayed alone in his office. He needed to reflect on the question that could no longer be ignored, the question that had been like a dull headache ever since he had recognized the drone of the plane's failing engines. What should he do? Busar and the others would keep their promise not to tell. Even among non-Christians such as Busar's travel companions, a Lun Dayeh's promise was sacred.

But news of the American airplane crash was bound to reach the Japanese occupiers, and Makahanap's current boss, the *ken kanrikan* (Japanese regional administrator) would no doubt be sending a party upriver from Malinau to look for survivors.

Makahanap's Chinese trader friends here in Long Berang had all kept telling him that the war would end soon, and that the white people would win. That might be so, he thought, but at the moment the Japanese were powerful and close by whereas the Allied forces were not. Nor had the white men shown themselves ready to try to recover the territory that had fallen so easily from their grasp. And even if the Japanese were to lose the war, who knew for certain that white rule would return to this part of the world?

The nearly three years that the Japanese had been in control of the Dutch East Indies had been hard for Makahanap to bear. Yet he was aware that he and his wife were among the few East Indians who regretted the departure of the Dutch. Under Dutch rule, Christians from his home islands, the Celebes, had been privileged above other natives. This favoritism was resented by the people of Java, who constituted the great majority of Dutch East Indians and who were Muslim, at least nominally. The Dutch had encouraged Christian outer islanders like himself and the "Indos," those of mixed European and Asian blood (who were also Christians for the most part), to attend Dutch colonial schools. Unlike the Muslims, they had been taught to read and write not only Malay but also Dutch, and had followed a Dutch curriculum. They finished school knowing more about the rivers of Holland than about those here. Thus qualified, they were able to find desk jobs in the Netherlands East Indies armed forces and in the Dutch colonial administration.

But now, the Javanese—all eighty million of them—were enjoying a nominal rise to power under the Greater East Asia Co-Prosperity Sphere. Makahanap suspected that the Co-Prosperity Sphere was just another colonial regime with a new name. But if, after the war, the white men did not return, the Javanese might really come to power, and people like himself and his family would lose their privileges. Prudence dictated, therefore, that he and his wife and other Christians keep their heads down now if they wanted to stay out of trouble later on.

As a former missionary teacher, Makahanap knew his loyalties were already suspect to the Japanese and their local allies, especially the coastal Malays, whose history and Muslim religion gave them no reason to like the white man. What he ought to do, surely, was turn the airmen over to the *ken kan-*

rikan. It was his civic duty. No one could blame him if he did that. It was also the best way to ensure the safety of his district, his family and himself.

But doing this went against his Christian conscience. And he knew—even before discussing it with her—that his wife would be scandalized if he handed any Americans over to the Japanese. Yet, if he were caught hiding them, it would mean a hideous death for himself and his family and probably serious repercussions for his district.

He could not forget how the Japanese had killed his cousins in the Celebes three years before. At that time, the new masters had seemed to be trying to win the trust of the Celebes people. So when his cousins, who were pillars of the community, learned of Japanese soldiers putting a nice girl from their church group into a brothel for Japanese officers, they had complained to the Japanese civil authorities, expecting to have the matter rectified and the girl released. Instead, the couple's throats had been slit by one of the samurai swords the Japanese officers liked to display unsheathed, as a warning of their power.

When the news reached the Makahanaps in Long Berang, their first thought had been for Christiaan, the cousins' only son, an orphan at age fifteen. Frightened as they were, William and Theresia had gone back east to the Celebes to get him.

Makahanap's thoughts kept going off on tangents, but in his heart he knew why he was having such a hard time concentrating on what to do next. He was afraid. He feared the Japanese as he never had the Dutch, even the drunken ones.

He was haunted by the many stories he had heard of torture, rape and murder of white prisoners of war at a prison camp in Sarawak, to the west, and at another big camp in the British state of North Borneo. More terrible still, because it was closer to home, had been the murder two years ago in nearby Long Nawang of dozens of Westerners, including Kemah Injil missionaries, their wives and even their babies. And then there had been the execution of Long Berang's own American, Brother John Willfinger. Makahanap could not bear to think about that now.

Fortunately for his district, the people of upriver Borneo had been relatively unaffected by the Japanese occupation. The Dutch had rarely bothered with them, and the Japanese, after coming upriver to kill the foreigners living there in 1942, had not been back.

The biggest annoyance to Makahanap's district during the *masa Jepun* was the wartime disruption of commercial shipping. That meant imported goods, such as the brightly colored cotton cloth the Lun Dayeh loved to use for sarongs and loincloths, was no longer available. However, the Lun Dayeh had always been fairly self-sufficient, growing their own rice and vegetables and catching their own fish and game. They made their own weapons, as well as bamboo fish cages and fishnets. Their hand-drilled hardwood blowpipes and poison darts they made themselves or obtained in trade from the nomadic Punans of the deep interior rain forest. Some of the Lun Dayeh had their own dried springs containing iodized salt. The Lun Dayeh could even manage without the imported cotton cloth by pounding homemade fabric from tree bark or weaving threads spun from pineapple fiber.

But in recent months, tribespeople living nearer the coast had been coming upriver to demand rice from local Lun Dayeh farmers because the Japanese were taking theirs. Makahanap had heard that when these downriver people got back home with the rice, the Japanese took half of it. Farmers who refused to give up their rice were taken away, and some had not been heard from since.

And now, to complicate matters, there were American soldiers in his district. The Japanese would expect him to find and surrender them. Could he bear to court the risk to his family and his district—not to mention himself—of hiding American soldiers from the Japanese? His thoughts had come full circle without leading to an answer. He tried to pray for guidance but could not concentrate. He needed to consult the person who always seemed to have an instinctive grasp of the right thing to do. It was time to talk to Mama.

When he walked next door to his house, he found Mama and eighteen-year-old Christiaan having a cup of tea during the quiet time while the four little ones napped. Seeing him enter, Mama served her husband tea in a porcelain cup brought from the Celebes. She listened tranquilly as he told her and Christiaan all about the Americans and the alarming problems their presence in his district could pose.

As he had expected, Mama did not hesitate in finding an answer. She said she was convinced that the Allies would eventually prevail and that her husband would be held accountable for how these airmen were treated. "If the Americans die, William, you die," she said, exaggerating her argument slightly, as was her wont when her emotions were affected. Christiaan, when asked, said he could not imagine ever being on the same side as those who had murdered his parents.

When William started to protest about the risk to them all, Mama refused to be alarmed. Instead, having listened to his arguments without comment, she now urged William to rely on his own good sense in handling the Japanese. She knew he could do it. After all, he had been a senior administrative official of the region for more than four years and had shown a great ability to judge character, even in foreigners. She argued that in dealing with Dayaks, both animist and Christian, his instincts had proved sound in determining whom to trust, how people would behave. Now, despite his doubts, he was proving just as skillful with the Japanese. His new bosses, they were leaving him alone, weren't they, to administer his district?

Makahanap took heart from Mama's remarks. He suddenly realized that he did, indeed, know precisely how to handle his Japanese supervisor at Malinau, whom he judged to be both cowardly and ambitious. When dealing with any supervisor, Makahanap had always found it advantageous to appear more stupid and less well informed than his boss. But especially this supervisor, the *ken kanrikan*, must get all the credit, whatever the circumstance. If Makahanap kept that in mind, he could manage the man perfectly.

He had little time to plan. In all probability, the Japanese had already learned of the plane crash. Fortunately, it took three times longer to go upriver than downriver. That meant he could safely count on the Japanese not arriving in Long Berang for at least a few days more. The thing to do was to use that time wisely. He left Mama and went back to the office.

Blinking his eyes against the shimmering brightness above, he stood on the office steps, a slight and slender light brown-skinned man whose coarse, curly hair, betraying his Celebes origins, was thinning. He was barefooted and dressed for everyday chores in a dingy white shirt threadbare from frequent washing and an old pair of wide-legged tan drill shorts. As he was well aware, he would not have cut an impressive figure in the Netherlands East Indies capital, Batavia. But he knew he was a person of great influence here among the Dayaks.

Makahanap and his family had arrived in Long Berang in late 1937, charged with taking over the mission school. A year earlier, his predecessor had tried but failed to start a school there.

In early January 1938, the Dutch D.O. once again sent out

messages to the longhouse leaders ordering parents to send their children to the school. It was then that Makahanap gave proof that he had found his true calling. He convinced the D.O. to ask the parents to come along that first day of school, and to bring with them the tools to build a schoolroom and a small house for the new teacher, his wife and their little daughters Mientje and Rika to live in.

Construction from local materials was one area where these Dayaks excelled, and they came from longhouses all along the various branches of the Mentarang, bringing twenty-five of their daughters, fifty-five of their sons and their machetes. They all worked together to build an open-sided schoolroom—with a pitched roof of woven leaves and mats, supported by wooden posts above a raised plank floor—and a little hutlike house next door, both buildings slightly raised aboveground, in case of floods. Within a couple of days, the buildings were ready for use and the parents left their children in the Makahanaps' care with mutual expressions of satisfaction. The Dayak pupils and their parents by then had begun to call William Makahanap *Ama* (Papa) and his wife, Theresia Manis, *Mama*. The names stuck.

By September 1940, when the Netherlands East Indies (N.E.I.) government made Makahanap the D.O. for the Mentarang District, he had become so loved and respected that he could count on the local people to do virtually anything he asked. He felt that his primary responsibility was to keep the welfare of the people of his district always in mind, an enlightened attitude he had come to acquire under the guidance of the Kemah Injil missionaries, American and Canadian pastors of the Christian and Missionary Alliance, who had made clear to him that the Dayaks must be treated with genuine respect—an idea not current in the Dutch colonial schools in which the Makahanaps had been educated.

The Dutch, though they had been the colonial masters of the southeastern two-thirds of Borneo for a hundred years, had paid almost no attention to this part of their tropical empire. Borneo was the third-biggest island in the world, bigger than England, Spain and Portugal put together, but it was sparsely populated and its interior lacked an obvious source of riches. To the best of Makahanap's knowledge, the Dutch had waited until at least the 1920s before assigning a handful of colonial administrators to Borneo, most of them scattered along the coast, where there was oil. They had left the interior uninterfered with, preferring to lavish their attention on more profitable islands. Proud as Makahanap was to have been one of the few "natives" to be named a district officer by the colonial government, he knew the Dutch would never have left a district in Java, Sumatra or the Moluccas in the hands of an East Indian like himself, no matter how Christian, conscientious or competent. And probably not even a district in Borneo, in peacetime.

Long Berang's reason for being the district seat was that it was the authorized place for the Dayaks of two East Borneo districts—Mentarang and Krayan—to sell their forest products, under the direct supervision of the district officer. When the D.O. declared a market day, the sleepy little hamlet was transformed. Hundreds of people wearing tattoos, loincloths and little else would appear. They came with woven reed baskets hanging from rattan poles balanced across their backs. The baskets carried heavy loads of rattan, cakes of damar resin, balls of wild rubber sap, camphor, snake gall, various parts of monkeys and orangutans wanted by Chinese for use in their traditional medicine and, of course, surplus hill rice. Those nights, the usually empty Dayak rest house would pulsate with the sounds of Dayaks chattering, laughing, preparing dinner and occasionally dancing to the beat of drums and gongs.

The next morning, Makahanap gave a Dayak messenger a brief, businesslike report of the plane crash. It included word of the appearance of some American airmen in his district. He told the messenger to deliver it to the *ken kanrikan* at Malinau Town.

He then hastened upstream to Long Kasurun accompanied by Christiaan, Yakal, Busar and Busar's two companions. Despite his worries, Makahanap enjoyed being in a *perahu* on the wide Mentarang. Taking their cue from Christiaan, who was aware of his stepfather's preoccupation, the normally ebullient Dayaks soon gave up trying to point out sights to the D.O. and engage his attention the way they usually did.

Makahanap appreciated the quiet. This stretch of the Mentarang was almost the only place in this part of East Borneo where the dense vegetation gave way for more than a few yards, allowing an uninterrupted view of the sky and a chance to appreciate how high the giant trees were. Makahanap could pick out the distinctive summits of various mountains, some marked with a square, empty space (*tafa*) where the Lun Dayeh had cut away all the brush to make a natural monument to a dead nobleman. He cared less for the nearer view. Looking at all these different shades of green around him, he could barely distinguish one plant from another. The Lun Dayeh, he knew, would be eager to point out which plants to use to make roofing, siding, fishnets or sleeping mats, which ferns were edible and which vines and pitcher plants held the most rainwater for drinking. Makahanap had no such knowledge. To Makahanap it was all just jungle.

He could hear the sound of falling water from mountain

streams and, beyond the shrill din of the insects, the calls of many kinds of birds, only a few of which he could identify. He could distinguish the sounds of the hooting gibbons and the chattering monkeys but they were hard to see, though they occasionally made the higher branches of the tall trees sway under their weight. Once in a while, a stretch of the river would be temporarily covered with brilliantly hued, velvety butterflies, but such bursts of color were rare.

People traveling by *perahu* were advised to keep an eye out for crocodiles. There were fewer of these giant reptiles than in the old days, but sometimes you could see a few sunning on the mud banks. The problem came when someone mistook them for logs floating on the river. They were such impressive, powerful beasts that Makahanap found it understandable that some of the Dayaks who resisted conversion to Christianity still worshipped effigies of these reptiles.

It was a pleasure to observe the paddlers' economy of motion as the river sped by. The water was low in places, obliging them to get out and carry the *perahu* on their shoulders through the shallows or where big rocks were too plentiful. The paddlers were able to keep such portaging to a minimum. They seemed to know how to avoid every submerged rock that could tip the narrow dugout over or damage its fragile keel. Still, someone drowned every few years on the river, and great care was always required. The biggest nuisance of wading through the high, wet grass was spending the next hours picking off leeches.

After two days, Makahanap and his party, now on the Kinaye River, approached the Lun Dayeh longhouse at Long Gavit, Yakal and Busar's home and the last village downstream before Long Kasurun. It was an hour before sundown.

The men of the village were mooring their dugouts nearby; they shouted a welcome to the newcomers. Coming back from a hunt, the villagers were in high spirits as they continued with their early evening routine of a quick bath in the river. It had been a good hunting day—a fact especially treasured because it might be their last before the rains made jungle travel nearly impossible for months. Now there would be plenty of meat—wild pig, monkey, deer and jungle fowl— for the longhouse and its honored visitors. After their bath, the villagers carried the game and forest products they had collected up the hill to the longhouse, all the while continuing to boast and laugh about the hunt. The dogs, near delirious with the scent of fresh meat, were barking, growling, snapping and swirling around the men, making it a minor miracle that neither man nor beast fell off the log ladder into the malodorous mud beneath.

By the time Makahanap, Christiaan and their Dayak companions had bathed and climbed up to the veranda, the men of Long Gavit were already sitting cross-legged, ready to smoke, chat and exchange news with the newcomers while their women prepared dinner. Makahanap regretted that he had to worry these villagers, who had clearly been looking forward to a pleasant, boisterous evening. With his letter perhaps already in the *ken kanrikan*'s hands, there was no time for idle chat, and the need for secrecy made a boisterous longhouse evening too risky. As soon as he had replied to the ritual greeting, he allowed the worry to show on his face while he asked the longhouse chief to send out runners to call the elders from the other longhouses along the Kinaye River to meet him there. Normally, the runners would have carried a knotted string made of vine tendrils, each knot representing a day until the rendezvous. This time the messengers were told to ask the headmen to come to Long Gavit right away.

The strain visible on the D.O.'s face and his not volunteering the reason for the hasty meeting changed the atmosphere on the veranda. The longhouse men discarded their unfinished tobacco and went off to their separate fires to eat their dinners. Instead of the usual teasing questions and the booming laughter at the answers, conversation gradually came to a halt. This being a teetotal Christian longhouse, there was no *borak*, the Lun Dayeh homemade rice beer, to ease the atmosphere. After the children had been put to bed and a quick evening prayer said and hymn sung, the D.O. excused himself and wandered out to the veranda.

There he lay, wrapped up in a reed mat for warmth, listening to the night sounds of the longhouse: the scraping noise made by the log ladders being pulled up onto the veranda for the night; the grunts of the pigs settling in below; the harsh, hacking cough of one of the old women; a sudden puff of soft laughter from the group of young men whispering before sleep in the bachelors' quarters on the veranda; the tittering of the teenage girls in the loft above; the occasional surreptitious sound of someone finding his way in the dark to the edge of the boardwalk to relieve himself. Eventually, Makahanap slept.

Served breakfast the next morning by the headman's wife before she and the other women went off to weed their rice fields, Makahanap waited as patiently as he could for the men he had summoned to arrive. The able-bodied Lun Dayeh left to go fishing on the river, taking Christiaan, Busar and Busar's friends with them to help handle the big traps. In the now nearly empty longhouse, the district officer idly watched the little children totter about under the supervision of a bossy girl not old enough to help in the fields or go away to school.

The children, accustomed to playing host to visitors during the daylight hours while their parents were away, came up to greet him and offered to include him in their play, but he did not respond. The only adults present were the headman and villagers too old or too ill to work. Makahanap sat quietly with the old men and looked forward with as much patience as he could muster to the arrival of the other headmen. He had learned that, although the position of longhouse headman among the Lun Dayeh was inherited, a headman had to keep proving his worth. He had to be the hardest worker, the best rice producer, the most successful hunter, the most farsighted trader of cattle, the bravest in battle and the most adept in dealing with emergencies, such as a fire in the longhouse.

Until about fifteen years before, one way a leader could prove his worth was by how many heads he had taken. Makahanap had to concede that the best change the white man had brought to Borneo had been accomplished shortly before the missionaries had arrived: an end to headhunting. It had not been easy to do. The British and Dutch governments had conducted campaigns, using both force and diplomacy. The Dutch had declared headhunting illegal in their territory in the 1890s but it had taken decades to make the ban stick.

Although no new heads had been taken since 1930, nobody was ready to declare this age-old Dayak practice entirely dead, given its intimate connection with the Dayaks' traditional animistic beliefs. As far as Makahanap understood those beliefs, they involved a bewildering variety of benign and malign spirits in the natural world who had to be propitiated, avoided or fooled.

It was annoying enough when auguries and omens, believed to have come from these spirits, would sometimes interfere with hunting trips or harvesting crops. But what was most disturbing to the colonizers about the Dayaks' religion was the belief that ambushing and taking the head of someone from a rival group and bringing it back to one's own longhouse could turn the head into a spirit that conferred health and good crops on the people of its new home. The Dutch colonial service had encouraged Christian missionaries to come to Borneo, fearing that without wholesale conversion of the Dayaks to a different religion, headhunting might start up again.

Sitting on the veranda at Long Gavit, Makahanap's patience was gradually rewarded. The headmen and a few elders from the Lun Dayeh longhouses at Long Bisai, Long Kiangen, Long Metuil and Long Kafun began to appear. Makahanap greeted them in the standard way.

"You have come?" he asked Pangeran Lagan, the headman of Long Metuil, an animist longhouse. Lagan's title of *pangeran* meant he was the senior native official of Makahanap's district and, as such, the D.O.'s immediate subordinate. The D.O. felt pleasure and relief at seeing him come up the log ladder. Without him, no firm agreement among the elders would be possible.

"I have come," the *pangeran* answered slowly, as he reached the veranda and shook Makahanap's hand. There was a special warmth between the two men.

"You have come from where?" continued Makahanap, taking his time.

"I have come from Long Metuil."

"You are many?"

"We are three."

"All is well where you come from?"

"All is well."

"Good. All was well on the journey?"

"All was very well on the journey."

So it went with all the visitors.

After there had been enough small talk to satisfy the Dayaks' sense of etiquette, Makahanap took the leaders aside, where they could not be overheard, and spoke to them about the American soldiers. He took pains to make clear the danger that these foreigners might pose to the longhouse communities once the Japanese learned of their presence. Looking at them one by one, he quietly asked the headmen what should be done.

The *lun mebala* (aristocrats—literally "good people") spoke among themselves quickly and in the local dialect, so that Makahanap could not really follow the conversation. Then, turning to him, Pangeran Lagan said that the longhouse leaders wanted to know who would win the war. Makahanap had expected the question, and answered it with another: "What if the white people win and we have *not* helped these Americans?"

He knew that an important element in the elders' thinking—even among the animists—was their great respect for the North American missionaries who had behaved with such courtesy when they worked among the local people. The Lun Dayeh remembered when the Japanese had appeared at Long Nawang (farther to the south), where the Dutch, British and other Westerners had gone to hide from the Japanese. Within a few days, the *heitai*s (Japanese soldiers) had killed forty of the men, including two Kemah Injil missionaries. They had taken the women and children prisoner and "visited" them often. A month later, they had quietly bayoneted the women and children.

The Kemah Injil's John Willfinger, normally based at Long Berang, had been away up north, over the border in British Borneo, when the Japanese had killed the other missionary men and women. The Lun Dayeh and other Dayaks had all urged him to stay where he was. But Willfinger returned to Long Berang and gave himself up rather than have his flock try to hide him. He was beheaded on Christmas Eve of 1942. The Lun Dayeh had been greatly touched by the fact that this foreigner was willing to die for them.

Makahanap discussed what to do about the American fugitives with the elders for the rest of the day and evening and the next day. Almost every time he thought he had gently but clearly delineated the problem, the question would be temporarily pushed aside by the elders as they pursued other topics. These men, who saw one another only a few times a year, had much to discuss and were prepared to take their time. They talked of old rivalries, new marriage negotiations and forthcoming funeral plans. Where would the new couple live? Which longhouse would become the home of the bride's wealthy uncle with the coveted dragon jar? When would one particular longhouse have enough *borak* prepared and pigs, chickens and buffalo assembled to properly celebrate an ailing nobleman's expected death? What hilltop would the hosts and guests cut a swathe through to honor him? Who would care for his crazy old wife when she became a widow?

Or they might discuss another favorite subject among Lun Dayeh men: hunting. How many wild pigs had one longhouse chief's son and his friends brought home from the hunt last year? How many days had another longhouse hunting party been away and come back with nothing but one small mouse deer with almost no meat on him? Tales of hunts in the days of their own youth could spin out for many hours among this highly competitive group. Most of the leaders prided themselves on being good storytellers and some were brilliant animal impersonators. They all loved a good laugh at one another's expense. But Makahanap persisted. After each digression he would tactfully try to return the elders to the subject at hand. After just two days—a triumph of speed—he was rewarded with the group's decision: The *lun mebala* would do whatever was necessary to protect the Americans.

In that case, the district officer insisted, lowering his voice for emphasis, they would all have to follow his orders exactly and execute his instructions punctually. He would help as much as he could with supplying the Americans with food, firewood and other necessities, but the fugitives must be kept hidden. And, he emphasized, dropping his voice still further, the whole operation must be kept secret. Only after the headmen had agreed to this was Makahanap ready to face the Americans.

CHAPTER FOUR

"Good-bye, Mister"

W hen Phil and Dan awoke in the longhouse at Long Kasurun, they felt sore from sleeping on a hardwood floor cushioned only by a thin grass mat. They could hear a cock crowing below as they stretched and looked at the unblinking hosts who still surrounded them. They did not realize that the men of the longhouse had been up for a long time and had already eaten breakfast.

Phil and Dan were given big servings of rice again and, being hungrier than they were the night before, made a respectable dent in the white mound wrapped in the packet of leaves in front of them. Over breakfast they tried to convey to the Dayaks that they wanted to go back to the plane wreck. Although the Aussies had told them to stay away from a crash site, the airmen were hoping to pick up the trail of some of their crewmates. They must have felt they looked silly doing arm-and-hand imitations of an airplane crashing, but the Dayaks seemed to understand. Soon Phil and Dan were following the Dayaks out of the longhouse to the riverbank. They walked single file upstream along the muddy banks until the river was merely a creek.

Phil and Dan were young and fit, but they were no match for their barefoot guides in speed or endurance. Leeches covered the airmen's legs and crawled up inside their underpants, leaving trails of blood that showed through their trousers. The Dayaks also had leeches on their legs but showed no inclination to slow down because of them. Phil and Dan were wearing G.I. boots that slipped in the mud, making it difficult to go uphill and even harder to keep from sliding downhill. Phil was feeling the familiar pain of his shin splints. And he and Dan were still burdened by the items they had collected from the wreck, which they did not want to hand over to the Dayaks.

But at least it would be as hard for the Japanese following them, the airmen thought. And they realized they had another advantage. They were tall enough, especially Phil, to see farther above the dense brush than the Japanese probably could. Not that lack of visibility seemed to slow down the Dayaks. They were the best walkers the flyers had ever come across. Phil and Dan did not know that their Lun Dayeh hosts were renowned throughout the island as jungle walkers and mountain climbers, but they did notice how strong their leg and thigh muscles were.

On the way to the crash site, Phil, Dan and their guides came across a solidly built lean-to. The Dayaks gestured to Phil and Dan to go inside. There, astonishingly, were Jim Knoch, their flight engineer, and Eddy Haviland, the young nose-turret gunner whom Phil had helped out of the nose wheel hatch. For a brief moment, the Americans could almost forget their fear of the Japanese and their native guides' headhunting proclivities. In less than twenty-four hours, all the men who had jumped from the front of the plane were together again—except for Tom Coberly, for whom they had little hope. They did not yet know what had happened to those crewmates who had parachuted from the back of the plane: John Nelson, Franny Harrington, Tom Capin and Elmer

Philipps. But at least they could rejoice that half of the plane's surviving crew was reunited.

For an hour or more the airmen stayed in the hut and caught up with what had happened since they left the plane. Eddy, half blinded by the Plexiglas that had entered his eye, had fallen first into a tree where his parachute had caught, then had dropped a hundred or more feet to the ground after the chute came loose. He said some Dayaks had found him half limping, half crawling, protecting his almost certainly broken ribs, and had carried him on a litter to the hut where he found Jim, who was in good shape.

Jim took up the story. He, too, had landed in a tree and had half climbed, half slithered his way down to the ground, where the Dayaks had found him and brought him to the hut. Then, other Dayaks had appeared carrying a litter and set Eddy down on the floor next to him. When the two airmen realized they were hungry and brought their fingers to their mouths, the Dayaks had reached into the small reed baskets on their backs and brought out neatly folded palm-leaf parcels containing sticky white rice. The rice tasted like library paste, but Jim and Eddy had been so hungry that it hardly mattered.

The airmen would learn that the Dayaks had different kinds of huts they called *sulap*. One type was a lean-to that could be quickly thrown together to shelter three or four hunters for a night. A layer or two of sticks kept the hut floor off the ever-moist ground, and taller sticks or tree branches at the four corners held up a few layers of big palm leaves, which kept the rain out. But other *sulap*s, made of bamboo and reeds, were a bit bigger and were semipermanent, built on stilts. A family would stay in such a hut throughout the weeks of the rice harvest if the fields were too far from the longhouse. The airmen were now inside a hut of the more permanent type.

Rough-hewn and small as it was, its roof was high and it kept the men fairly cool even after the sun came out from behind the usual morning cloud cover.

Once the airmen had exchanged their news, Phil took out the first-aid kit he had recovered from the plane wreck and began to apply some ointment to Eddy's eye. It did not seem to help much, but they had better luck with the bandages Phil made from torn strips of parachute silk, which he used to bind up Eddy's ribs. Eddy, a smart, soft-spoken and stoic young man from suburban Maryland, found he could hobble alongside the others as they continued their walk to the plane wreck.

The next discovery was no cause for rejoicing. Hanging from parachute lines entangled in the upper branches of a tall tree was the battered body of Tom Coberly. The parachute was still in its cover and the pilot's clothes and body showed the effects of having crashed through the jungle canopy. Perhaps the parachute had malfunctioned or maybe Coberly, in his morphined state, had not been able to pull the cord. It was a shock for the airmen to see their leader like that, but it was not really a surprise. They knew there was nothing they could do for Tom now. The Dayaks made signs that seemed to mean that they would bury the body. Phil gestured that he wanted them to bring him back the parachute when they were done.

The survivors were submerged in contradictory emotions as they absorbed the fact of their pilot's death. They were genuinely sad and shocked. But they were also full of the rush of adrenaline that always seemed to follow the loss of a buddy in combat. Here they were, perhaps in grave danger, but at least they were still alive.

Soon the party reached the plane's fuselage. The flyers sat quietly a moment to contemplate the total wreck that the plane now was. Airmen generally feel that their planes are living things, but this one was clearly stone-cold dead. Fred's and

Jerry's bodies were gone: The Dayaks presumably had taken them away for burial. They all began poking through the debris to see if there was anything left worth saving, but Phil and Dan had found it all. The Dayaks urged them to move on, though they could not convey precisely where they meant to take the airmen next. The Yanks stood up wearily, as aware as the Dayaks were that the Japanese already might be looking for the fallen plane.

Their guides led them on a new path, and the airmen found it increasingly hard going as they tried to keep up. Walking through the jungle was not at all like strolling through a forest back home. Dark green and tan foliage surrounded them, blocking the view in every direction beyond a yard or two. Close-up, there seemed to be nothing but leaves, vines and stems, though the screams of a million insects assaulted their ears from all direction. The airmen had always heard that jungles teemed with life. If so, little of that life was visible in this one.

Pooling their limited knowledge of Borneo, the airmen were just as glad they weren't running across any animal life. Dan remembered from the *National Geographic* articles that the island was home to a great variety of snakes, from giant pythons and big king cobras to the small but even more deadly banded kraits, similar to the coral snakes of the Southwest. Somebody else, maybe Eddy—who also was a reader—remembered learning about honey bears with slashing claws nearly a foot long. The airmen also would have been half expecting to come across orangutans, such as they had seen in zoos, apes as big and strong as a man. Wary as these thoughts made them, the airmen pressed forward as best they could. Dan and Jim, glad to be together again, could walk with relative ease. But Phil was feeling increasing pain from his shin splints and Eddy, still blind in one eye and in great pain from his ribs, was breathless with the effort of moving fast enough to keep the Dayaks' slim backs in view.

The airmen were hauling their weapons and the items salvaged from the plane, including the one-man inflatable raft. Phil and Dan also still had their chutes; they wanted to be ready to spread the white silk out and signal their presence to friendly aircraft, if any appeared overhead.

Eventually the guides paused; they had reached their destination: a bigger hut on a hilltop in the middle of a burnt-off rice field. The Dayaks gave the men a few days' supply of raw rice and firewood and then slipped off into the jungle.

That evening was the airmen's first one spent trying to cook for themselves. They saw the light from torches in the valley and felt their own isolation. It was remarkable how far away the light from a fire could be seen. Afraid to draw attention to themselves from unfriendly men or beasts, the four barely spoke above a whisper. Using water from a nearby stream, they tried to cook the rice as fast as possible to prevent their fire being noticed. Their efforts were, in Dan's words, "pathetic." They had to force down the gray, soupy gruel. After dinner, time passed slowly as they lay in the dark. The damp air grew almost cold.

"No sign of rescue," Phil wrote in his diary the next day. "Natives very friendly. Food plentiful. Ed's eye a little better, ribs same. When Ed can move, we plan to travel river to coast."

Looking at his silk map of Borneo, Phil thought their best plan would be to go north to Kudat, on the northern tip of Borneo, to find one of the submarines that the briefer had said were supposed to be on the lookout for downed airmen. If they could not reach the Philippines by sub, maybe they could get there by one of the Black Cats (Catalina flying boats) that the briefers had said were based in several locations along Borneo's north coast.

They spent another long day in the hut, resting up and thinking of how to get back to their base. The following day, November 19, was notable for the sound of a plane overhead, but they could not see it well enough to tell if it was one of theirs or the enemy's. On November 20, another plane flew overhead: a B-24! It passed almost directly over them, so low that Phil thought anyone standing in the waist window would have seen them. The men scrambled to spread out their parachutes to make a big patch visible from the air, but no one onboard seemed to notice the splash of white or the men's frantic shouts and wild gestures. The plane passed from view; Phil and the others quietly refolded the chutes, hoping they had not drawn the attention of the Japanese or their collaborators.

A welcome break in their isolation came later that day. An old man from the longhouse where Phil and Dan had stayed the first night stopped by to see them. The man, like the other Dayaks they had met, was nearly naked, except for a loincloth. But today he also wore a black oval felt hat. It was as if Charlie Chaplin had come on the scene. Inside the hat was a newspaper. The Dayak let them examine it. It was a copy of the *Los Angeles Evening News* for February 19, 1939. It was their first new reading material since dropping from their plane and they read it hungrily. But how did their visitor happen to have it? The airmen shook their heads at yet another bizarre event in a world that had changed totally for them after they landed in the middle of Borneo.

Five days after their drop into the jungle found Phil, Dan, Eddy, Jim and their Dayak guides—who had returned with more food—trying to get help for their journey north to the coast at Kudat. Phil had found that some local words were like the Malay words on the survival kit's word list, and had managed to understand that the nearest town not in Japanese hands was called Long Berang. From what he could make out, it was not too far away, perhaps a day's travel downriver by dugout canoe.

Although the airmen were now letting the Dayaks help carry their things, the trek was still an ordeal. When they reached the river, Phil tried to figure out how to get hold of a canoe. He and Dan remembered that at the first shelter, with the green banana stalk, they had seen long, carved pieces of dugout tree trunks leaning against the walls of the hut. They told Jim and Eddy their idea and then managed by acting out a kind of charade to convey to the Dayaks their wish to go back to the first *sulap*.

It was a hard walk but the guides led them back to the right place; the hulls were still there and the airmen began to bargain with the Dayaks for one of the dugouts. But bargaining was something the Dayaks had done all their lives and the young Americans were greenhorns by comparison. Over the next hour or two, while a group of Dayaks from the rice fields gathered to watch, the airmen handed over fishhooks, the collapsible machete and much of the remaining contents of their survival kits. For good measure, Eddy threw in his Loyola High School ring from Govans, Maryland. Eventually, a deal was struck.

Next, they and their Dayak guides tried out the vessel on the river, but the trial set the Dayaks to laughing. The airmen had bought only the bottom piece of the longboat. Without the upper sides to keep the water from swamping it, their hull barely stayed afloat. The exuberance the airmen had felt doing something that might lead to their getting out of Borneo faded. They were hot, tired and itchy from sand flies and gnats. They had traded away just about everything they were willing to give up for this "boat" that was a joke. Still, there seemed nothing to do but keep to their plan of paddling to

Long Berang and hope for the best. They bunked down in the *sulap* for the night.

The next day, the airmen set out, along with two Dayak paddlers who were "laughing up a storm" as Dan recalls. Within a quarter of an hour, as the Yanks' half boat wobbled precariously around a bend in the river, a proper dugout canoe came toward them with its elegant sidepieces in place. Despite going against the current, this oncoming boat was moving briskly, paddled by a half dozen experts. There were a few Dayaks as passengers, but the place of honor was occupied by a man dressed in a dirty store-bought white shirt and wide-legged cotton shorts—the first set of Western-style clothes the airmen had seen on anyone in Borneo. As the boat drew closer, they could see that the man in the white shirt had curly black hair—not straight, like the Dayaks'—and pale tan skin. With his big sad brown eyes and a more protuberant nose than was typical for a Bornean, he looked like he might be Malay or Filipino, or possibly even Eurasian.

"Good-bye, mister!" they heard him shout.

It was William Makahanap, greeting the Yanks with one of the few English phrases he knew.

Makahanap, making his way upriver from Long Gavit, had seen the Americans from a distance and all he could think was that these were not soldiers, they were boys. As tall as they were, they did not look any older than Christiaan—and were probably not as mature. His heart sank. He had to wonder: Would they be able and willing to follow his orders? Could he trust them not to do something foolish that would cost them all their lives?

Makahanap was unused to acting bossy. It was not his style, and the Dayaks recognized his authority without his having to make a display of it. But he thought he ought to appear as masterful as possible to these white men. Once the two boats drew close enough, he immediately took charge, telling the Dayaks to moor the half boat and bring everyone to the Long Kasurun longhouse.

When the airmen reached the longhouse, Makahanap led them up the notched log onto the veranda and sat down with them across from the Long Kasurun longhouse chief, who, after the ritual exchange of greetings, told the D.O. how he had sheltered two of the foreigners the first night after they had fallen from the sky.

Drawing on his days as a mission teacher, Makahanap managed to get across to the airmen in a mixture of gestures and with a few English and Dutch words—and the help of Phil's Dutch/Malay/English word list—that he was a government official and that he spoke Dutch and Malay but not English.

He could sense the young foreigners' uneasiness. Perhaps his own doubts about the course of action he had embarked on were showing. He knew they must be hungry, and he had an idea how far the Dayaks' food was from the Americans' usual fare. With permission from the chief, he took food from the Lun Dayeh stores to prepare a meal of broiled spareribs, rice fried in pork fat, boiled pork and coffee with sugar. The airmen wolfed it down.

Although Phil found the official's gaze shifty, especially compared to the unblinking, forthright stares of the Dayaks, he wanted to trust this man who had made such a wonderful meal for them. In any case, he felt he and his men had no other option. He wrote out the names and ranks of the four airmen and gave it to the official. He also gave the man a typed description of their squadron's general mission, with the most important words in both English and Malay. Then he showed him the blood chit in Dutch that promised a reward to anyone who helped the Allied forces.

All this exchange of names and documents, not to mention the soothing effects of good food, produced a somewhat more cordial mood. Phil pulled out his silk map. With it and a map that Makahanap produced of the Dutch East Indies, Phil was able to tell the district officer about the successful battle of Leyte Gulf and that the airmen's home base was in Allied hands. Makahanap managed to convey that he came from Long Berang and had known American missionaries there.

The airmen tried to ask if there were still Americans living at Long Berang but could not understand the answer. Americans in Long Berang—that would be almost too good to be true.

Then Makahanap led the airmen back to the river, where they boarded his boat. Within an hour or two they moored at Long Gavit. There, with Busar's help, Makahanap arranged for a celebratory dinner to welcome the Americans. This time, Makahanap's adopted son, Christiaan, did the cooking: pork fritters, fruit, fried rice.

"If only G.I. chefs had recipes like this," Phil remarked. His and the other airmen's spirits rose as their stomachs filled.

After the flyers were sent off to sleep in a nearby hut, Makahanap again took out his map of the Dutch East Indies. By the light of damar resin torches, he showed the headmen where Morotai was and told them the Allies were based there. The Lun Dayeh elders could see that the Allied forces were not so far from them. They discussed the whole matter again for hours. Makahanap knew he must not rush, that he must allow the Dayaks plenty of time to turn over the subject in their minds. In such a discussion, everyone who had something to say had to say it. If the argument grew heated, there was always someone in the group—often one of the highest noblemen—who would play the clown, make faces and dance about or do animal imitations to make the others laugh and restore the group's equilibrium.

Finally, everyone seemed in agreement that the Americans should be hidden and protected. Makahanap then suggested that they all swear an oath so that nobody would betray the plot. The Lun Dayeh agreed. To seal the oath, the Long Gavit elders took a dog from the longhouse down to an amphitheater-like area nearby that had delicately carved and ornamented log seats. This was where the longhouse noblemen slaughtered their pigs and water buffalo for a big feast.

The men tethered the dog to a post and quickly slit its throat, catching the blood in a wooden basin. Everyone had to lick a small amount and smear a bit of the blood on his chest. This was the Lun Dayeh's most solemn oath. Makahanap knew that a man would think long and hard before daring to break this oath because it would mean his death. That fulfilling this oath might also lead to their deaths was a thought Makahanap kept to himself.

The elders eventually went off to sleep, but Makahanap stayed awake on the veranda. At midnight, when everyone else was asleep, he woke the four flyers and Christiaan. This was a time of day when no one would normally venture out of doors. Even hunters in the forest would stay inside their huts until just before dawn, to avoid the nocturnal wildlife that prowled unseen.

Makahanap and his son dropped the notched log down through the hole and led the airmen through the tall grass to the edge of the Kinaye River in front of the Long Gavit longhouse. There, the former mission aide held an evangelical prayer meeting such as he remembered Brothers Willfinger and Presswood doing, with "kneeling, sobbing and praying to

the Almighty God, asking His mercy, and pleading with Him
to spare us all." He wanted to ask God's blessing on this haz-
ardous enterprise, but he probably was looking also to bind
the airmen to him the way drinking the dog's blood had
bound the Lun Dayeh to him. He later remembered it as "an
unforgettable moment in my life."

He must have felt he had done the right thing when the
Christians from the longhouse, hearing the noise, came out
and joined them. The Lun Dayeh, with Christmas approaching, sang hymns into the dark to the tune of "O Come All Ye
Faithful" and "Silent Night." They sang a song to the tune of
"My Country 'Tis of Thee" that the Americans found com-
forting. The flyers sang their version while the Dayaks sang
theirs, to everyone's apparent satisfaction. But there was one
song unfamiliar to the Yanks that the Lun Dayeh appeared to
like even better. The chorus went:

> *Alla ngimet moejoe,*
> *Anid atjo; ngimet do' do'*
> *Ie ngimet moejoe,*
> *Alla ngimet moejoe.*

William (as Phil and the others were beginning to call Makahanap) had learned the English for it from the missionaries. It
meant:

> *God will take care of you.*
> *Through every day, o'er all the way;*
> *He will take care of you.*
> *God will take care of you.*

CHAPTER FIVE

Another Part of the Forest

After the dying copilot shouted, "Hit the silk," John Nelson had been the first to jump out of the plane. "The first part, when you leave the plane, is like stepping off of a porch. Next you hit the slipstream and then you realize what it is like being in a 150-mile-an-hour windstorm," he later said. After slowing down a bit, he pulled the rip cord but the chute stayed in its pack. Desperately throwing the rip cord away, he clawed at the flap until he got the chute out. The shock of its opening caused his antimalaria Atabrine tablets, his first-aid pack and a variety of small tools to fly out of his unbuttoned pockets. Fortunately, his .45 was in its shoulder holster and two clips of ammunition were in his flying suit.

Once he recovered from the shock of his chute opening, he experienced "a moment of silence and loneliness such as I have never had before or since." He could not see any of his crewmates, not even Franny Harrington or Elmer Philipps, who had been chuted up and standing just behind him. Above him, the plane still seemed to be flying. Had he jumped too soon? Below, some distance away among the seemingly solid cover of dull green mounds of treetops, he could make out a few plumes of smoke. Smoke had to mean human life of some sort. As the trees came up to meet him, trees that seemed to be on top of a mountain range, he tried to keep in mind where he had seen the smoke coming from. Then he crashed into a very tall tree. Unable to work his chute free, he managed to wriggle out of his harness and did a combined slide and fall a hundred feet down to the ground. His experience working one summer in the Idaho forests had been good for something after all.

It was midday, and the sun was at its highest. John crawled around in the undergrowth in the steaming heat, hoping not to surprise snakes or other dangerous creatures while he re-trieved what he could of his fallen gear. He did not find much. Then he started down the mountain alongside a small stream, heading in the direction of the no-longer-visible plumes of smoke. Though John found it slow going through the thick jungle, the stream beside his path gradually widened and led to what was clearly a river. By now, he had been tramping through the leech-ridden brush for a good five hours. A bit farther on, he could see a large native structure. But what to do now? He had heard from the Aussies about headhunters, and he did not want his own head to become one of their trophies.

It was nearly dark, so John decided to wait and watch be-fore taking action. Meanwhile, he tended to the leeches that were covering his ankles and the lower parts of his legs. He re-membered being told during the three days of jungle survival training in New Guinea that tobacco juice would make the leeches fall off. He chewed up a couple of cigarettes from one of the two packs that had survived the drop and tried spitting the juice on the leeches. This did not work.

He looked up from his ministrations to see a fierce-looking dark man carrying a spear outside the house a short distance away. The Dayak dropped his long weapon and bowed down. John called out to him in his best high school Spanish that he was an "Americano." After the initial shock of seeing each other had subsided, John pointed to his bloodied legs and feet. The Dayak (a Lun Dayeh, as John would learn) approached with his machete in hand and flicked off the leeches with the tip of the blade. He then grabbed a hunk of moss from a nearby tree and wiped the places on John's legs where the leeches had been. This cleaned the blood off and stopped the bleeding.

The Dayak led John up a notched log into the longhouse, some twelve feet above the swampy ground. (Though John did not know it, the longhouse was at Pa' Inau, in the northern part of the Krayan District.) It was smoky and dark inside the two-hundred-foot-long by fifty-foot-wide structure. The only light came from resin torches and cooking fires burning in the stone or clay hearths scattered about the floor of the one big room. There seemed to be about thirty men, women and children, and they were visibly excited by John's arrival. John kept telling them that he was "Americano." He took off his .45 in its shoulder holster and hung it from a peg on the wall before sitting down.

He had arrived at dinnertime. He was offered a place by one of the cooking fires and was given a lot of rice and a little bit of boiled greens and meat to eat. After eating what he could, he pulled out one of his wartime brown packs of cigarettes and passed it around. John could see that the gesture was greatly appreciated, although he mistook one old man for a woman and did not offer him a cigarette—a huge social error, he later learned, but one he was forgiven because of his foreignness.

As the evening wore on, John learned that these people knew a lot about foreigners from his part of the world because the Krayan District had been proselytized by North American

Protestant missionaries, whom the Japanese had murdered two years before. After terrifying the Dayaks and killing all the white people in the interior, the Japanese had gone away.

John learned this because, after dinner, the Dayaks brought out paper and pencil and a Malay/Lun Dayeh/English glossary the missionaries had left with them. To supplement this word list, the Dayaks kept pointing out things to John and giving him their word for it so he could write it down.

Using gestures as well as his growing command of the Lun Dayeh vocabulary, John tried to tell his hosts where he had come from. "I finally got them to realize that I had been in a plane that had flown over their village. They knew what planes were, but they could not believe that such a big person as myself could have possibly been in that small an object."

It was getting late, and his hosts stretched out a woven fiber mat by the fire, indicating he should sleep there. Exhausted by trying to sort out the jumble of hopes, fears and memories of this extraordinary day, John quickly fell into a deep sleep, not waking till the roosters underneath the longhouse started crowing at dawn. The Dayaks were sitting around him, waiting for him to wake up.

John conveyed to his hosts that he wanted to find his crewmates and that he had left his parachute up in the top of a tree. By midmorning he was part of a hunting party looking for his crewmates, his parachute or, ideally, both. Some of the dozen or so dogs that seemed to have the run of the longhouse came, too.

Although John had worked one summer in the high forests of his native northern Idaho, he had no experience of the oppressive damp heat or dense vegetation he now faced. "After we had spent about six hours going up and down impossibly steep and slippery mountains, we returned home empty-handed and I had a greater respect for the jungle."

Late in the afternoon of his third day at the longhouse, John heard a big commotion outside. Going out onto the veranda, he saw a hunting party returning with a short, stocky middle-aged man he immediately recognized as Franny Harrington. Franny was bruised and bloody from having slipped and fallen on the steep, wet paths in the jungle. His blond hair was covered with leaves, and his legs and feet were eaten alive by leeches. His flight suit was in tatters, and he was limping because one of his boot heels had been ripped off by the force of his parachute opening. That blast of air had also taken his sidearm, but he had managed to hold on to three or four clips of ammunition. Usually a tough-acting bantam cock of a guy, Franny was now weak and dehydrated after three days without food or water.

The Dayaks recalled that their dogs had made a lot of noise the night John had arrived, but they had not gone out to investigate. Nobody who can avoid it goes into the jungle in the dark, they explained to John. That is why the log ladders are pulled up at night. They surmised that the noise that had alerted their dogs must have been made by the new airman walking somewhere nearby, along the stream past the longhouse. They had found the man they called "Efrani" some five hours' walk downstream, and they had had to almost carry him home.

The next three or four days were spent nursing Franny back to health while both flyers tried to learn more about how to manage life among the Dayaks. The food was not too bad, if you didn't mind plain rice. Sometimes there was even a bit of fresh fish from the river or meat from a successful hunt. The women caught fish in shallow parts of the river or in puddles in the rice fields, often with just their hands, and the men caught bigger fish in the deeper water, using big fish traps made of wood, leaves and vines.

The biggest problem for the airmen was the total lack of privacy. With no walls between households, there was no way for anyone in the longhouse to be alone or out of sight, and certainly no way for these very interesting foreigners to screen themselves from view. John had already learned that urination and defecation were done along the edge of the veranda. He and Franny tried not to think about the fact that the pigs, which were being fattened for an eventual feast, were quick to swallow whatever fell down to them. The two Americans learned how to take a bath in the stream without exposing their bodies to the frank stares of the Dayaks. They noticed that their bath time tended to bring out many of the long-house women, who chose just that moment to draw water from the stream for cooking.

The Dayaks often sang in the evening after dinner. John and Franny could sometimes recognize the tunes of Protestant hymns, though the words were in another language. When it was the guests' turn to entertain the others, the two airmen had fun singing old camp songs and army ditties. There was a Sousa marching tune that was especially dear to John, who had tried and failed to get through Air Force officer cadet training, because of slightly below-standard eyesight. It be-gan: "Be kind to your washed-out cadet, for he may be your aerial gunner." But the song the Dayaks liked best was John and Franny's rendition of "When der Fuhrer Says We Are the Master Race" from the repertoire of comic songwriter Spike Jones. John and Franny's exuberant sound effects invariably brought the longhouse down with laughter.

The two men kept asking for news of their crewmates; Tom Capin and Elmer Philipps ought to have landed nearby. But nobody seemed to know what had happened to them, much less to the guys in the front of the plane.

A week or more after Franny's arrival, the season for visits

among the longhouse people began; the harvest was done and
the heavy rains had not yet started. The Dayaks told the Yanks
that one of their teachers, a native of Menado in the northern
Celebes who had been recruited by the missionaries to be
their aide, would be coming to see them.

His name was William Mongan, and John and Franny
found him to be a small, gentle man in his late thirties or early
forties, with a little knowledge of English and a lot of sympathy for their plight. He explained that he had been left behind
by the departing Kemah Injil missionaries to try to keep the
Christian spirit alive in the Krayan valley. The Japanese had allowed him to stay, with his Menadonese wife, Maria, and their
ten-year-old son and two little girls, so long as they did nothing disloyal to the Japanese or the Co-Prosperity Sphere. They
had not seen any Japanese since. The Mongans had lived and
worked first at the Kemah Injil school in Long Sempayang in
the southern Krayan, but they were based now at the village of
Long Nuat, to the north, on the Kemalu River. Mongan explained that Long Nuat was one or two days' walk (less than
one day's walk for a Lun Dayeh) east from Pa' Inau, the longhouse John and Franny now regarded as home. Mongan insisted that the airmen should come with him to Long Nuat.
They would be better off with him, he said. He and his wife
knew how to care for them.

As John and Franny prepared to leave the longhouse the
next day, their hosts were clearly not eager to see them go, and
loaded them up with reed mats and other gifts. The airmen
bade a reluctant farewell. Something like love had developed
between them and these generous-hearted longhouse people
of the Krayan.

By the time they actually got under way, it was midmorning, the beginning of the hottest part of the day. As with virtually all the Lun Dayeh mountain trails, the one they took

was steep. The air was damp and the path was muddy, except when it went through the middle of a stream, several of which had currents so strong that there was a real risk of being swept quickly downriver if one slipped on the rocky bed. Franny's age and infirmities were beginning to tell.

When they stopped for the evening, the Dayaks threw together a temporary *sulap* for the night. It seemed almost magical the way the Dayaks could collect vegetation from very nearby and quickly turn it into a lean-to. A fire was started to cook their rice and to temper the mountain chill—and to keep clouded leopards and honey bears from approaching.

Long Nuat, reached the next afternoon, was a surprise to the airmen. It was almost as if they were no longer in Borneo. There were several Western-style buildings there, chief of which were the Kemah Injil church and the Mongan house next door. There had been no Japanese or other outsiders there in two years, so Mongan invited them to stay with him and his family. Maria cooked for them the recipes she had learned from the American missionaries back home in Menado: fried chicken, pork roast (from animals that had not been raised under a longhouse) and, best of all, fried bananas for dessert, washed down with limeade sweetened with sugarcane juice.

Being at the Mongans' felt to John and Franny like staying with relatives, and the airmen naturally became involved in the activities of the church. There was some kind of service every day, and Sunday morning service was an all-village event. Mongan would ask the airmen to tell about their lives, while he translated for the congregation. The Yanks were happy to participate, and they would join in the singing of "Onward Christian Soldiers," "Down by the Riverside" and—a hymn new to them—"Fishers of Men."

While staying with the Mongans, John and Franny finally learned where they had landed and where they were now—

the northwest part of Dutch Borneo, near the borders of Sarawak and (British) North Borneo. Looking at a map, John saw they were near the center of the island, with the Pacific Ocean to the east and the South China Sea to the west. But the real question was: Where was the war?

CHAPTER SIX

Becoming Lun Dayeh

A week after jumping into the jungle, twenty-one-year-old Sgt. Tom Capin was alone and near death. At six foot five and a good 240 pounds, he had always cut an imposing figure, but now he was gaunt from dehydration and lack of food. Even his red hair, which stuck to his forehead in the overwhelming heat and damp, was beginning to fall out.

Tom had been the last to jump from the back of the plane, taking with him only his small handgun and a shoulder bag of ammunition. He had landed in the upper branches of a tall mahogany tree and climbed down using the vines that clung to it. Despite his height he was agile, and getting down from the tree presented no problem. Aside from some surface shrapnel wounds on his leg, his body seemed sound—nothing was broken.

Tom had no idea where in Borneo he was. He thought he heard the sound of airplane engines, and "I had this crazy notion that if there was a Jap base I would steal a plane." He had not walked far before he realized that the noise he heard was not an engine but rather water falling from a stream higher up on a nearby mountain.

With his handgun at the ready, he set out through the jungle, searching in vain for food, drinking river water that gave him diarrhea and trying to locate the other crew members.

A city boy, he would not have known how to catch fish or reptiles or other animals even if he had been able to see them. At night he slept under the trees on the damp earth. He could hear birds and other creatures calling in the mornings, but visibility was very limited by the tall underbrush that spread in all directions, even along the water's edge. Like his crewmates, he had bitter thoughts about the training he had received on how to survive in the jungle. It had all been designed for New Guinea, a very different world from the one where he now found himself.

"By the eighth day, I was too exhausted and starved to care what became of me; I knew I could not stand another mile of jungle. I found a well-fortified spot where I could hold off onrushing Japs for a while, set my clips nearby and loaded my gun." After sitting there a while, with insects crawling on him and biting him—the sand flies and the leeches were the worst—he felt he had to find somebody, either friend or foe, to bring an end to his untenable situation. So he let off one round from his gun. "If the Japs came, I intended fighting as long as possible, and make sure they would never take me alive. All Air Force men in the Pacific knew what had happened to American airmen forced down in enemy territory."

The only married man of that B-24 crew except for Franny Harrington, Capin thought of his wife, Betty, and how she would react when she got the inevitable telegram about his being missing in action. He could see her with that telegram, and the image so upset him that he tried his best to dismiss it. He listened hard in an effort to distinguish the different noises of the jungle, in case someone was approaching. As quietly as possible, he picked off a dozen leeches that had climbed up inside his trouser legs. He used his fingers like tweezers so as not to have the loathsome blood-bloated creatures break off under his skin and cause an infection. He noticed that his legs were covered with blood.

He stood up and tried to remain perfectly still. He was waiting for the enemy to find him when he heard someone call out: "Ho American!"

With no more warning than that shout, two natives in loincloths carrying blowguns and machetelike swords appeared out of the bush. Tom gave a weak "Hello." The Dayaks dropped their weapons immediately, smiled and ran forward to shake hands. Greatly relieved, Tom dropped his gun and gladly grasped their dark outstretched hands.

Appearing to recognize the cause of his weakness, the Dayaks took down the woven-reed pouches they wore on their shoulders, brought out leaf-wrapped packets of sticky rice and offered him some. They also had tobacco, which they rolled in a banana leaf to form a crude cigar for him. Tom relaxed as he savored his first food in a week, but he froze when one of the Dayaks reached into a little box for a match to light the cigar. The box was decorated with the emblem of the rising sun. With no Bornean vocabulary, Tom tried to learn from his rescuers where the matches had come from, but he could make nothing out of "their native gibberish."

After a short rest, when he was strong enough to walk, he let his rescuers lead him to a small hut in a clearing. No one seemed to be living in the hut, but he was given a piece from a length of sugarcane that had been stored there. Trying to eat the cane was like chewing on the business end of a broom until his laughing guides pantomimed that he should just suck the sweetness from it and then spit out the fiber. The sweetness was wonderful and gave him a fresh spurt of energy. Next, the Dayaks walked him farther along in the jungle through scratchy, dense brush, as tall as he was, that pulled at his hair and clothes. Mercifully, they soon emerged near a much bigger native house, high up on stilts above the river.

Climbing up the notched log to the veranda, Tom found this thatched-roof house full of people. They talked loudly among themselves, and every once in a while a woman or man would come up and touch him on the arm. At first he flinched at the contact, but soon he realized what an oddity he must be to the local people.

"I learned later that I was the first white man many of them had ever seen. One woman threw cobs of corn on a fire, and was feeding me the most delicious roasted ears, when Kibung, one of the natives who had first found me, refused to let me have more."

Kibung, a long-limbed young man with complicated black rosettes tattooed on the top of his muscled shoulders, took charge of Tom's welfare from then on. He supervised what Tom ate, letting him have only rice gruel seasoned with deer meat until Tom's system could stand more solid food.

Tom quickly saw that Kibung knew precisely how to care for a fugitive. It would take some days to learn why: Kibung was a fugitive, too. He was from the famous Iban tribe, the island's most notorious headhunters in the old days, the original "wild men of Borneo" and the biggest tribal group in Sarawak, the British-run territory over the mountains to the west.

The Iban were mostly found in parts of Borneo nearer the coast, not as far inland or as high up as the Lun Dayeh. The Iban were (to Western eyes, at least) a stunningly handsome people, for the most part taller and longer-limbed than the hill people, but, like them, they had nearly hairless bodies and honey-colored skin that was often tattooed. Unlike the socially hierarchical Lun Dayeh and other upriver people, however, the Iban are uncompromisingly egalitarian. They are also famously competitive and self-confident.

Kibung, who radiated Iban self-confidence and ease with this foreign red-haired giant, had fled over the border after killing some Japanese occupiers in his home village, which was in the Limbang District of northwest Sarawak, not far inland from Brunei Bay. Tom never learned exactly why Kibung had killed the Japanese, but the Iban were among the most anti-Japanese of Borneo's ethnic groups, being impatient with people who required subservient behavior of them. The frequent Japanese order that the natives bow before them would have been cause enough to engender murderous Iban thoughts. But this past year, as food had grown scarcer, the Japanese demands for the Iban's rice, and their commandeering of the young men for labor and the young women for sex, had made them utterly intolerable.

Once over the border into Dutch Borneo, Kibung had kept going inland until he found himself on the Pa' Ogong, a stream that joined the mountainous, uppermost reaches of the Mentarang River. He eventually came to the Pa' Ogong longhouse. There he met and married a Lun Dayeh woman. Their baby boy was now six months old.

While the headmen and the village elders were at the longhouse, Kibung and his wife and baby and many of the other longhouse residents were in individual family huts in the midst of their rice fields at this time in the farming year. They were weeding (chiefly women's work) and trying to protect the rice crop from the birds that feed on the rice grains and the fruit bats that steal the flowers and fruit from the fruit trees. Both men and women fought to protect their rice crop as it grew, trying to keep all sorts of vermin from feeding on the plant roots.

Tom was brought by Kibung to a hut near the one Kibung shared with his wife and baby. A woman—who he later learned was the sister of the longhouse chief—was designated to cook for him at the longhouse and bring food to his hut. She was able to speak Malay because she had attended a mission school for two years. That gave Tom the opportunity to use the Dutch/Malay/English word list that had survived his parachute drop.

Kibung would invite the American every evening after dinner to come to his hut so he could teach him how to speak and understand Lun Dayeh. Kibung's first instructions to Tom had been to stop wearing army boots and go barefoot. As Tom understood it, Kibung's pantomime said: "Boots mean white man; barefoot, just another Lun Dayeh." This was not strictly true. Tom's feet were too big and his toes not splayed enough for a Lun Dayeh, but at least his footprints would not leap out to a Japanese or coastal collaborator the way boot or shoe prints would have done.

The Iban, having learned the Lun Dayeh language himself so recently, was an ideal teacher. While his wife and baby slept, he would sit with Tom next to the fire and teach him one word or phrase at a time, using gestures and acting everything out. Tom found that vocabulary alone could take him further in this tongue than in Indo-European languages, there being no genders, cases, tenses or plurals to complicate matters. With Kibung to help him, Tom made rapid progress.

Tom was, in a sense, benefiting from the fact that his parents had been dirt-poor throughout much of his childhood. During the Great Depression, his father, a hardworking electrician, would find himself without a job each time the plant where he was working closed down, obliging the family to move. Tom had learned quickly how to adapt to new surroundings.

One of their homes, in Fort Wayne, Indiana, had been destroyed when the St. Mary's River overflowed its banks. Tom recalled being rescued by his uncle Wilbur, who came by their house in a beautiful car with the water up to the running boards. His parents took in another uncle to help pay the rent, and he stayed with them for years, accompanying them from house to house. Another time, he and his parents moved in with his grandmother until a family quarrel forced them out on their own again. Once, they lived in a mostly black neighborhood where Tom found that most of his black neighbors "were much the same as I was."

All through his childhood, Tom had few friends because he tended to try to disguise his unease as an outsider by being bossy. But he had been a good student. He had managed to complete high school despite all the moves, which had put him a year behind. Thanks to his excellent physical coordination, he had excelled at running and swimming, solo sports that rewarded endurance. His mother was a conscientious housekeeper and his father was a handy amateur carpenter. Tom had absorbed from them some useful survival skills, though those skills had not included how to find food in the jungle.

With Kibung to guide him, Tom was determined to be "the best Lun Dayeh I could be." He noticed that at mealtimes while he sat on a mat on the floor with his legs stretched out before him, the others squatted on their haunches, with their posteriors an inch or two off the floor. This crouching position, which looked so comfortable when the Dayaks did it for hours at a time, was less so for Tom. It took long practice before he could stay that way for more than a few minutes without his legs and thighs aching.

It was easier to learn how to eat the way the others did, using only two or three fingers of the right hand, with a stiff leaf as a plate and a gourd as a serving spoon. Eating what was served him was harder, but he soon found he could manage swallowing one of the Lun Dayeh delicacies, roasted grasshoppers. Tom found they weren't that bad if he didn't think about what he was eating. The hunters would bring back meat from a dozen different kinds of jungle animals. The meals might also include a bewildering variety of strange fruits and vegetables. Few of them appealed to Tom, but he did his best, quickly realizing that good manners required his appearing to eat a lot and enjoy it, though one was expected to end the meal with a little bit of rice left uneaten.

Rice was the mainstay and sometimes the only food in a meal, and he could never work up a hunger to match the enormous mounds the chief's sister brought him. Still, he found even rice could be appetizing when stuffed with raw sugar into a section of bamboo and cooked to a perfumed tenderness in glowing charcoal.

The next problem for his hosts was how to clothe a giant. Tom's uniform had not survived the week of continual dampness in the jungle; it was torn everywhere, the fabric was full of mold and rot, the seams full of lice. An extra-long loincloth was made for him out of bark cloth. Kibung taught him how to put on this loincloth and how to undo it in the river when he bathed, twice a day. He watched Kibung and learned to keep his genitals modestly from view while he cleaned himself with suds from a particular tree bark. He then wound the long cloth again around his waist and between his legs before leaving the water. In the heat, the loincloth dried quickly.

The sun was not very strong in the early morning and near dusk, and there was generally so much rain and cloud cover that Tom soon learned he need not worry about sunburn, redhead though he was.

Often, when Tom went to the stream to bathe or swim, Kibung's baby—now called Tom in the airman's honor—would cry to come with him. The baby had been covered with sores when Tom first had seen him, but now, thanks to some Palmolive soap from Tom's flight kit, the baby's skin was smooth.

It warmed Tom's heart to see the baby reaching out to him. Tom had taught swimming at a YMCA, though never to anyone so young as little Tom, and he would bring the baby along in his arms and play with him in the water if there seemed to be no danger of the Japanese or their henchmen coming by.

There were no signs yet of anyone nosing around looking for Tom, though Kibung said he had heard that the Japanese were looking for four other airmen who had landed on another branch of the Mentarang, near Long Kasurun. Tom was anxious about the safety of his crewmates, but he did not want to leave Pa' Ogong where he felt so well looked after.

Kibung, who worried that he himself still might be a target of the Japanese, was anxious to show Tom how to hide in a thicket without being seen or heard. First, though, he had to show Tom how to get around in the tropical mountains. It seemed almost impossibly complicated to Tom. The Lun Dayeh never seemed to take a straight path, except up and down hills.

Kibung could sympathize with Tom's problem. The Iban were not great walkers like these Lun Dayeh hill people. The Iban preferred to travel by dugout canoe and had good, wide rivers that made such transport relatively easy. The rivers here were full of rocks and waterfalls and the land had many unexpected ridges and gullies that twisted back on themselves.

With few exceptions the hilltops all looked alike to Tom, as did the rest of the landscape. Kibung, who had recently been taught by his father-in-law how to find his way in this unfamiliar landscape, eagerly passed on what he had learned to Tom. He warned Tom that in this terrain it was easy even for Lun Dayeh to get lost or at least to engage in long, heated arguments about which was the right way to go. He pointed out the different kinds of soil under their feet. It was soft and slimy and covered with moss if they were higher up the mountains and sandy if they were lower down. He made Tom notice where the stones were big and few or small and many. He said that often the name of a river or stream or mountain accurately described what the place was like, so that the more Lun Dayeh words Tom learned, the easier jungle travel would be.

In the midst of what seemed to be total wilderness, Kibung would occasionally point out a fruit tree only to warn Tom that the fruit of that tree could not be taken without permission of the owner. How did he know that someone had claimed that tree? Kibung would point to the mark of ownership, a main stem with a branch twisted perpendicular to it at the base of the tree. Or the owner might have formed a cross with two sticks and stuck it into the ground at the foot of the tree. If Tom and Kibung came across a tree with four sticks intertwined to form a square, Kibung would smile and offer Tom a fruit if it were ripe, saying that the sign meant the tree belonged to the nearest village and anybody from that village could help himself to the fruit.

Kibung showed Tom different kinds of plants and explained their uses, some to make sleeping mats, some to make string or rope, some to make baskets, some to make fish traps. He showed Tom a sago palm. Its leaves could be used for thatching, while the pith of the young palm shoots made a delicious vegetable and the mature pith could be boiled to make a starchy pudding. He said that the sago palms were so prized that an indignant owner of a tree had once speared a young man for taking some of the shoots without permission.

Once, when they saw a beehive up in a tall tree, Kibung said it was a pity that they could not risk attracting the attention of possible enemies by using a torch to drive out the bees. He said that anybody was free to take a single honey hive. But if there were many beehives together, high up on a very tall, straight tree, collecting them would become the object of a joint expedition by the men of the village.

Kibung put his greatest effort into making clear that if Tom could learn to be still and quiet in the jungle without being distracted by leeches or ants or flies or mosquitoes, he would be invisible to the Japanese or people in league with them, such as the Malay police sent upriver occasionally to spy for Mustapa al-Bakri, the Malay administrative official based in Malinau. He said Tom would also be able to hunt animals this way.

Tom practiced keeping still, and the day came when Kibung took him hunting. They headed for higher ground, bringing a few of Kibung's dogs with them. Tom had had German shepherds as a boy, a compensation for having no siblings, but these dogs were much wilder. If Kibung put their noses in a puddle where a boar or a barking deer had been, the dogs could track the animal for miles. When the dogs located the prey, they would chase it tenaciously until the animal was exhausted or fell into a trap. Kibung showed Tom how to make a camouflaged pit with bamboo splinters hidden underneath and how to coil a tree limb like a spring that, when tripped by unsuspecting prey, would drive a bamboo spike through its body. They would sometimes have success by merely shaking a tree trunk long enough to dislodge smaller animals, usually a big-eyed slow loris or a small monkey. But often the best way to catch an animal was to stay perfectly still in a place where they knew an animal was in the habit of coming, such as one of the upriver salt springs. Kibung told Tom that if the hunter was in his hiding place by midafternoon, he could hope to see a whole parade of animals come to the salt spring before nightfall. First would be the birds, then the monkeys and gibbons coming down from the tall trees and, finally, the land animals: mouse deer, wild boar, barking deer and maybe a honey bear.

When they set off to hunt together, Kibung strapped a machete onto a holster that hung from a woven beaded belt around Tom's hips. He said no Dayak man left home without his knife. He also instructed Tom in the use of a blowpipe (*sempit*). Seven feet long and made of ironwood with a quarter-inch-diameter hole hand drilled down its length, this blowpipe was a work of art. It had been made by a Punan, one of the small, pale-skinned nomads from the far interior jungle who slept in trees, had no houses and were known to have almost no material possessions but who, nonetheless, were the very best in Borneo for making fine blowpipes and beautiful woven-grass mats. As usual, the blowpipe that Kibung gave Tom had an iron spearhead lashed to the end of it. As Kibung would explain, a Dayak always carried a blowpipe with a spearhead when hunting animals, but he would carry a real spear if he were hunting for human heads.

To complete Tom's hunting equipment, Kibung gave him a bamboo case to hook onto his loincloth. He opened the case to show Tom a handful of needlelike darts, each about ten inches long. Before Tom could reach for one of them, Kibung held up his hand and told him to hold the dart by its wood or cork end, and never to allow the dart's poisoned tip to touch his skin. With an almost silent puff of breath, a man could force one of these darts down the core of the blowpipe and as far as 150 feet. It did not matter where the dart hit the animal or how big the animal was. The poison, made in secret rites from herbs and the bark of a special tree, was so strong that the prey would almost immediately experience convulsions and paralysis. Death often came even before the hunter could make his way through the brush to the stricken animal. Using the blowpipe was a good way to kill game because the poison did not affect the meat—except in the area near where the dart entered, which was cut out during butchering. If Tom had remarked that it would make a good weapon of war, Kibung would have made clear that the blowpipe was used only on game, never on man.

When Tom grew proficient at hiding in the forest and using the *sempit*, Kibung and a couple of his neighbors took Tom out with them to hunt wild boar. Using their dogs, they trapped a young boar and Kibung killed it. By late afternoon they made their triumphal way home. Meat was a special treat. Except for the chickens, the Dayaks never seemed to eat the meat animals they kept under the longhouse: the pigs and the goats, or their free-grazing water buffalo. Kibung explained that those animals were fattened up by the Dayaks and kept for a big party—a funeral, a child's naming day or, in the old days, when they brought back a head.

Thanks to the successful hunt, several families would have boar meat at dinner that night. Tom looked forward to eating meat with his rice, but this was not the only reason for his sense of well-being.

Looking back on the day, Tom experienced a moment of pure elation. Barefoot, loinclothed, moderately competent in the Lun Dayeh language, able to stay still enough so as not to scare away game and carrying deadly weapons he knew how to use, Tom had been able to act like a man again, in control of his own life. He had not felt like this since he had jumped out of the B-24 more than a month earlier.

CHAPTER SEVEN

A Letter from the Japanese

Makahanap rose well before dawn the morning after the prayer meeting by the river. Then he, Christiaan, Phil, Dan, Jim and Eddy and their Lun Dayeh boatmen hastened into his dugout canoe and glided downstream until they came to where the rushing water foamed past rocks so big and dangerous that even this proper longboat had to be portaged along the riverbank.

Farther downstream, Makahanap could see the airmen enjoying themselves as the *perahu* picked up speed. Speed demons all, the young men smiled into the wind as it slapped their faces. Makahanap did not tell them how often boats were overturned or swamped on this stretch of the river.

By midmorning, with the current running quickly, they were at Long Berang. Makahanap had been thinking throughout the trip about how to keep the Japanese and their spies from knowing of the airmen's presence. At this time of day, the waterfront was empty as usual. He took the men quickly to his house. Luckily, Binum, Yakal's wife, had arrived while Makahanap and the others were upriver meeting the Americans. Like Yakal, Binum was someone Ama could trust to be discreet and helpful.

Binum, like Yakal, had been the Makahanaps' student. She had then gone to work in Malinau for some years for a

Dutch family, a contact made through the Makahanaps, after it had become evident that she and Yakal were not going to have children. Ama and Mama had been glad to help Binum find such a good way to deal with the shame and sorrow of being barren. Also, she could earn money that her husband could use for the church once he became a pastor; each Kemah Injil church group was supposed to be self-financed. When her Dutch family left Malinau just before the Japanese came, Binum had gone to help her elderly parents. But now her husband had called her home to him and she came gladly.

For Makahanap it was a pleasure to see Binum again. Among the inland hill people of Borneo, paleness of skin is admired, as is slimness and height. Binum was nearly five foot eight, with a light, Chineselike complexion. With her long blue-black hair neatly tied up in a chignon like a Javanese, she had the kind of looks that both the hill people and the Dutch of Malinau admired. But Makahanap was sure she was a good girl, and it was clear to all that she had stayed faithful to her beloved Yakal. She was too old at twenty-five to receive unwelcome advances from any Dayak man, and she was efficient at cooking and cleaning for Westerners. If she agreed, as Ama knew she would, she could be the go-between from his household to the police barrack where he planned to hide the airmen.

Across the river and accessible by a swaying bamboo-and-vine footbridge secured to trees on the riverbanks, the police barrack had been empty for years. The "Malay" (the Borneo term for coastal Muslims and immigrant Javanese) police had run away when the Dutch left.

Makahanap was relieved to see the airmen behave politely when he introduced them to his family and Binum. The airmen were clearly well brought up, and Makahanap saw no trouble ahead in letting Binum take care of them. Sitting in his dining room, they seemed to him less like soldiers than like children at a birthday party as Binum and Mama served them a meal at a proper table with a tablecloth. They seemed impressed by the finger bowls—something Mama always insisted on when chicken was served. Tensions all but disappeared as the airmen relaxed in the warmth of Mama's kindness and in the gracious courtesy of the beautiful Binum. The men scraped the plates with their forks until there was nothing left—a bit of bad manners in East Indies circles but, as Makahanap, his wife and Binum all knew, a sign of appreciation among white people. The soldiers held their forks and knives in the same odd way that Brother Willfinger had done, switching the fork from one hand to the other to cut something, but otherwise they ate like Dutchmen.

As soon as the meal was over, Makahanap took advantage of the quiet—the active adults of the longhouses had already gone to the rice fields, their vegetable gardens or the hunt, and the children were at school—to walk his charges across the swaying vine bridge and deposit them in the police barrack. This big, bare, wooden shed had been built by the Dutch administration. It had housed the police who had worked for the district officer. Makahanap gave the airmen the food Mama had assembled for them, together with some of his own old sarongs and undershirts.

In a mixture of Dutch and hand gestures, Makahanap tried to convey to his guests that they must stay quiet and out of sight. He planned never to contact them in daylight or if anybody in the village was awake. The Japanese were just a few days downriver.

Makahanap was no doubt glad that the soldiers had been too dazed to notice a dazzling white American-style clapboard house near the barrack that could have been at home in suburban Connecticut. The Presswood house had been built in the early 1930s by Ernest Presswood, the first North American Protestant evangelical missionary to live in Long Berang. Ernest Presswood had been one of a handful of missionaries from the U.S.-headquartered Christian and Missionary Alliance (known locally as the *Gereja Kemah Injil*, literally, Church of the Gospel Tent) who had introduced Christianity to this part of Borneo. Presswood and the other Kemah Injil pastors had quickly learned local languages and had converted nearly half of the longhouses in the Mentarang and Krayan districts in less than a decade before the Japanese had come upriver and taken the white foreigners away. The Presswood house, though empty now, had housed visiting North American missionaries in normal times, and it would have been a good place to lodge these Americans but it was too conspicuous to serve as a shelter for fugitives.

Makahanap brought back the airmen's dirty uniforms for Binum to wash by the big flat rock in the river in front of the Presswood house. He told her to do it when no one was around and repeated what he had already told Yakal, that she should tell no one about the white men.

Of course, someone did know about their presence in Borneo—the *ken kanrikan*, to whom the D.O. had sent his report before heading upriver to meet the airmen. Now the D.O. was pleased to learn that the *ken kanrikan* himself was on his way to Long Berang. It suggested that his boss had risen to the bait.

If Makahanap had guessed right, the Japanese administrator would take his time getting to Long Berang. The *ken kanrikan* would hope that by the time he reached the district seat any shooting would have stopped, and the airmen would be all trussed up for him and ready to be brought down to Malinau. The timing of the Japanese official's travels suggested Makahanap's theory was correct, but he tried not to be overconfident. With the Japanese, he could never be certain.

Three days later, Makahanap's informants told him that the Japanese administrator was less than a day away. This was closer than he had expected. The Americans had to be moved immediately, but where to?

One factor weighed heavily in his decision: Thanks to the missionaries, the Christianized Dayaks were convinced that the road to hell was paved with lies; any lie, for any reason, was simply intolerable.

An illustration of how absolute the ban on lying was involved the preacher Brother John Willfinger. When the Japanese had ordered Willfinger to come out of hiding and give himself up, the thirty-two-year-old American had done so, even though his friends had urged him not to. To explain his decision, Willfinger had sent an open letter saying that he had come to Borneo to bring the truth to the people there. If they had to tell lies to save his life, he would have failed them— "drag[ged] them into sin." Makahanap had held the very letter in his hands. He would never forget its message, nor would any of the Dayaks.

Makahanap admired such honesty but he could not emulate it. Try as he might, it was not in his nature. Sometimes telling the truth did not get you what you wanted or needed. Had he not won Mama through an act of deception? A series of deceptions? No time to think of that now.

But Makahanap knew he could not ask the people of the Christianized longhouses to be untruthful even for the best of reasons. If Japanese soldiers were to ask the Christian Dayaks about the airmen's whereabouts, they would get a truthful answer.

Among the D.O.'s headmen, however, was Pangeran Lagan, the resourceful and reliable longhouse chief who was not yet a Christian. (Among the Lun Dayeh, social hierarchy counts for a great deal, and so no one in Lagan's two longhouses at

Long Metuil would convert to Christianity until Lagan had done so.) Makahanap had just seen Lagan in Long Gavit, and the pagan headman had unhesitatingly licked the dog's blood. Makahanap could safely put the young Americans in Lagan's hands. The former mission employee had to smile at the irony of it.

Around 3 A.M. on the fourth day of their confinement, the Yanks woke up in the Long Berang police barrack to see a group of armed Dayaks walk in noiselessly, accompanied by William Makahanap. The Dayaks had crept in as silently as if they were approaching a rival longhouse where they hoped to kill someone and take his head. This time, however, their aim was to escort the foreign soldiers to their longhouse village.

The party's departure was nearly as silent as its arrival. The Americans, despite wearing boots, did their best to imitate the stealthy movements of their Dayak guides. Before they left, Makahanap managed to convey to Phil that the lead Dayak, a tough-faced man with a confident stride and a piece of cotton cloth bound around his head like a crown, was Pangeran Lagan and that he was a friend of the Allies. He presented the departing Yanks with a bottle of ketchup, some tea, coffee, sugar, salt, peanuts and raw rice—partly as a farewell gesture, partly as an effort to keep the soldiers from being too great a burden on the Long Metuil villagers.

It was still pitch-black outside. In the dark, walking through the jungle was safer than traveling by canoe, but it was still a novelty for the Lun Dayeh.

It was the time of night when the owls stopped sounding and the jungle grew almost silent. The badgers, civet cats, lemurs, tarsiers, great hill otters and the many kinds of bats had retired for the night; even such nocturnal birds as the nightjar and the frogmouth were quiet. The Dayaks' main concern in this unaccustomed nighttime walk was the danger of crashing into the den of a honey bear.

The Americans were even less accustomed than the Dayaks to walking through a jungle in the dark. The *pangeran*, sensing everyone's unease, decided to wait for sunrise in a house belonging to a close friend of his, the Chinese trader Ah Tin. Ah Tin came to the door and let them in without waking his wife or children. As the dark grew more transparent, birds began calling and the party started on its way north.

The Dayaks spotted a young barking deer across the river, on the good side of their path, fortunately, auguring well for their journey. Had it been on the wrong side, these Dayaks, being believers in the old religion, would have made a long detour around it or even returned to Long Berang to stay another day and night and avoid ill fortune for themselves and their longhouse.

Dayak hunters often used their dogs to kill a deer, but that method is noisy. Sometimes a hunter presses his mouth against a leaf and imitates the deer's cry, luring the animal within reach of a blowpipe's poison-tipped dart. This time, seeking to move fast, with as little noise as possible, the *pangeran*'s men quickly fashioned a trap from the underbrush along the path they expected the deer to take. The trap worked; they finished off the struggling creature with a blow from a machete. They butchered the deer quickly and roasted it on a fire. Eaten with the cold, sticky hill rice the Dayaks had brought with them, the grilled meat gave them all strength to continue their journey in the increasing heat of the morning. There were several hours of hard walking ahead of them through the mountains to Long Metuil.

Back in Long Berang, Makahanap was relieved to have the Yanks gone so that he could concentrate on playing his big fish. Summoned by a message November 26 from the *ken kanrikan* to come downriver to Tamalang, the next village below Long Berang, the district officer replied in a deceptively truthful letter that he had moved the Americans from Long Berang to Long Metuil. Choosing his words carefully, he wrote that Long Metuil would be a good place to ambush the airmen, and that Long Metuil's headman was under orders to keep a close eye on them.

Makahanap hoped that the *ken kanrikan* would feel safe enough to come upriver when he read that the possibly armed Yanks were no longer in Long Berang. He was therefore pleased to see the *ken kanrikan* arrive by dugout canoe the next day, accompanied only by two local messengers. The Japanese administrator announced that they would be joined by the district officer of the neighboring Krayan District and the headmen from several nearby villages. Makahanap, who had already been in contact with his Krayan District counterpart— he was also a Christian from outside Borneo—managed to avoid serious conversation with his Japanese superior until his colleagues were present. When they were all finally assembled in Makahanap's Long Berang office, the *ken kanrikan* asked in Malay for ideas on how to capture the enemy airmen.

The Krayan D.O., having been coached by Makahanap, took the floor to say that his colleague, the district officer for Mentarang, would surely be the best person to advise the *ken kanrikan*, would he not? Was it not Makahanap who had met the airmen, had brought them to Long Berang and had arranged for them to go on to Long Metuil? But Makahanap, bowing low, hands at his sides the way the Japanese had taught them, said he must defer to the *ken kanrikan*, whom he had kept informed of every step along the way. And now—Makahanap smiled at the company—the Japanese administrator was here "in our midst, to decide what to do."

The *ken kanrikan,* seemingly torn between wanting to take any credit for success and to avoid blame if something went wrong, continued to insist that Makahanap tell him how to capture the airmen. But Makahanap kept shaking his head gently and saying that he, in his lowly position, could merely make suggestions. Ultimately, he said, it was the *ken kanrikan* who had to make the decisions and accept the responsibility.

Having read in his superior's face that he had won this point, Makahanap went on to try to win the next. He had noted with satisfaction that the *ken kanrikan* had arrived without a military escort. Now he asked him when they could expect the Japanese soldiers to arrive. The *ken kanrikan* replied stiffly that it was not certain the *heitai*s would come. "Only if it were deemed necessary," he added.

Makahanap tried not to gloat. The decision not to involve the soldiers could only mean that the *ken kanrikan* wanted to keep for himself all the credit with Japanese headquarters in Tarakan for having captured the Americans, rather than share the honor with the army. In the cheerful certainty that his advice would be ignored, Makahanap then said that it would be better if the *heitai*s could get there soon because capturing armed Americans was a soldier's job, not a civilian's. The *ken kanrikan* did not deign to reply.

So far, so good, thought Makahanap, who then spoke at length about how difficult life in the jungle must be for these soft young Americans. He argued that the Yanks, if they did not fear being killed immediately, as they would be by the *heitai*s, would probably be ready to surrender to a Japanese civilian official, such as the *ken kanrikan.* Then, as if the idea had just occurred to him, he added: "If they surrendered to us, that would be better than to be hunted by the soldiers. If they surrendered to us, there would still be the possibility of surviving in an internment camp, but not if they had to face the *heitai*s."

He broke off, as if embarrassed. "I would like to explain this to the Americans but I can't speak English. But what if the *ken kanrikan* himself were to write a letter inviting them to give themselves up?" Makahanap knew his boss was vain about his mastery of English. Afraid to say another word, he waited for the *ken kanrikan*'s response.

He did not have to wait long. The Japanese leaped up, called for pen and paper and quickly wrote out a letter, which he ordered the pair of Malay messengers to deliver to the airmen at Long Metuil. The letter read:

> *Mr. Soldier:*
> *I am Japanese. I think you did fillful yours mission.*
> *You permissive and pistol gun give to this man, it*
> *consent and come to Long Berang.*
>
> *R. Iwasaki.*

The *ken kanrikan* told the messengers to use two canoes so they could bring the airmen back to Malinau, via Long Berang and Tamalang, properly supervised. Meanwhile, he would take a third canoe and go back to Tamalang. (He was never comfortable in the presence of the district officers.)

The messengers reached Long Metuil the next day and brought the administrator's letter to Pangeran Lagan, explaining what it was about. The Lun Dayeh chief told them in broken Malay that he could not deliver the letter himself. The foreigners had guns, he said. He did not dare approach them. (People who knew Pangeran Lagan would have been amazed to see him acting like a timid, incompetent government servant.) But, he added, if the messengers wished, they could give him the letter and he would try to see that it reached the

Americans somehow. The messengers should wait on the front veranda.

Pangeran Lagan went inside and gave the letter to one of the longhouse people with instructions to pass it to the airmen. He could not read the letter nor write a message, and he did not want to risk being seen with the airmen right now.

When the letter reached Phil, he didn't read farther than the first sentence. He and his crewmates snatched up their belongings, rushed to the back veranda and headed into the jungle. They moved awkwardly, encumbered by the things they were carrying, including their parachutes. As they ran out, one of them dropped a metal piece of their stricken plane that he had kept as a souvenir. It clanged against the veranda boardwalk.

The messengers heard the noise from the back and thought they were being fired on. They fled from the veranda at the front of the longhouse and hid in the brush nearby. They were not soldiers, after all, merely messengers.

The escaping Americans had no idea where to go but were determined to do anything to avoid being caught by the Japanese. Phil, however, had not taken into account how badly his legs were hurting. His shin splints were acting up dreadfully. His doctor would have told him to avoid stressful activity until the pain subsided. God knew this running uphill was stressful activity, and he had just completed the exhausting trip from Long Berang. Partway up a mountainside an hour north of Long Metuil, he called out to his companions. He was in terrible pain and could go no farther. Go ahead, he told them. He would deal with the Japanese by himself.

Flight engineer Jim Knoch had been very quiet since landing in Borneo, but he still saw himself as the ranking enlisted man. With the same cool judgment he had brought to other emergencies, he estimated the chances of any of them surviving if one of them were left behind to be tortured by the Japanese. He knew from reliable stories circulating in the Pacific theater that the Japanese were not taking fallen airmen as prisoners.

Jim drew his gun from its holster and calmly turned it on his superior. He told Phil to keep walking. If Phil insisted on staying behind, he would not be left alive. Dan and Eddy, who had stood by while Jim defied officers over matters of far less importance, raised no objection to his defying one now, when all of their lives depended on it. Phil slowly stood up and resumed walking.

The messengers came back to the front veranda and waited several hours for the airmen to surrender, but finally they took their canoes and went back to Long Berang. After they left, Pangeran Lagan and a few of his men followed the airmen's trail. Although the airmen had several hours' head start, the Dayaks soon caught up with them. It was child's play for experienced Lun Dayeh to track the fugitives. For one thing, the airmen's boots left distinctive marks in the mud. Nor did Lagan worry about the Japanese or their collaborators following him and his men. No other Bornean, much less a Japanese, could track a hill man through the jungle unless the hill man wished to be followed.

Lagan and his men approached the soldiers cautiously. Having no language in common with the strangers, they could not explain that they were there to help. Then Pangeran Lagan finally thought to order his men to throw down their weapons, and the moment of tension passed. The winded airmen stood and watched with relief as the *pangeran*'s men built them a lean-to and then moved away silently in the direction of Long Metuil. A couple of other men from the longhouse discreetly approached toward evening to bring the Yanks a little food cooked by the *pangeran*'s wife in secret. The Dayaks showed the Americans how to use lengths of bamboo for glasses and cups.

The next day the airmen were moved for the eighth time in two weeks. Now they were taken to a better hut, which Lagan's men had built for them nearer the Long Metuil longhouse. The hut was very well hidden but there was no water nearby. Some Dayaks brought them more food, some water in earthenware pots and some firewood cut into logs. The Yanks tried to start a fire the way they had seen the Dayaks do it, by striking a section of bamboo with a broken piece of porcelain until sparks began to smolder in a handful of pulverized wood bark. The Dayaks would then place the smoldering bark within a pile of more coarsely shredded bark and blow on it gently until it flamed. But the airmen couldn't manage it, not even Jim. Eventually they went back to using their few matches that would still light in the overwhelming dampness. In any case, fires were to be used rarely, since they could be seen from a distance. The *pangeran* had managed to make the airmen understand that they should make fires only at night, when everyone else was indoors. The airmen readily accepted this advice. They had noticed how far away a plume of smoke was visible above the jungle brush.

The following day, Phil, who had been keeping a daily diary, announced that today was November 30, Thanksgiving Day. Their dinner consisted of boiled rice, boiled cassava root with sugar, pineapple, two K-ration "dog biscuits," a quarter bar of chocolate and, as a special treat, an American cigarette apiece. Phil wrote in his diary: "We four have a lot to be thankful for."

CHAPTER EIGHT

Polecat Gulch

Makahanap quaked inwardly as he saw the *ken kanrikan* turn red in the face with anger. He had been dreading this meeting the whole way down to Tamalang with the empty-handed Malay messengers. He bowed low before his boss and mumbled a reminder that he had warned him to wait for the *heitais*.

The Japanese administrator contemptuously dismissed his subordinate and demanded to see Pangeran Lagan. The next day, the *pangeran*, still wearing his cloth bandana, arrived at Tamalang. The men with him were fully armed, although he himself left his weapons out of sight. A well-built man with an air of command that perhaps reflected his status as a prolific headhunter in earlier days, Lagan put on an expression of innocent puzzlement as if to ask the *ken kanrikan* what he could have expected, after having sent the Yanks a letter warning them of the Japanese presence.

The *ken kanrikan* was beginning to be suspicious and had his informers try to find out if there was collusion between the pagan longhouse chief and the former mission teacher, but no one would betray the *pangeran*. Meanwhile, in Long Berang, Makahanap took great care about what he did and said in front of others. His caution, already so ingrained in him, increased after he learned from visiting Lun Dayeh that a planeload of

American airmen had been killed in a gun battle with the Japanese after crash landing near Brunei Bay the same day that Phil and the others had parachuted into Borneo. (That was the squadron's lead plane, with Major Saalfield aboard.) Some thirty Japanese had reportedly been killed in the fire-fight, a toll that Makahanap reasoned would make the occu-piers more determined than ever to hunt down and kill any remaining enemy aviators.

Still more worrying was the news from various Dayak vis-itors that there were three other American airmen now scat-tered about the Krayan District, no doubt from the same plane as the four he was protecting. Makahanap's informants told him that two were up north at the Lun Dayeh village of Long Nuat, where they were being cared for by another Celebes-born mission aide and his wife, William and Maria Mongan. The third American airman was described by the Dayaks as a redheaded giant. The Dayaks said the giant was now staying at the Lun Dayeh longhouse of Pa' Ogong. That accounted for three of the four men whom Phil had asked his help to find. No word on the fourth as yet. Meanwhile, Phil and the others were in the *pangeran*'s care.

But by now, Phil and the others with him were not sure they were in anybody's care. After Thanksgiving, five days went by with no sign of the *pangeran* or his helpers. The four airmen, too weak from lack of food and water to talk much, even if it had been safe to do so, began wondering if they were simply going to be left to die. By December 4, after another B-24 passed above their hut hidden in the thick jungle without see-ing their spread-out parachutes, the airmen were out of water and almost entirely out of food.

To their great relief, they had a visit the next day from a few of Pangeran Lagan's people, who had come to help the

Yanks move to yet another shelter. Weak and ill though they were, Phil and the others immediately saw that the new location was much better. Nestled within a small canyon, it was invisible from any distance. Not only did it have water, but the Yanks could also make a fire there without fear. It was really well hidden; even sunlight had difficulty trickling down into the canyon. The only way the airmen could see the sky was by looking straight up.

Aided by gesture, the Lun Dayeh let the airmen know that more than fifteen Japanese had come upriver to look for them. They pantomimed the need to stay out of sight and make no noise. After the Dayaks left, the Americans tried not to think about their helpless dependence on the natives. Although they were immensely grateful for the food and shelter they had received from the Dayaks, they had no way of judging how trustworthy they were. Would they still keep the Yanks hidden when the Japanese began to put pressure on them? After all, this wasn't their war.

Under Phil's guidance, the airmen devoted themselves to making their new home as comfortable as possible. They guessed that they might be staying there a while, so they gave it a name—it may have been Eddy who suggested it—Polecat Gulch, after a place in Al Capp's L'il Abner comic strip. Phil recalled that American airmen who made an emergency parachute jump from an aircraft were ex officio members of the Caterpillar Club, and they constituted themselves the Polecat Gulch branch, called "Club Borneo."

Meanwhile, in Long Berang, Mama was continually asking Ama if he was sure the young men were being fed properly. Makahanap felt nearly overwhelmed by the responsibilities that had fallen to him. He felt he could not take on any more fugitives for the moment, so he kept to himself the news about the three other crewmen and merely asked the Dayaks to tell those protecting the three airmen that they should encourage their guests to stay well hidden, because he was certain that the *ken kanrikan* from Malinau would be sending Japanese soldiers to the Mentarang and Krayan districts.

Once again, Makahanap was right. On December 5, thirteen *heitai*s arrived in Long Berang. Leading them was a chief officer (*taicho*) named Takahashi, and he was accompanied by the *ken kanrikan*s from Malinau and Bolongan prefectures and a Japanese/Malay translator named Sakata. With three such high-ranking officials heading this mission, it was clear to Makahanap that the Japanese were taking the matter seriously.

At a dinner for the senior Japanese visitors that night, Binum served at table, just the way Mama and her Dutch employer had taught her. Through the interpreter, she overheard Takahashi praise Makahanap for his good work. The chief officer then said, "The Americans have escaped temporarily but surely they will be captured. I hope that the Dayaks under your supervision will know what to do."

But Mama privately assured Binum (who had come to like the airmen when she had been in charge of feeding and caring for them at the police barrack) that Ama would never allow the Americans to be captured and brought to the Japanese. Binum's husband Yakal explained to her that the Japanese did not like walking in the jungle, particularly while trying to find enemy soldiers known to be armed. He predicted that the *heitai*s would not hunt for the Americans, so long as they could send someone else to do it. In the morning, Binum was relieved to see that the *heitai*s stayed in Long Berang, sending the Dayaks off in their stead.

Every day for the next six weeks, a number of the Long Berang Dayaks were paid, solemnly accepting a Japanese-occupation paper guilder from the soldiers, and moved off quickly and purposefully to the east, in the direction of Mount Basakan, where the Japanese said they thought the Americans might be hiding (and where the Dayaks had earlier left bits of parachute cord, boot prints in the mud and other signs to encourage the *heitais* in this belief). But as soon as it was safe to do so, the Dayaks followed the D.O.'s advice to turn off the path and go to work in their rice fields or vegetable gardens and spend the night in their garden huts.

The thought of the Japanese army paying the Dayaks for this deception could not but amuse the D.O. and his family and would have seemed comic to Pangeran Lagan as well, were it not that the presence of Japanese in the area made it dangerous for him to get food to the airmen.

None of the airmen knew what the Dayaks were doing on their behalf. Up in Pa' Ogong, however, Tom Capin was realizing that Kibung's training in the art of concealment had been accomplished just in time. By mid-December, Kibung received word that the Japanese were searching for downed American airmen and were using as their base not only the prefectural capital at Malinau but also the district seat at Long Berang, just a few days' walk downriver from the village of Pa' Ogong.

Kibung, unaware that Makahanap had been informed, assured Tom that nobody beyond the village knew where he was. Nonetheless, Kibung stressed, Tom must lie low for the time being and spend much of the day hidden in the bush. Tom did not need urging. Added to his instinct for self-preservation was his determination not to expose Kibung, his family or his village to Japanese reprisals for sheltering him.

Over the previous month, Tom's self-confidence had grown as his competence increased. "The enemy was within twenty feet of me on Christmas Day and didn't know I was there. Kibung had taught me well. I could always hide in a thicket, and my backup—my back door—was always the river. I knew if I could reach the water alive, they would never catch me. I swam in the river all the time."

Word that there were enemy spies in the neighborhood and Japanese nearby had sent Tom and Kibung into the bush that day, interrupting the best meal Tom could remember having eaten since leaving the Morotai air base. He hoped his crewmates were also enjoying Christmas somewhere and he thought especially of John Nelson, the youngest of the crew and the mascot, who had jumped out of the camera hatch before he had.

For hours Tom and Kibung squatted in the damp, itchy underbrush. But now Kibung decided that he and Tom could leave their hiding place, after seeing what he took to be an enemy patrol go past hours earlier. Since their conversion by Kemah Injil missionaries more than ten years earlier, the people of Pa' Ogong regarded the Christmas feast as a big event, not to be interfered with by a contemptible enemy. "Let's go back home," the Iban said, standing up. "I kill if they come."

Farther north, in Long Nuat, word came to William Mongan from visiting Dayaks that the Japanese had sent patrols through the Krayan and Mentarang districts looking for fugitive American aviators. Mongan and his church people rushed John and Franny to one of the small empty huts in the rice fields. They gave the Yanks mats to sleep on, as well as rice and other essentials.

Franny and John were later told by the Mongans that the Japanese or their Malay agents had appeared in the area, but that the Dayaks (presumably without telling an actual untruth) had convinced them that no Americans were there. John and Franny had stopped wearing boots when they were in or near the village and had left no obvious trail for outsiders to follow.

Being stuck inside together while the rain fell ceaselessly proved an unexpected hardship for the two men. They had so little in common. Franny was a short, garrulous, profane, citified, middle-aged Irish-Catholic postal worker from New Bedford, Massachusetts, who would get out his rosary four or five times a day and repeat the prayer in his flat New England accent but would casually sprinkle his ordinary conversation with the usual G.I. obscenities. John was a tall, very young, quiet, polite, outdoor-loving mountain man. Franny, a staff sergeant, had joined Coberly's at the last minute, replacing the crew's young tail gunner. He had been looking for a way to get on a combat mission, not because he was eager to fight but because he had figured out that he was going to remain overseas until he had enough combat missions under his belt. His war-weary attitude was at odds with John's more idealistic outlook. During the long days and evenings in the abandoned hut in the empty rice field—especially when the mosquitoes and the sand flies were biting—John and Franny would sometimes say things to each other that they then had to try to forget.

Learning how to survive on their own took a lot of time at first, but it provided welcome occupation for their otherwise empty days. The Dayaks cut them a great pile of firewood and left sacks of hulled rice but warned them not to expect a return visit until the Japanese or their spies had left the area. It took John and Franny several attempts before they learned how to cook rice, beginning with learning how to keep a fire lighted with their dwindling supply of matches. There was a nearby stream for water and bathing, but many leeches lurked in the tall grass along the water's edge. Luckily, the men came across nothing more deadly, although they temporarily had to cease swimming when there were crocodiles around.

During daylight, when there were not more important tasks, they often played cards, using a deck they had made from paper the Mongans had given them. Hearts was their main game, although it could get quite adversarial. Reading was more peaceable, but they sorely lacked reading material. John had managed to hold on to his G.I. New Testament, endorsed by President Roosevelt. He read it through, including the psalms and hymns at the back. At first, he dog-eared it daily in an attempt to keep track of the calendar. When he realized that he had missed a few days, he gave up the effort. What difference did it make what day it was, since they weren't going anywhere?

The nights—twelve hours long at the equator—seemed even longer. They used as little light at night as possible, not only because their stock of resin torches was small but also to avoid calling attention to themselves. Sitting in the dark after their unsatisfactory dinner, they told each other their entire life histories; Franny's years gave him a distinct advantage.

Illness soon gave them other things to think about. When their Atabrine wore off—they had had their last dose before boarding their B-24 on November 16—they both came down with malaria. As John recalled, "One minute we would be so hot that we could hardly stand it. Next, the chills would come on and we would be shaking so bad the whole hut would tremble." These bouts were typically preceded by days of strong feelings of self-pity and depression, and would come to an end in three or four days, leaving them slightly weaker but otherwise back to normal. In the extreme humidity, they were also prone to skin infections that would not heal. They had rare bouts of dysentery, but these were very frightening, bringing excruciating intestinal cramps and dehydration.

Uncomfortable as their time in the empty hut was, their next place of shelter proved to be in some ways worse. When the Mongans learned that some of the Japanese had moved to Long Sempayang in the southern Krayan District, their Dayaks moved John and Franny into a small longhouse in a remote valley above Long Nuat. There was only one old man living in this house, and he seemed to be sort of a hermit. He tolerated the newcomers' presence, but the utter filth of his surroundings alarmed them. He tried to cook for the airmen but his rice was always burnt and his way of preparing chicken was to pull off the fowl's big feathers, singe the rest of the bird by holding it over the fire and then throw the singed carcass into a pot of boiling water to cook for a while.

The old man lived with about a dozen hunting dogs, and one day he returned with the dogs and the carcass of a wild boar he had caught and killed. The airmen watched as he took his knife and butchered the wild pig right in front of the hearth a foot from the snarling, snapping jaws of the dogs. Occasionally he would throw a scrap of meat or gristle to one of the Cerberuslike creatures. When he wanted to wipe his knife clean, he would grab the nearest hound and wipe the blade on its rough coat before proceeding with the carving. The airmen were hesitant to touch this meat but found that boiled pig liver tasted pretty good.

For Phil, Dan, Jim and Eddy at Polecat Gulch, December 7, the third anniversary of the Japanese attack on Pearl Harbor, came and went, and the airmen's food was running out again. At this point, morale was so low that Jim later recalled "if I had had the strength to reach for my .45 I'd have blown my brains out." By December 10, when a few Dayaks came again with food, the airmen had been entirely without food for forty-eight hours. The young men, who were of an age when they might normally be expected to wolf down a quart of ice cream standing at the fridge, passed the time making up lists of their favorite foods. Phil's was a chocolate malted milk shake—so luscious, rich and satisfying. Thinking of it, he could almost feel the bubbles of the foaming liquid against his lips. As each man described his dream meal, the others listened appreciatively, drawing some satisfaction from imagining the smell, texture and taste of the dish described.

Phil and the others searched for anything edible within the canyon, where they felt relatively safe. They tried gathering ferns and roots and boiling them, the way their survival book recommended, but they felt more ill after eating the plants than they had felt before from hunger. They did not find fish in the stream, and there was nothing nearby that resembled the plants the veteran Australian airmen in New Guinea had pointed out to them. The Aussies had gone on at length about the versatility of the coconut palm, but the men had not seen one since dropping into the hills of Borneo.

On December 12, one of their usual Lun Dayeh visitors arrived at Polecat Gulch in the early evening with rice, tobacco and firewood. He was a young man whom the Yanks called Skeezix after an American comic-strip character whose hair stood out from his head. Pointing, Skeezix made it clear to the airmen that the Japanese were looking for them upriver and downriver. For days afterward, the Americans stiffened involuntarily at every unusual sound coming from outside their narrow canyon.

Their supplies had run out again by the time the Dayaks came back a week later, but the new supplies were worth waiting for. "Pork, a big bag of rice, bananas, sugarcane and ten ears of fresh corn. Delicious!" Phil wrote in his diary. Sugarcane at first puzzled the airmen; they did not realize that they should not try to eat the fiber. The first time they were given sugarcane and tried to swallow it, the Dayaks found their efforts hilarious. The airmen took the laughter at their expense in good part, but they hated being so dependent on others for their every need.

All soldiers in a war feel a certain separation from the real world, but here in the jungles of the Pacific there was nothing to remind them of anything they had ever known, only what one historian has called "a green and threatening mystery." Moreover, with no radio or other reliable source of news, the airmen were utterly cut off from what was happening in the world they knew.

Again and again, Phil thumbed through the USAAF-issued jungle survival pamphlet he had taken from the plane. It was supposed to deal with precisely their present situation, but he and the other men found it an infuriating document, with its airy pronouncements that "good food and good water are fairly plentiful in the jungle if you know where to look for them" and "wood is plentiful, and even in rain forests comparatively dry wood can be found hanging in the network of vines and rattans." They eventually found a use for it: its pages, cut in two, made a good deck of cards. Phil and Dan taught the others to play bridge and sometimes they played pinochle, as they had done during slow periods on the air base at Morotai.

Other times, they varied their entertainment with a game of gin rummy or hearts, although hearts is a game where ganging up on one person is encouraged, and sometimes this led to bad feelings within the group. Later on, picking out lice from the seams of their disintegrating garments—their boots had already rotted away—proved a productive way to spend a few hours each day.

Eddy, who could see out of both eyes now, would have given up his favorite meal to have been able to find something new to read. He was the only Easterner of the four and although he liked them all, he had little in common with the others. He missed John Nelson who, though also a Westerner, was the same age as he and had been his companion for off-base adventures back in California.

An account by each of the four men of their lives up to now provided some entertainment for the others, but not much. They were not the type of young men to feel comfortable unburdening themselves of their deepest desires, fears or family secrets. Phil and Dan were guarded in their choice of subjects and words. Coming from privileged backgrounds, they had grown up believing that it was good manners to assume the vocabulary of the common man as protective coloration, and to avoid standing out from the crowd. If one of the army's primary functions is to regiment men and make them as alike as possible, in World War II it succeeded. The American forces in World War II comprised, in the words of one acute participant, Paul Fussell, "the largest, most uniform army ever fielded by the United States."

Phil Corrin had grown up the only child of an Englishman from the Isle of Man who had immigrated to California and married Ruby, a rancher's daughter with a zest for life that she passed on to her son. Phil's father had landed a job early in his California days in the print shop at Bullock's, a Los Angeles department-store chain, and had gradually worked his way up to vice president of the company. Twenty-one-year-old Phil, though not as ambitious as his father, was a natural if diffident leader. Tall, fair and slim, he had been looked up to by his friends since childhood. He had just been voted president of his college fraternity before he left to join the air force. Phil would never have mentioned any of this to his crewmates. He merely said he wanted to get back to college, though he still had not decided what subject to major in. After college, he thought he might go into advertising but he wasn't sure.

Phil could be decisive when he needed to be but he did not often take a leading role; he preferred encouraging others to do well. Now he prompted the others to talk about their plans for the future when the war was over.

Radioman Dan Illerich never liked to talk about himself. He enjoyed reading and loved to play chess with his father, a civil engineer with the state of California. Describing himself as "not much of an athlete," he had still been chosen to head his high school air force cadet program—where he had tried in vain to keep the authorities from removing Japanese Americans from the corps. When he was at Sacramento College, where he had joined the enlisted reserve corps while he waited for a West Point appointment, he had attempted to learn cribbage but not bridge. He was still at the stage of regarding girls more as friends than as sweethearts, and would not talk about them. The only thing even vaguely personal he would tell the others was that his grandfather had invented a burn ointment and that he was torn between wanting to become a pharmacist to exploit his grandfather's invention, and wanting to go into the restaurant business. Everything about food interested him hugely at the moment.

Jim, who was keeping constantly alert for danger and thus was very quiet, may have been thinking of his girlfriend, Maggie. Five foot two and 112 pounds soaking wet, Maggie, the child of Yugoslav immigrants, had caught his eye when they were both fifteen-year-olds growing up in the same Sacramento neighborhood. The day he met her, he had gone home and told his mother he had found the girl he would marry. Maggie was taking a lot of convincing, but Jim was confident he would win her over if he ever got out of Borneo. He would have died rather than tell his mates about his feelings for her, but he would admit to dreams of owning a cattle ranch where he could be his own boss and have lots of land and not too many people about.

Eddy, who was hiding from the others the amount of pain he still felt from his broken ribs, was even quieter than the others. Pressed by Phil to speak of his plans after the war, he said he wanted to get back East, to Maryland or Washington maybe, and find a good office job where he never had to be out of doors again, except possibly for a game of golf.

Phil, the only officer of the four, wore his rank lightly, which was fortunate, given the attitude of the other airmen. Perhaps because they were so close in age, and also perhaps because most of the crewmen had started out planning to be officers, there had been from the beginning a feeling among the enlisted men that they were every bit as good as the officers. The officers, for the most part, had shared that view; certainly Phil did. He bore no grudge—quite the reverse—for Jim's having forced him to continue walking the day they fled Long Metuil after the Japanese letter came.

This egalitarian view had already become clear during their training as a crew at March Field. The four officers were in the habit of jumping into Tom Coberly's Ford the moment they had any free time and heading for Los Angeles. Partway through their training there, Jim and Dan, the two enlisted Californians, asked: "How about letting us ride, too?" Although officers and enlisted men were not supposed to fraternize off-duty, Coberly and the other officers agreed to give lifts to town to any enlisted men of their crew with passes. Later, when the crew was transferred to Hamilton Field, near San Francisco, Dan had invited all of them, including the officers, for a day at his grandparents' house near Oakland.

Jim, with his father's strongly worded views on bosses and bureaucrats still ringing in his ears, had an attitude toward rank that was openly confrontational, almost hostile.

One memorable time when all the squadron's crews had been assembled in the Morotai briefing room, Jim had called out in a loud voice to an overly rank-conscious officer, "Hey, you need to go take a shit. You look a little full in the face." On that occasion, Jim's crewmates had not known where to look.

The airmen sitting in Polecat Gulch liked to recall the time when they had taken part in what, in effect, had been a mutiny. It had been brought about by an announcement that the newly arrived trainees, unlike their predecessors, would not be given ten days' furlough after their March Field training was done. Instead, they would go directly to Hamilton Field and wait there for dispatch overseas. Coberly's was among the crews to be affected by this elimination of home leave. Most of the men had not been able to get home to their families in more than a year, and they were all incensed at the new measure.

Cannily making use of the army regulation that stated that no one could be ordered to fly against his will, the entire class of new trainees had gone to the commanding general of the air base and said, in effect, "No leave, no fly." They did not wait for an answer before taking off for their homes. The general, recognizing the limits of his options, revoked the objectionable ruling and did not punish the men except to delay their promotions.

Jim, of course, had pushed the powers of a mutineer to their limits, by turning up dressed in civvies at the Sacramento home of a horrified Dan Illerich. Being out of uniform while officially AWOL was grounds for court-martial, and Dan and his parents had urged Jim to go home and put on his uniform, which he grudgingly did.

The airmen liked to think back on that mutiny. They had, by a combined force of will, made the AAF back down. That victory was a stark contrast to their situation now, where they were powerless, and there was nothing to do but wait through the onslaught of biting insects for whatever William and the Dayaks would do for or against them.

Christmas Day was miserable at Polecat Gulch. It had been six days since they had had visitors. Christmas dinner consisted of the last bit of rice and their last four squares of chocolate. At the end of the meal, Phil passed out the last four American cigarettes—saved for this occasion and disappointingly foul tasting because of mildew. The men smoked them nonetheless.

But the next day was better. The flyers had three Dayak visitors who brought rice, cassava root, sugarcane, bananas, coffee, sugar, salt, fresh fish and tobacco. Five days later, the Dayaks were back with more rice. The following day was New Year's, and their Long Metuil visitors arrived in the afternoon with rice, bananas, roasted peanuts and tobacco. The Yanks had been in Borneo six weeks by then and were pretty weak from their poor diet and lack of physical activity, but Phil tried to keep their spirits up. He wrote in his diary: "Happy New Year and it certainly will be a happy one for us and our families." The Dayaks were clearly doing their best to help make it so, with six surreptitious nighttime visits to the Yanks between New Year's Day and January 18, despite their constant warnings that the region was swarming with Japanese soldiers.

Since the Yanks at Polecat Gulch had no idea of their benefactors' names, they invented monikers for them. In addition to Skeezix, there was Alice the Goon, whose torso earned him the name of a hulking cartoon character. And then there were Fido, who was small and wiry, like a dog; Old Chris, who had come the day after Christmas and who the airmen later found out was one of the aristocrats of the Long Metuil longhouse; and Charles Atlas. There was also Indigestion Joe, an older man so named because he twice insisted on bringing them moldy pork rind and urging them to eat it. Later, the airmen learned that he was chief of a nearby longhouse. The other regular visitors were the Butcher, another longhouse chief, who once had chopped up some meat for them, and Herman, Sherman and Vernon, three Long Metuil teenage boys who often came to Polecat Gulch together, bringing whatever treats they could find for the airmen.

The Dayaks would grin and try to cheer up the airmen by acting out the rumors they had heard of Allied attacks against Tarakan and campaigns against the Japanese on the Borneo mainland. The Americans wanted to believe their visitors' tales, and they did their best to pick up some Lun Dayeh vocabulary. They wrote down lists of words spelled the way they sounded, with guesses as to what the words meant. These word lists were constantly refined, and helped make their conversations with the Dayaks more than just pantomimes.

In addition to firewood, the Dayaks would bring whatever they could find that the Yanks might like: rice, pork rind, fat, tobacco, salt, pepper, sugarcane and (in season) corn on the cob. They made special trips into the jungle at lower elevations for bananas, knowing how fond the Yanks were of them.

Despite the Dayaks' best efforts, the airmen continued to lose weight. In the six weeks they were in Polecat Gulch, they each lost close to thirty pounds. Dizzy with hunger, they would sometimes faint if they stood up quickly.

It was also a difficult time for the Japanese who had been sent upriver to find them. These six weeks had gone by with no results. As the four Japanese officials and thirteen *heitai*s at Long Berang grew more frustrated, they became ruder and more demanding, slapping people in the face without warning, hitting villagers with their rattan sticks and becoming a nearly intolerable burden on the Makahanaps and the Dayaks. Sometimes when the Japanese soldiers were bored, they would pick at random a couple of Dayaks from one of the longhouses and tie them both to the same length of rope, making them fight each other with their bare fists. If one of them fell over, the *heitai*s would beat him with a stick to make him stand up and continue fighting. When there was a clear winner, the loser would be flogged. In such conditions, the question was, Whose patience would snap first?

Finally, the senior Japanese military officer, the *taicho*, said that the Americans were never going to be caught this way, that the Dayaks must be playing a game. The Americans had been sent to Long Metuil first, so he would go there himself to pick up their trail. He would bring the interpreter, Sakata, and three *heitai*s with him, and they would make that disloyal Pangeran Lagan help them. By the time the *taicho* arrived at Long Metuil, though, Lagan had prudently disappeared, perhaps warned by Makahanap.

Before the *taicho* left Long Berang, Makahanap heard him order the two *ken kanrikan*s to take five soldiers and go to the Krayan District, to the village of Long Sempayang, where there was a Christian mission school and a big Lun Dayeh longhouse. The other five *heitai*s were to stay at Long Berang, and they should not just sit there, the chief officer shouted, but must go hunting for the fugitive white soldiers with the Dayaks.

It was easy for the local Dayaks, following the secret orders of the D.O., to lead the five Japanese soldiers still in Long Berang on a merry chase, strewn with false clues, across the nearby hills and back home again when the Japanese grew tired. It was certainly better at Long Berang with only the five Japanese there than it had been with all seventeen. But the word Makahanap was receiving from Long Metuil and Long

Sempayang was that the Japanese were behaving badly. If things were not done precisely the way they wished, or sometimes for no reason at all, they would order some of the Dayaks to beat other Dayaks and then they would beat the beaters.

One day, a messenger from Japanese administrative headquarters in Tarakan delivered sealed letters to Makahanap with instructions that they be passed on, still sealed, to the *taicho* and the two *ken kanrikan*s.

Makahanap felt he had to learn what was in those letters before sending them forward, but who could read Japanese? He worried about the sealed letters all that evening. The next morning, as he said his usual prayers next to Mama, a verse from the book of Jeremiah came back to him:

> *Call unto me, and I will answer thee*
> *And show thee great and mighty things*
> *Which thou knowest not.*

Suddenly, he knew what to do.

Along the village's only street were a few narrow, shuttered, two-story shop-houses, where Chinese traders (known in pidgin as *towkays*) had set up businesses in Long Berang early in the century. The *towkays* bought the Dayaks' produce and sold them a motley collection of inexpensive imported goods. They stocked cotton shirts, lengths of colorful cotton sarong cloth, kerosene pressure lamps, buttons, pencils, paper, cooking pots, sandals, tiny colored glass beads for ornamenting Dayak ladies' skullcaps and other odds and ends—though not many goods were available now, with maritime shipping disrupted by the war.

Right after breakfast, Makahanap went to two of the Chinese *towkays*, Ah Piauw and Ah Kun, who were the most literate people in the area. Chinese and non-Chinese were rarely on friendly terms downriver but happily that was not the case upriver, in Makahanap's district. The Dayak children who came from distant longhouses to attend school at Long Berang often lodged with one or another of Long Berang's three Chinese families, in return for which the students would help load and transport trade goods up- and downriver or help in the vegetable gardens. The children of the Chinese and the Dayaks, as well as the Makahanap children, all played together and remained friends for life.

The district officer appreciated that the Chinese were deeply conscious of their delicate position in relation to the Japanese occupiers. Any and all Borneo Chinese could be regarded as enemy aliens whenever the Japanese chose to do so. On the coast, the Japanese had seized Chinese property using that excuse. Furthermore, a Chinese-led anti-Japanese uprising in the state of North Borneo in October 1943 had not only ended disastrously for the rebels, hundreds of whom had been tortured and executed, but also left a residue of suspicion in Japanese minds about all Borneo Chinese. The Chinese were understandably careful to avoid being implicated in the effort to hide the fugitives.

But with no other options, Makahanap brought his Chinese friends the letters from Tarakan. He watched while Ah Kun steamed the letters open. Because the Chinese written language shares many characters with written Japanese, Ah Piauw and Ah Kun were able to more or less decipher the letters' contents.

It was just as Makahanap had feared. The Japanese headquarters in Tarakan had understood what the *taicho* and *ken kanrikan* had not: that Makahanap had fooled them. The letters, after scolding the addressees for their stupidity, instructed them to bring the Mentarang district officer and his entire family to Tarakan. As Makahanap knew, that was another way of saying that he and his family would be executed. (A favorite way to deal with disloyal subordinates was to throw them into a pit filled with sharpened stakes.) Trying not to show how unnerved he was, Makahanap burned the letters and his two Chinese friends promised to keep quiet.

Makahanap went back to the messenger from Tarakan and told him he had arranged to have the letters delivered. In his haughtiest voice, he ordered the messenger to return to Tarakan with the news that the Americans were almost in his grasp, that the region where they were hiding had been located and that "the master in Tarakan had to be patient."

The next day, after the Tarakan messenger had headed downstream in his long canoe, Makahanap got word to Pangeran Lagan in his hiding place. The headman arrived secretly at Long Berang late the next night and made no attempt to hide his feelings. He had heard from his longhouse people that the Japanese were showing no respect, not even to people of rank. He said that the Japanese had threatened to take as hostages eight men from Long Metuil until Pangeran Lagan gave himself up and led them to the Americans.

They were also threatening to interfere with the women. As Makahanap knew, unmarried women in an animist longhouse were free to sleep with any unmarried men they liked, but no one could force them; that was unacceptable.

Moreover, Lagan continued, the Japanese were treating the longhouse people as one would a dog—actually worse, because hunters loved their dogs. It could not be borne any longer. The D.O. sympathized and told his friend of the letters he had intercepted.

Early the next morning, when the *pangeran* left to return to Long Metuil, the two men were in tacit agreement that the present situation could not be allowed to continue. As these two old colleagues exchanged their ritual phrases of farewell, they did not need to say more.

The same day, January 18, the *taicho* came back to Long Berang, bringing with him, as his aide, one of the Japanese soldiers who had been with him at Long Metuil. The chief officer asked to see a letter from headquarters in Tarakan that he had been told would be waiting for him.

CHAPTER NINE

The Pangeran Forces the Pace

By the morning of January 18, despite rain so heavy that it threw a thick curtain across his path, Pangeran Lagan was back in Long Metuil. He learned quickly that the Japanese visitors had gotten very drunk on *borak* the previous evening. Made indiscreet by the alcohol, they had let slip the fact that they planned to take eight hostages, some of them the *pangeran*'s nephews, to Long Berang within the next day or two. The previous night, Lagan had reached a tacit agreement with the D.O. on what had to be done. And now he knew when he had to do it.

He called his best men together. He said that they could not tolerate their Japanese visitors' behavior any longer. It was time to take heads. There was no time to consult the omens the way they had done in the time of Lagan's youth. Nor was there time for erecting a sacred shrine, where permission could be asked of the protecting spirits by the village shaman. This time they would have to act immediately, in stealth, without even consulting the longhouse elders. Lagan and his warriors paused only to put on cloth sarongs over their loincloths to hide their knives underneath.

The Japanese/Malay interpreter Sakata and the two remaining *heitai*s were moving slowly that morning, thanks to the effects of the *borak*. They were cooking a late breakfast when Lagan and his longhouse warriors rushed into their hut with a whoop, swinging their machetes. The heads of the two *heitai*s fell to the ground by the fire. Blood spurted out of their necks. Sakata was wounded but leaped from the hut into the river. He did not get far. Wading close behind, one of the Dayaks stabbed him from the rear while another lopped off his head, and the river turned dark with blood.

With those few sword strokes, the Long Metuil animists had revived the sacred rite of headhunting after a gap of more than a decade. Or had they? As Pangeran Lagan and his men were anxiously aware, this morning's head-taking, though providing a welcome supply of fresh heads, which had long been missing from important feasts, was not according to customary law.

In the earlier days of headhunting, the object had been (according to a leading ethnographer) "to *hunt*, get and *bring back* one or more heads; normally one per operation." But the purpose had never been to decapitate a specific person. The idea had been simply to take a head from a rival group or one that had caused trouble to one's own longhouse, and use its spiritual powers for the good of the longhouse.

But, in the final decades before headhunting was effectively banned, the rivalry and revenge motives faded; by the 1920s, obtaining a head for an occasion that demanded it, such as the funeral rites of an aristocrat, had become an end in itself. Any head would do, from any other longhouse not closely tied to one's own or not on the same river branch.

But today, it had been done simply to kill enemies. This was not really headhunting, and some of the longhouse elders expressed their concern that the appropriate rites had not been carried out beforehand. Might not these heads, obtained without the correct ceremonial preparations, bring misfortune to the longhouse?

Lagan agreed that all they could do now was see that the rites for bringing a head back to the longhouse were observed. Such rites were protective measures, meant to ensure that a head's powers did not cause trouble in its new home.

So, in conformance with the old rituals, the heads were washed and wiped dry on the ground near the river. In former days, the longhouse girls would form a circle around an earthen, crocodile-shaped mound and pass the severed head from one dancer to the next. Normally, the head would then be stuck on a pole and smoked, a process that might take a week. This time, Lagan insisted that the head feast take place sooner, before the Japanese had time to learn of the deaths and mount a reconnaissance party from Long Berang.

Without enough time to smoke the heads properly, the Dayaks peeled them to keep down the odor and make the heads ready to be carried about in the festive procession that would follow in the next few days, after the guests arrived.

As usual after a head-taking, the elders of Long Metuil sent out word by runners to all the surrounding villages to come to a head feast. Normally, the runners would have brought knotted strings made of vines to the guest longhouse headmen, with a knot to be untied each night, the last knot to be opened the night before the feast should begin, perhaps five or ten days hence. This time, the Long Metuil hosts asked their guests to come the following day.

This shortening of the interval between head-taking and feast brought problems for the women of the longhouse. Even before the runners had left, the women had started preparing vast amounts of *borak*. Soon, the longhouse was filled with the sour stench of rice that was first half burned and then spread out on mats to cool. When the rice mash was cool enough, the women sprinkled a powdery, ginger-root yeast on it and put the mixture in giant, high-shouldered Chinese or Thai dragon jars made of porcelain or earthenware.

While making the *borak,* the other women followed the lead of Lagan's wife. She was, both by protocol and in fact, the best *borak* maker in Long Metuil. This time, though, she was under more pressure than usual to produce adequate amounts of the brew. She had been more than willing to cook secret meals to be delivered to the airmen in their hiding place, and she was in full agreement with her husband on the need to rid the village of the Japanese. But with guests coming so soon to the head feast, there would not be enough time for the *borak* to brew. Fermentation normally took four or five days; this brew could not possibly be ready to drink in one day. She asked the other women to check out the longhouse's current supplies. If there was not enough *borak,* the longhouse would be disgraced. Perhaps they could get additional stocks from longhouses nearby, though it would be hard for anyone to carry a lot of it. The *borak* itself was heavy, not to mention the great jars, many of which weighed more than seventy-five pounds empty. Besides, people often used their best jars to make the *borak,* and nobody would be willing to bring them to another longhouse. Such jars were the wealth of a long-house, worth a fortune in trade, or used to settle scores if members of one longhouse had caused the death of someone from another village. One could just hope that there was enough brew on hand until the new *borak* was ready to drink. A good party ought to last at least four or five days.

Normally, the last day of the party was the proper time for a favored guest—often the chief of another longhouse—to be invited to kill the biggest water buffalo available. The hosts thereby paid off a previous debt of hospitality or obliged the honored guest to reciprocate soon. Lagan's wife looked around at the full jars. The new *borak* would be ready for the slaughter of the buffalo.

On the morning of January 19, more than two months after their unceremonious landing in Borneo, the Yanks in Polecat Gulch were awakened by the youth they called Herman and another young man. Their visitors managed to explain to Phil and the others that they had killed three Japanese and it was now safe to return to Long Metuil. That day, Phil recorded in his diary: "We ate a hearty breakfast of rice, root, bananas and sugarcane, packed our belongings and said goodbye to 'Polecat Gulch' and 'Club Borneo.' It was breathtaking to reach the top of the first ridge where we could see for a great distance, without having to look straight up."

It was a hard walk, uphill and down. As Phil and the other flyers had long noticed, the Lun Dayeh never went around a mountain if they could go up it and down the other side. Going through tall brush, the Lun Dayeh wanted to see as far ahead in all directions as they could. But if they had been up on a plateau where they *could* see far, they would still have wanted, whenever possible, to arrange their route so that they could climb to the top of any ridge that had a *tafa* (memorial swathe) cut through it. This square of space, cut into the profile of a hilltop or mountain peak, was a favorite Lun Dayeh way of honoring their noble dead. It was cut by machetes wielded by the fittest (and often the drunkest) of the longhouse men after they rushed up to the top of the peak on the last day of a funeral feast. To walk through it was to honor the dead nobleman and also the longhouse that had hosted the sumptuous feast that had preceded the making of the *tafa*.

The Yanks were so weak they could barely walk, but they could hear drums and gongs and voices shouting long before they reached Long Metuil. Some of the Lun Dayeh from long-houses miles away were there to greet them, and the Yanks had to shake hands for what seemed like at least ten minutes. The neighbors had all bathed in the river and changed into fresh clothes after arriving, and they were in a festive mood.

The airmen were first shown where the three Japanese had been attacked, where two of them had lost their heads. The blood was still fresh on the hut's floor and the fire was still smoldering down by the river, where the Dayaks had burned the bodies. The airmen had never been that close to enemy dead before. The smell of the burned flesh almost made them ill. After smelling that, bathing in the river did not seem to get them really clean, but it refreshed and cooled their bruised, leech-covered bodies and aching leg muscles.

The Americans were then invited up the notched ladder to the main longhouse floor where they were presented with their best meal in weeks: rice, sugarcane, bananas, pork and what Phil described as "some kind of fruit [a yellowish squashlike vegetable known as a *timun dayak*, or Dayak cucumber] which tasted like a cross between a cucumber and a watermelon." Four chairs (no doubt made for the use of prewar Dutch colonial officials) were found for the Yanks and, once seated, the airmen were shown the Japanese souvenirs their hosts had acquired along with the heads: pistols, rifles, bayonets, money, gold teeth, cartridge boxes, pencils and clothing.

The airmen, dazzled by the noise and the presence of so many people, sat and watched while the celebration preparations continued. From the veranda, they saw a pig being slaughtered below. This was done without any ceremony, except for each man's dipping his finger in the blood and touching his chest, seemingly a gesture of courtesy to the dead animal. A few days later, they may have witnessed the ceremonial sacrifice of a water buffalo. The slaughter of such a beast by the highest-ranking guest would take place out of doors, in an amphitheater with elegantly carved wooden seats circling the post to which the beast was tied.

When evening fell, the Lun Dayeh hosts and their neighbors formed a big circle. Three big iron drums kept the beat as they had throughout the day, their deep vibrations echoing for miles through the jungle. While the airmen looked on, Dayak men wearing capes ornamented with feathers or fur and lots of beading slowly took turns coming forward in the flickering torchlight to dance a warrior dance. In a strange, jerky rhythm, the dancer would hop first on one foot and then the other, stamping the wooden floor each time as hard as he could. At the same time, he would wave a ceremonial machete in the air but close to his body.

The airmen noticed that a few of the men had put on colorful loincloths made of imported cloth, but most of them were wearing loincloths made from the usual dark, beaten bark. Some of the men wore in their upper earlobes earrings carved out of the scarlet-and-yellow crest of a hornbill bird or from the ivory-colored, curved fangs of a clouded leopard. A few men also had brass rings in their lower earlobes.

Meanwhile, the women stood and formed a long line. Some were bare breasted above dark bark-cloth skirts that covered them from the waist to ankle. Others wore a Javanese *kebayak* (tight-fitting long-sleeved bodice) or a Western-style blouse, while still others wore a bib woven from pineapple fiber. Many of the women wore close-fitting skullcaps covered with hundreds of colored, glittering glass beads. Each cap (the Yanks were told) represented the life savings of its wearer. The resin torches reflected the glint of the heavy brass rings distending the long loops of the women's lower earlobes. The women, unlike the men, merely shuffled along the veranda singing a chant over and over. Their movements were paced, perhaps, to meet the need for their dance to continue without interruption for days.

An enormous amount of food had been prepared for all the attendees, though not all the guests took part in the ceremonial banquet for the village aristocracy and their noble counterparts from other longhouses. On a slightly raised section in the middle of the longhouse floor, special foods in blue-and-white Chinese dishes were laid out on mats. The women had spread out beautifully woven seating mats and little resin lamps instead of torches. The Yanks, having watched the slicing of pork from the sacrificial pig, were taken to look at these banquet arrangements before being politely escorted to the far end of the longhouse, where they were asked to stay while the ceremonies continued. Curious though they were to see what was going on up by the leaders' seats, they found it perfectly proper that they had been consigned to the sidelines. After all, they were not aristocrats. Left to eat by themselves, they enjoyed the pork and gravy they had been given with their rice. They were also supplied with enough tobacco to last them a month, and coffee, a rare treat.

Later, when the formal part of the banquet was finished, the Yanks were invited back to the party. At their hosts' urging, they started in on the *borak*—which tasted to Phil surprisingly like a California wine. Served the Lun Dayeh way, *borak* was sipped through reed straws from the tall Chinese jars in which it had been brewed.

When offering a guest a drink of *borak*, as Phil describes it, "Your host will take you by the hand and lead you to the jug. The two of you stoop over the jug facing each other and then both drink through the straws at the same time. The host must drink as long as the guest. The basic law of Borneo society is that the last one on his feet is the best man." The airmen soon learned to pretend to be sucking in the drink rather than imbibing every time. In their weakened state, they could not hope to hold their liquor the way a Dayak could.

While the dancing and chanting continued, two Dayaks went down to the river and brought back a pair of heads on poles that were then hung up over the fire. The Dayak men formed a long line and did another dance to the beat of the drums.

Phil thought, "I'm a God-fearing person," but realized he was "happy to sit in on the end of two members of a race of people who brought so much suffering to so many people throughout the world." Neither he nor the other Yanks felt disgust at such treatment of the *heitais*' corpses. The stories they had heard of Japanese behavior toward the natives and toward Allied prisoners precluded any sympathy for these dead men. And what they were seeing was clearly not an act of disrespect. On the contrary, the Dayaks were performing a sacred rite; the airmen felt privileged to be witnessing it.

What the airmen probably did not realize was how completely their attitudes toward the Dayaks had changed in the months since they had dropped into Borneo. When they had left Polecat Gulch that day, their primary emotion had been, not surprisingly, exhilaration at being free of their enforced isolation. But now, well fed, feeling comparatively safe and sitting on chairs for the first time in months, they were filled with feelings for and about the Dayaks that they could not have predicted.

They had started out in November thinking of the Dayaks as barely human. By now, they had come to feel not only respect for the Dayaks' competence in the challenging tropical mountain world, but also gratitude for their generosity and a genuine liking for their straightforward manners and their cheerful courage during trying times.

In the crowd of celebrants, the Yanks recognized some of the men and boys who had come to Polecat Gulch to bring them food, firewood, tobacco and moral support. Indigestion Joe (who they now learned was the longhouse chief from Long Kafun) came during the first night of the feast with some of his people, bringing another pig and other foodstuffs to add to the feast. The Butcher was there, too, and he and Indigestion Joe, Phil noted, "make a grand pair." As the *borak* began to take effect on them all, great oaths of mutual affection were pronounced between the Dayaks and the Yanks and grand gestures were made. The Butcher and Indigestion Joe each urged the Yanks to come live in his longhouse. The Butcher offered them wives if the men would come to live with him. At some point well into that first night, Phil gave his lapel wings to Indigestion Joe as a gesture of friendship. Joe, equally moved, declared he wanted to go to America with the Yanks.

Two and a half days of heavy rain followed, but this did not dampen the spirits of the partygoers. On the night of January 21, Pangeran Lagan reappeared. He had with him ten of his chosen warriors, his best marksmen. They were wearing their most elaborately ornamented sword belts and carrying their blowpipes and poison darts, and their spearheads were on their shafts, a sign they were going headhunting.

They were leaving for Long Berang, they pantomimed, where more Japanese were to be killed. Lagan asked Phil and the Yanks to go down with his group to help kill the seven Japanese still there. He showed them a rifle and two muzzle loaders belonging to the Japanese soldiers whose heads he and his men had taken three days earlier. For Lagan, who had not witnessed the Yanks' weeks of deprivation in Polecat Gulch, it must have seemed normal that the airmen would want to take part in an attack on their enemy.

Phil and the others tried to talk Lagan and his friends out of making the trip that night. They knew it was risky even for such skilled walkers as the Lun Dayeh to travel at night in the rainy season. The Yanks hated the idea of the Dayaks, who had already done so much for them, running such risks on their behalf.

But when Lagan remained determined, Phil shook his head. With the weight of command on his shoulders, Phil was grown-up enough to recognize that this was not the time for amateur heroics by the Yanks. For one thing, they would be no good at moving down a sopping-wet mountainside through the jungle at night. They would just be in the way. For another, they were weak from their weeks of semistarvation, during which time none of them had fired a weapon.

Reluctantly but firmly, he told Lagan that neither he nor his men would go with him. When it was clear the Lun Dayeh were going to go anyway, Phil took off his bombardier wings (the only medal-like object he had left). He pinned it on Pangeran Lagan's boar-skin hat before watching the "bravest man I ever knew" go off to fight the Yanks' battle for them.

The head feast at Long Metuil was a historic event both for the region and Borneo, but Makahanap and his people at Long Berang did not yet know of it. Pangeran Lagan had managed to get word by runner to the headman of the village at Long Kafun and to the people of other nearby longhouses, who were all invited to the feast. But he had not been able to get a message to Long Berang, now that the *landas* (rainy season) had arrived in earnest. In inland Borneo, yearly rainfall exceeds two hundred inches, with heavy bursts of rain every day;

but during the four months of the *landas* (November through February) it often rains hard *all* day, especially in January and February. Walking for any great distance during the heavy rains was virtually impossible, and the swollen rivers and streams were no longer navigable.

There was a pause in the rainfall on January 22, and Indigestion Joe, the headman of Long Kafun, who had left the party hours ahead of Pangeran Lagan and collected more warriors from his own longhouse at dawn, hastened downriver to Long Berang. He arrived midmorning with additional warriors, who had joined him en route. They made an imposing crowd in the small street of Long Berang. Indeed, the only time Makahanap had seen a bigger crowd there had been Easter 1941, when more than a thousand Dayaks had assembled for three days of prayer and feasting led by Reverend Willfinger. To accommodate them for two nights, every bit of space in every longhouse had been occupied, as well as in the government rest houses and the Chinese stores. This time the Dayaks were here for a very different purpose.

Joe had a quiet word alone with Makahanap, to tell him of the head-taking in Long Metuil and to ask the D.O.'s permission to do the same here. Makahanap was still reflecting on the matter when the *taicho*, who had spent four days waiting impatiently for the expected letter from Tarakan, appeared with his soldier aide and two of the Long Berang–based *heitai*s to demand that the D.O. furnish him and his escort transport back to Long Metuil.

The *taicho* also wanted to know why there were so many Dayaks gathered in Long Berang. Makahanap explained that they were there in such numbers to conduct their usual market day, postponed till now by the heavy rains. He provided the *taicho* with four canoes, one for each of his party. The Japanese official would appreciate the extravagance of the ges-

ture, but the district officer saw this as the easiest way to eliminate these four on the river. The Long Kafun warriors would
be granted their wish.

Once the Japanese were on the river and out of sight of
Long Berang, the paddlers launched their attacks. The *taicho*
was stabbed first, with a machete. Badly injured, he fell out of
his *perahu*. The current was running so fast that the Dayaks,
anxious though they were to have his head, were unable to
catch hold of the dying chief officer. They could only watch as
the current sailed him downstream. The boatmen in the other
three dugouts quickly beheaded the other Japanese. They
took the heads and, after beaching their boats, they slogged
cheerfully through the mud for hours, returning in triumph
to Long Metuil. The head feast there was still going on and the
new heads greatly enhanced the occasion. Phil wrote in his
diary, without being aware of the cause: "The people and food
are really pouring into this place. Another pig and a young
water buffalo, another celebration in the making."

Makahanap realized that, now the seven Japanese had been
killed (assuming the Long Kafun people had been successful),
he must somehow eliminate the remaining three *heitai*s at
Long Berang, who knew nothing yet of what had happened.
The problem was that these remaining Japanese soldiers were
more cautious than the others had been. They never went
anywhere without their weapons—and one of them had a machine gun.

It was time to employ other means—and quickly. Makahanap called Binum to him. As he looked at her with the eyes
of a man—and not as her teacher and protector—Makahanap
knew that her fair skin, long black hair, slim body and white
teeth would make her tempting to the Japanese. Perhaps because she had never had children or perhaps because she had

had an easier life working for a Dutch family than she would have had as a Lun Dayeh longhouse woman, she looked much younger than her twenty-five years.

He told Binum that seven of the seventeen Japanese who had come upriver to catch the Americans had been killed by Lun Dayeh in the last several days. It was only a matter of time before Japanese headquarters in Tarakan learned of these killings. Tarakan was already calling for Ama and Mama and the children to be brought back there. Binum must know what that meant. He asked her: Could she find a few girls as beautiful as she was to go out to the big flat rock in the middle of the Pa' Paru and take off all their clothes and lure the *heitai*s?

Binum found herself torn between the traditional Lun Dayeh and more Western concepts of what was the right thing to do, the right way to behave. To show herself naked in public was totally against both social codes. To appear entirely naked, even before one's husband, was as shocking to the Lun Dayeh as having sex in public would be. But Binum knew her Bible stories, thanks to the missionaries, and she remembered the story of the beautiful Jewish widow Judith who had dressed in her finest clothes, gone to the Assyrians' camp to seduce their general Holofernes and had emerged from his tent with his severed head. This was just like that, wasn't it? Although it might involve trickery, even treachery, it was not actual lying. Surely these Japanese who had killed Reverend Willfinger and the others, and now wanted to kill Ama and Mama Makahanap and their children, were the enemies of the God-fearing. Also, she was confident that Ama would not ask her to do something wrong. Indeed, she would not have felt right questioning the orders of her acknowledged superior; the Lun Dayeh obeyed their leaders. She felt she had no choice—nor did she want one.

She thought Ama's plan was a good one for distracting the *heitai*s. She had lived among foreigners long enough to know the effect of a naked woman's body on the imagination of foreign men. She knew the flat rock Ama mentioned. It was a favorite place for the Long Berang women and girls to bathe and wash their clothes. She had washed the American soldiers' uniforms there. Eager to go ahead while she had the courage, she immediately went to ask a few of her closest friends in the Long Berang longhouses to do this with her: Ganit and Kafit, who were young and single, and Ilau Padan, who was already married. They were all beautiful by anyone's standards. The three young women admired Binum, who was older and very knowledgeable but also kind and generous. They readily agreed to this extraordinary request without sharing with Binum their worry that, if there were a firefight, they might also be "bathed in bullets."

The river glittered in the midday sun, although the water was coffee brown from the mud. It was more than waist deep by the big flat rock, deep enough to slow down waders. At Makahanap's request, several Dayak men brought heavy iron and brass drums and stationed themselves on either side of the river. Some of these instruments had taken hundreds of years to reach the interior from coastal Brunei and had oral histories telling of their transfer from one person or tribe to another. Now, they would have a new story to tell.

Binum and the other girls waded out to the flat rock and let their sarongs slide down to their feet; they began to dance naked to the sound of the drums. While they danced, Makahanap's son Christiaan and some of the Long Berang Dayaks silently slipped under the bridge and swam to the shore near the Presswood house, where the *heitai*s were staying.

A houseguest of the Makahanaps' named Santoni, a middle-aged Javanese woman, was in on the plot. She walked across the swaying bridge to the Presswood house and spoke in Malay to the *heitai*s, who were staring out of the window, transfixed by the sight. She encouraged them to join the girls in the river. It must be terrible for the *heitai*s to have been without a woman for months, Santoni said. She assured them that they would be allowed to have sex with the girls, after the dance was over.

Binum, seeing that the Japanese had not yet approached, slid off the rock like a mermaid and waded toward the river-bank nearest the Presswood house. Her satin-pale body, dappled by the sunlight coming through the overarching trees, was covered below the waist by the opaque water. Calling out in Malay, she urged the *heitai*s to join her: *"Mari, mari, mandi dan menari"*—Come, come, bathe and dance—she said, before turning back toward the flat rock.

"She was so beautiful," Makahanap later recalled, "too much for the poor men." One of the soldiers gave a deep-throated shout, pulled off his outer garments and ran out of the door to join the girls in the river. He waded out awkwardly in his underpants and was about to reach the flat rock when a Dayak stabbed him dead from behind. By then, Christiaan and his Lun Dayeh accomplices had crept inside the Press-wood house.

Christiaan seized the machine gun from the room where the other two *heitai*s were still staring out the window while Santoni discreetly left the scene. The two Japanese turned to see him and tried to grab him, but there were Dayaks every-where. Quickly, the *heitai*s were stabbed and their heads cut off.

The *heitai*s' blood pumped out and stained the hardwood floor and the whitewashed walls of the Presswood house. No one bothered to clean it up.

The Coberly crew at March Field, California, July 1944.
Back row, enlisted men (left to right): Jim Knoch,
Dan Illerich, John Nelson, Eddy Haviland, Tom Capin and
Charlie Burnette (who did not fly on November 16). Missing is
Franny Harrington. Front row, officers (left to right):
Tom Coberly, Jerry Rosenthal, Fred Brennan and Phil Corrin.
Used by permission of Jean Corrin Morris

William and Theresia Makahanap and their young children, circa 1948.
Used by permission of Emma Makahanap

Some of the Coberly crew on jungle training in Neumfoor, New Guinea,
October 1944. Tom Capin is in the front at left; Tom Coberly is in the
middle, smiling; and Jim Knoch is next to him, looking down.
Used by permission of Betty Capin

William Makahanap,
seated, circa 1945;
Christiaan is behind him
in the striped T-shirt.
The two other men are
unknown but they might
be two of the three
Chinese *towkays* at
Long Berang.
Used by permission of
Emma Makahanap

Pangeran Lagan (on right) and his family, circa 1945.
Used by permission of Jean Corrin Morris

The interior of a Lun Dayeh longhouse, circa 1944.
Used by permission of the Christian and Missionary Alliance

A Dayak drinking
borak from an ancient
Chinese dragon jar.
Used by permission
of Guy Piazzini

The Presswood house across the river at Long Berang, 1945.
Used by permission of Ruth Presswood Hutchins

A Dayak dancer at a head feast, 1945.
Used by permission of Ruth Presswood Hutchins

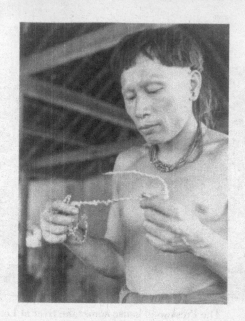

A Dayak opening one
of his calendar knots.
Used by permission
of Robert Pringle

Tarakan Town in 1945 or 1946.
Used by permission of the Christian and Missionary Alliance

Mr. Soldier

I am Japanese. I think you did fillful yours mission. You permissive and gun leave *pistol give* to this man, it consent and come to Long Brang.

R. Iwasaki

The letter written at Long Berang by the *ken kanrikan* from Malinau and sent to the four airmen at Long Metuil. Used by permission of Jean Corrin Morris

Left to right:
Dan Illerich,
Eddy Haviland,
Phil Corrin and
Franny Harrington
showing off their
souvenirs in Labuan,
June 1945, after
their rescue.
Used by permission
of Jean Corrin Morris

Phil Corrin
on his first day home,
September 1945.
Used by permission of
Jean Corrin Morris

CHAPTER TEN

The D.O. Declares War

Now in the fourth day of the head feast, the Dayaks at Long Metuil were sleeping off the night's *borak* during the quiet time of the day. Suddenly, the Yanks heard the barks and grunts from below that announced visitors. They looked up to see Makahanap and Pangeran Lagan and his warriors coming toward them. Lagan, with the bombardier wings still pinned to his hat, caught Phil's eye and grinned. Makahanap, also looking pleased, announced that all the Japanese in Long Berang—and, indeed, in the entire Mentarang District—had been killed, and that the next morning he would help the airmen move back to Long Berang.

When the Yanks had first met Makahanap, they had figured him for an extremely cautious, ambivalent man who was working for the Japanese. They now could see that he had linked himself, his family and his district to an Allied victory.

The next day, when the Yanks reached Long Berang in the driving rain, they could see how much things had changed since their previous stay there. This time their arrival was expected, even welcomed. Before they could moor their *perahu,* Santoni rushed up to the water's edge to greet them carrying a waxed-paper umbrella and an enormous smile on her moon-shaped face. Phil remembered her as a nice, middle-aged woman who had come briefly to the police barrack to see them. He would learn from Christiaan that her husband had disappeared at the time of the Japanese invasion, leaving her with no place here and no way back to her home in Surabaya on the eastern end of Java. Her husband, also Javanese, had been in the Dutch colonial police and had accompanied Makahanap on his official trips through the district. When Phil saw her come up to the boat now, she looked so excited that at first he thought she was going to kiss him, but instead she settled for a hearty handshake. She patted him on the back several times, shouting, "Very good, very good"—possibly the only English words she knew. The Yanks came to think of Santoni as being like themselves, waiting for things to change so she could get back home. Never before had a war impinged so deeply on so many lives in this part of the world.

Christiaan was on the riverbank to greet the airmen and walk them back to the house. They could see a Dutch flag flying from the D.O.'s office flagpole, where the Japanese flag had been. Christiaan had prepared his wonderful fried chicken for lunch, but the absence of Mama at the dining table was palpable.

Makahanap explained over lunch that he had sent Mama and the little ones out of harm's way the day before. Binum managed to describe how she had carried three-year-old Thea on her hip while her girlfriend Iwak had carried five-month-old Victor in a basket on her back. Binum said she would never forget that journey: "We were so afraid and we held Thea and her brother up and down the mountains." They had run through the heavy rain along the banks of the Pa' Paru to where it joined the Pa' Silau, and on to a longhouse in a hidden valley at Punan Silau.

Binum had left Mama and the children with Iwak and had rushed back to help with the Yanks—and to bring the news that Mama and the children were safe, though Mama was sad not to see "her boys" again.

Makahanap told the Yanks that he and Pangeran Lagan and his warriors would be going to Long Sempayang to kill the Japanese there. He also told them what news he had of the other airmen from their plane who were currently scattered about the Krayan District. He promised that once the whole upriver region was free of Japanese he would arrange for the three airmen to join them.

The Yanks were thrilled to know that three of the four men from the back of the plane were alive and well. Phil wrote letters for Makahanap to get to them somehow. He wanted to insist on the D.O.'s helping to arrange for them to join their group now, but he sensed that their host could hardly wait to be on his way. And indeed, the D.O. and his group left right after lunch; Makahanap had learned that the two *ken kanrikan*s and five *heitai*s who had been staying at Long Sempayang were about to leave for the village of Pa' Silau, not far from Punan Silau, where Mama was.

Makahanap and his party made good time to the longhouse at Pengutan despite the rain. Makahanap received confirmation that the Japanese had arrived at Pa' Silau, a couple of hours upriver. Quickly inventing a plan, he asked Apui Sia, the longhouse headman of Pengutan, to invite the Japanese to come visit his village. He asked Apui Sia, an animist, to tell the Japanese that district officer Makahanap was already in Malinau with the other ten Japanese and the captured Americans.

The pagan headman was not only willing to lie to the Japanese but was evidently good at it. The Japanese at Pa' Silau, delighted at the news, readily accompanied him back by boat to Pengutan, since it lay on the route to Long Berang and Malinau. Makahanap, with help from Pangeran Lagan and Christian longhouse chiefs of the Krayan District, had stationed

Dayak forces by the river. There was one spot where there were rapids, obliging the Japanese to get out of their canoes and wade across the river. Makahanap and Pangeran Lagan's combined Krayan and Mentarang forces were in place there and offered to help the Japanese across. Once the Japanese were midriver, holding their guns overhead to keep them dry, the Dayaks, on a signal from the hidden Makahanap, rose up and quietly speared the Japanese one by one—the *heitai*s first, and then the *ken kanrikan*s. None of the Japanese reached the Pengutan side of the river.

The Krayan Christians, who were generally more devout than their Mentarang counterparts, had taken part in the massacre with reluctance, and only out of respect for Makahanap. They were horrified by the sight of so many dead bodies and the blood that colored the water everywhere. (Years later, Buing Udan, a Lun Dayeh who had been a teacher at the Long Sempayang school at the time, admitted that he had stood back at the fatal moment, unwilling to use his spear, because he had heard that one of the *ken kanrikan*s—probably the English-speaking one from Malinau—had been raised a Christian.) To Makahanap, all that mattered was that the last of the seventeen-man Japanese contingent sent upriver nearly two months earlier had been eliminated.

To Phil and the others, now staying at the Makahanap house, things felt very different from the last time they had been in Long Berang. They were no longer fugitives, but members of the community. Seeing that there were Dayaks patrolling day and night on regular guard duty, Phil offered his services and those of his men. Christiaan agreed and asked the Yanks to contribute their sidearms to an armory that now held Japanese rifles, pistols, mortars and the famous machine gun that Christiaan had taken and Jim showed him how to use.

A welcome diversion for the airmen came with the arrival that first day of a Malay doctor named Moli and a young Dutch-Javanese Eurasian, Edward Safri. The two visitors spoke some English and brought precious news of the world beyond the Lun Dayeh hills. They had both been staying in Malinau but had escaped upriver to avoid being captured by three Japanese soldiers who were suspicious of them. Safri, who was an expert in explosives, said he had come north from Java in December 1941 to work for a Dutch company in the oil fields on Tarakan Island. He had been there barely a month when the Japanese invaded and forced him to work in a sawmill.

Conditions were now bad on Tarakan, and no more oil was being pumped out. The Japanese paid Safri only thirty-five occupation guilders a month for his work at the sawmill. That was not enough to live on but, worse still, there was almost no food to buy. The townspeople were rationed to eight cups of rice per person for ten days, forcing them to live on cassava and mice. The Japanese had control of the news and told the people that they held Hawaii and were fighting inside the continental United States. Safri asked the Yanks if that was true.

Safri had eventually escaped upriver to Malinau, where he had met Dr. Moli, and the two men headed farther upriver, hoping to meet up with Allied forces that were rumored to be up north and west, maybe near Brunei.

That night, while Moli and Safri stayed with the Yanks, some other Malays arrived in the dark by dugout canoe. They explained that they had started out from Malinau with three Japanese *heitai*s (perhaps the ones who were chasing Moli and Safri). The Malays had agreed to be their boat paddlers and had offered to help carry things for the *heitai*s when they all had to portage the boat through the rapids. At first, the Japanese soldiers had held on to their weapons but, at the third

portage, where the leeches were particularly thick, the soldiers had handed the boatmen their guns to carry. The Japanese said they had been told that the Malays were on their
side. If so, these Malays proved to be an exception to the rule.
First they shot their passengers dead, then they pitched the
bodies overboard and now they had a boatload of Japanese
supplies. Did the Yanks want any of them?

Receiving an affirmative response, the Malays carried in
some of their impressive haul: 50-kilo (110-pound) sacks of
rice, a few barrels of salt, sugar, fish and pork, cloth towels,
loose tobacco, cigarettes and several bottles of Japanese sake.
There were even mattresses, which the Yanks were happy to
keep. The airmen had developed sores and calluses over their
protruding hipbones from sleeping on the ground or on very
thin mats on the longhouse floor. Lying on the mattresses that
night, the Yanks took extra satisfaction in thinking that these
supplies had undoubtedly been meant for the ten Japanese of
the Mentarang District who had been dispatched the week
before.

The next morning, January 24, was like Christmas. Christiaan and Binum appeared with new clothes for the Yanks:
shirts, pants, towels, even handkerchiefs. The towels may
have come from the Malays' boatful of Japanese stores but the
rest of the clothing was made by Ah Tin, who was not only one
of Long Berang's three import-export merchants but also a
skilled tailor. He had a pedal-powered Singer sewing machine—one of a number of such machines that had somehow
penetrated the inmost reaches of Borneo in the late 1920s,
ahead of the missionaries. Even more surprising was that Ah
Tin had used imported cloth to make the clothes. It emerged
that he and the other Chinese traders had put aside some dry
goods for a special occasion. That occasion had now arrived.

Phil and the others remembered Ah Tin, who now also brought them tobacco and fresh eggs, as the man in whose house they had stayed for a few hours of darkness on their way to Long Metuil back in November. Christiaan, with interpreting help from Safri, explained that Ah Tin had been a close friend of Pangeran Lagan's since their youth and had always helped the *pangeran* whenever he could, getting him semi-refined cane sugar and other scarce commodities for the Long Metuil longhouse people. In return, the *pangeran* had always helped Ah Tin get Dayaks to load and unload his merchandise.

The airmen put on their new clothes. It was only then that they realized how ashamed they had felt when they had had nothing to wear but rags all those weeks.

Christiaan and Binum prepared them a meal of string beans, pumpkin, stewed chicken and a dessert of fried bananas. At the table, Edward Safri passed along the rumor that there were American forces in Brunei that were spreading out to Sarawak. Dr. Moli said he had heard that Tarakan had been bombed and that Allied forces were on the Malay peninsula and in Hong Kong. Phil wrote in his diary that he thought this all was wishful thinking—it was—but it added to the airmen's good spirits. Toward evening, Safri brought out a Hawaiian guitar and played and sang many old American favorites and tunes from films. He had a pleasant voice and a good memory, though he clearly did not understand half the words he sang. The airmen sang along. The music ended by evoking a strong sense of melancholy, because it made them all think of their families and friends so inconceivably far away. Nonetheless, it had been a wonderful day.

That night, it was Phil's turn to do guard duty, and the heaviest rainfall he had ever witnessed brought the level of the river up some thirty inches. But he felt on top of the world as he sat on the porch of the Makahanap house in a comfortable chair, wearing his new clothes, smoking Japanese cigarettes, eating banana fritters and drinking hot tea. It made quite a contrast to the spartan conditions under which he had done guard duty with the air force cadets. Eighteen-year-old Christiaan, who shared the watch with him, said he wanted to learn enough English to be able to go to the States. In the morning, after a breakfast of eggs sunny-side up prepared by Binum, Phil gave Christiaan an English lesson, using the expanded Malay/Lun Dayeh/English word sheet he and his men had put together during the weeks at Polecat Gulch.

After the lesson, when the new shift of guards took over, Christiaan went away briefly and returned with a windup Victrola record player that had been in the Presswood house. Its arm was broken but Jim knew how to fix it. Out of its brass horn eventually came the strains of "Stars and Stripes Forever," "Silent Night," "The Star-Spangled Banner" and "When Irish Eyes Are Smiling." "This place will never cease to amaze me," Phil wrote in his diary.

Uncomfortable with the fact that Makahanap and the Dayaks were off to the west fighting their war for them, the Yanks took some of their own tools and some borrowed ones to build a pillbox to protect the machine gunner and dig out a perimeter trench. Their objective was to make the Makahanap house and the district office next door more defensible in case the Japanese should attack. It was exhausting work for the Yanks, but they wanted to feel they were contributing to Makahanap's war effort.

That afternoon, Christiaan took them across the vine-and-rattan bridge to see the Presswood house, which was surrounded by gardenia bushes and a crop of fresh pineapples— one of which was served at dinner that evening. Inside, however, the beautiful hardwood floors and the whitewashed walls were stained with blood. It was a shocking sight, and it brought back the horrors of this war to the men.

Since the Yanks' return to Long Berang, the Lun Dayeh from the longhouses ranged along the Pa' Paru had done their best to make the strangers feel welcome. They were fascinated by them and liked touching the Yanks' hairy arms and watching them as they went about their daily activities. They gave the Yanks Lun Dayeh names: Phil was called Ya-Kong ("pig trap"—for no reason the Dayaks ever explained); Dan was Lagan (the same name as the *pangeran* from Long Metuil); Jim's name was Pangeran ("chief") and Eddy's was Farung ("foreigner").

Singing served as a common language. Phil, who had a good baritone voice, got his crewmates to join him as he marched around the longhouse singing "Onward Christian Soldiers." The hymn had a strong beat to it, and the longhouse people were quick to join the Yanks marching around the outside veranda and indoors past the cooking fires. They all sang the stirring words—or a Dayak approximation of the English lyrics—at the tops of their voices, with the ancient iron drums beating in rhythm.

When sitting down in the evening with some *borak*, the Yanks' rendition of the old camp song "Hallelujah, I'm a Bum" was a great favorite with both sides. The Yanks enjoyed the mild impropriety of singing this parody of a religious revival song and were tickled by the way the Lun Dayeh, recognizing the one word, "hallelujah," took on a pious expression.

The airmen's youthful playfulness, dimmed since Morotai, now resurfaced. They liked to swim, though they first had to convince the anxious Dayaks that they could stay afloat. The Dayaks, fearing that the airmen would drown, had tried to discourage them from entering the deeper parts of the river. But once the airmen showed that they were competent in the water, the Dayaks relented and the river became their favorite playground. At Phil's insistence, they had been carrying a one-person rubber life raft since the day they had dropped into Borneo. Phil, who had often wondered whether it made sense to hold on to it, inflated the raft on the river one day and the Lun Dayeh were intrigued. They had never seen anything like it, and they would play with it on the river for hours. At night, Dayaks from one of the Long Berang longhouses would sometimes ask to borrow it, and a few men and boys would take turns lying on it on the veranda, where the bachelors slept, to the accompaniment of cackles of laughter from their friends and neighbors.

When the airmen went on visits with their hosts to nearby settlements, the first thing their companions did upon reaching their destination was to take the raft to the river in front of the longhouse and show it off to those who had never seen one before.

Makahanap returned home after stopping off in Punan Silau to see Mama and the children. Mama had told him a fascinating story. While she had been alone with Iwak and the children earlier that week, some Japanese had come by to pay a social call on her and the Dayaks of the longhouse. At Mama's suggestion, the Dayaks served their visitors their strongest brew, an *arak* (brandy) made from distilled *borak*. The Japanese tossed it back as they were in the habit of doing when offered *borak*. The effects came quickly, and soon they were stumbling and laughing, trying to dance with the Dayak women.

Throughout the evening, they kept asking Mama where her husband was. Mama, at her most flirtatious, said in Malay that she had no idea. But if he was doing something naughty, they should try to find and punish him. After all, "I am still young. I can get married with a Japanese." The Japanese had "laughed and laughed, and then they left."

Makahanap thought about Mama's story all the way back to Long Berang. Among other things, it reminded him of how young and lovely Mama still was, and how it was that she had become his wife.

He had been a proud young man of good family, who thought he deserved the best wife he could find. He was the sixteenth generation of heirs to the title of rajah of his native Sangir Islands, which were in the northernmost part of the Celebes island group. Sangir was famous in the old days for its sorcerers, but Makahanap's parents were Christian. His father, Pololot, was the pastor of the Lutheran church and *kepala kampong* (the Dutch colonial government's appointed head) of the Protestant community of Taruna, the capital city of the Sangir Islands. His mother was of Arab descent, her ancestors having come to the Sangir region in the early days of the Spice Islands trade, but she had become a Lutheran when she married Makahanap's father. Pololot's widowed cousin Beslar had moved to Makassar, the capital of the Celebes island group, and had joined the Christian and Missionary Alliance, the Kemah Injil. Makahanap stayed with this cousin in Makassar after high school in order to study at the teacher-training school there and he, too, had converted to Kemah Injil.

Before going to Makassar to study, Makahanap had already found the woman he wanted for his wife. She was Theresia Manis, the fifteen-year-old daughter of the *kepala kampong* of the town of Kaluwatu. Makahanap had come to the attention of Theresia's father by being the best bamboo-flute player in Sangir, and he was also the top student at the Taruna high school. When the young man made his interest in Theresia known, her father encouraged the suit. He saw Makahanap as coming from a suitable family, and he had brains—and he shared the father's love of music.

But Theresia had other plans. Young as she was, she had already fallen in love with a man named Herman who was off working in the Dutch half of the island of New Guinea. Unbeknownst to her father, she and Herman were exchanging letters.

Somehow, Makahanap found out about the young lovers' secret correspondence and bribed the postman in Taruna (at the only post office on the island) to give him the letters that Herman sent Theresia. When he had collected a few, he took them to Theresia's father, who forbade his daughter to continue the correspondence. Makahanap knew that Theresia never loved him as she had loved Herman, but she eventually consented to an engagement to Makahanap when she turned nineteen. When she could delay it no longer, she married him in 1935, when Makahanap was twenty-six and she was twenty-five.

Makahanap loved her enough to make up for the lack of reciprocity, and he knew she was a good woman who would never betray him. His own faithfulness was another matter. While he and Theresia were studying at the Kemah Injil schools in Makassar in preparation for assignment to Borneo, William had an affair with a Celebes Muslim woman, by whom he had a son, Hassan. Makahanap still did not know why he had done it. Perhaps because he felt insufficiently loved by his wife. Perhaps because it was always hard for him to stay on one side of any question. He was like a gambler who always needed to hedge his bets.

But this time, he told himself, this time, with the blood of so many Japanese already on his hands, this time, he prayed to God, this time he would prove worthy to be Mama's husband and God's servant. He would do right and not count the cost.

With that vow in mind, he arrived in Long Berang, eager to pursue the war against the Japanese. The visit to his wife in

Punan Silau had confirmed that the Japanese had not yet given up trying to find him. He would be unable to hide himself or avoid danger to his family much longer. The best defense would be to attack.

As for his American charges, he could not make up his mind which option made the most sense: To use them as fighters or to hide them where they would be safe. For the moment they were a distraction, so he decided to move them across the river to the Presswood house.

Still focused on his vow to continue the war, he took advantage of the presence of so many Dayaks in Long Berang to summon a mass meeting of the inhabitants of the Mentarang, Pa' Paru and Kinaye rivers. To the crowd lining the near bank of the Pa' Paru a short distance outside of town, the district officer declared there was no longer an alternative to fighting. The killing they had done already meant the Japanese would show them no mercy.

He warned the people that anyone who opposed or refused to carry out his orders would have to be regarded as a deadly enemy. There was no room left for standing aside. Now that the people of his district were directly involved in the war, it was better to die fighting than to wait to be tortured and killed by the Japanese. He said this would be a guerrilla war and explained that, in a guerrilla war, the advantage would be clearly with the Dayaks, who knew the jungle. They could hide, whereas the Japanese could not.

Makahanap knew his Bible. As he looked over the crowd, he must have been reminded of Gideon's selecting his Israelite forces for the battle against the Midianites. The D.O. knew many men of this part of Borneo personally and easily picked out a hundred strong men to be fighters and another fifty who were smart and reliable, but not as strong, to be messengers and informants. He divided the fighters into two groups, placing

fifty under the command of Pangeran Lagan and the other
fifty under Christiaan's command. He called on the two com-
manders to organize oath takings. "Dogs must be killed
again," he declared. As for the others present, they were ordered to return home, but to see to it that the troops were fed.
The meeting broke up without dissent.

The next day, Makahanap wrote a letter to be sent to the
Japanese headquarters at Malinau:

> *I, William A. Makahanap, acting on behalf of the
> whole people of the district Mentarang, herewith decree
> that we are not willing to be governed by the Japanese
> Imperium. We have decided to fight hand in hand with
> the Allied forces who at this moment are already in our
> district.*
>
> *We, the people of Mentarang, in cooperation with
> the Allied forces, now are ready to crush the Japanese
> Imperial Army.*
>
> *On behalf of the people of Mentarang,*
> *The Chief Commander,*
> *[signed] W. A. Makahanap*

He also wrote to the heads of the Krayan District and other
nearby administrative regions that "We, the people of Mentarang, herewith inform you that we are no longer under the
Japanese government. It is forbidden for strangers to enter
our district without permission. He who guides the Japanese
*heitai*s to our district will be regarded as our enemy."

The four American airmen whose presence had sparked
the armed rebellion against the occupying power were unaware that it had begun. The day Makahanap wrote his letters
of defiance, Phil's diary speaks only of Christiaan giving them
their first haircuts and shaves in more than two months. Phil
and the three other Yanks were also unaware that a head feast

to rival the one they had seen in Long Metuil was taking place just across the bridge. Phil's diary notes, "Some Dayaks from other villages were in town for a celebration, parading and chanting throughout the afternoon, and a goat and several pigs have been killed. So I guess they had a big feast." The Americans also had a great dinner that night, with wine presented by one of the Chinese merchants and Christiaan's specially prepared chicken (described by Phil as "next to Mother Hartman's, the best I've ever had").

Phil, who had written to Tom Capin and John Nelson and Franny Harrington after Makahanap had brought news of them, now wrote another letter to Tom urging him to join them. Christiaan, armed with Phil's own .45 automatic, agreed to take the letter to Capin and bring him back.

Phil, Dan, Eddy and Jim were all feeling well enough to be restless. They were spending their time "eating, sleeping, reading the five or six English books here and swimming in the river," Phil wrote. By January 31, he wrote in his diary that he hoped that they would be leaving soon, "because, although it's been a valuable experience in a way, I feel that so much time is being wasted when you sit for hours at a time doing nothing."

Just before Makahanap's letter reached Malinau, the Japanese there received a concrete piece of evidence that they had lost control of the Mentarang District. A Chinese working for the Japanese administration reported seeing the bloated body of the *taicho* floating past the absent *ken kanrikan*'s office. That body plus the absence of news from the other sixteen men meant that Japan's occupation of Borneo's interior was being put into question for the first time. The administrators in Malinau sent to Tarakan for troops to come up to join in an attack on Long Berang. Knowing that Pangeran Lagan was the most influential Dayak in the region, they held him responsible. They had been hunting for him for weeks, ever since the *taicho* had decided to move to Long Metuil. Now they would try to smoke him out by taking hostage some of the Lun Dayeh children in the Japanese-run boarding school in Malinau.

Mustapa al-Bakri, the Malay official technically in charge of the Muslim community of Malinau District but who was merely acting as an aide to the Japanese administrator, protested against the arrest of the students. He argued that this was a bad way to try to obtain cooperation from the Dayaks, who were devoted to their children. Eventually, as the days passed with no sign of Pangeran Lagan or any other indication that the Dayaks were ready to cooperate, the Malay's arguments prevailed. After a week, the Japanese authorities released the children, who fled home to their families.

Mustapa al-Bakri's advice had been sound. Already, the jailing of the students had done damage to the Japanese image among people who, for the most part, had been ready to tolerate the foreign occupation. The arrests had also frightened many of the other students into fleeing the boarding school. Malay police rounded up the students and brought them back, but rumors continued to circulate that the Japanese had killed the child hostages.

On the afternoon of February 1, Makahanap and Christiaan returned home with a strange-looking redheaded giant in a loincloth: Tom Capin. The other Yanks were amazed to see the change in him. In some ways Capin seemed more Dayak than Yank. For the first few days, he often broke into Lun Dayah and at times stumbled for the right word in English.

Tom brought welcome confirmation that John Nelson and Francis Harrington were alive and well. He said he had learned that they were being cared for somewhere in the north where it was safe and that they were hesitant to come down south to join the others.

Makahanap, although he had agreed to it, now wondered if having Tom Capin with them might be a mistake, since every additional airman added to the risk for them all. He was still unsure what to do with the airmen but was coming around to the idea that their safety should be his first priority. When he and Christiaan had stopped off at Punan Silau on their way to Pa' Ogong to collect the other airman, Mama had burst into tears at not being able to cook for the Yanks. She told her husband again: "Americans dead, you dead. Americans alive, you alive." William always took what Mama said seriously.

Now that he had time, Makahanap tried to explain to the Americans what had been going on in his district and that he was leading a guerrilla war to push the Japanese back to Tarakan. For a few days he had the airmen stand guard duty at night as part of a Dayak-manned twenty-four-hour watch for miles beyond Long Berang.

While Makahanap wrestled with his problem, Eddy Haviland wandered up one day into the attic at the Presswood house, trying to find a little privacy. Eddy was the most intellectual of the crew members and longed even more than the others did for a quiet place to think. He was now seeing well enough to be able to keep an eye out for insects and snakes. Instead, he found a true treasure trove: piles of old American magazines.

Paging through *Reader's Digest* for June 1939, Eddy must have been amused to find an article giving various national columnists' views on whether the United States should enter the war. Heywood Broun (syndicated in 41 papers with nearly three million readers) favored entry, arguing "There are no caves in which men can hide when their fellows cry out in agony." Westbrook Pegler (in 117 newspapers with a combined circulation of more than six million) had another view: "Perhaps the American people, if consulted, would say that if Britain and France must fight such a war, that is just their hard luck and, after all, only another war in the long series of wars between jostling European countries." Pegler ended with the comment: "For God's sake don't anybody blow a bugle now."

Eddy shouted to the others to come upstairs and see what he had found. The airmen pounced on the magazines. For the first time in ages, the thought of their next meal was not uppermost. Jim sat blissfully amidst a pile of *Popular Mechanics*.

In an issue of *National Geographic* from 1939, there was an article entitled "I Kept House in a Jungle," by a young American woman whose perspective was a bit different from the airmen's. Her problem was that apples were unavailable and the oranges were neither orange nor sweet. The airmen would have found it hard to sympathize, nor could they appreciate comments like, "The people of Venezuela . . . have the happy hearts of children." But there was a long piece in another 1939 issue by another American woman who had traveled throughout the eastern part of the Dutch East Indies, starting in Bali. What a pity that their parachutes had not brought the airmen there. It sounded so beautiful and so interesting.

The next day, the men's spirits sank briefly after a squadron of seventeen B-24s flew directly overhead. When they first heard the planes in the distance, they had spread out their chutes and had used mirrors to reflect the sunlight in the hopes of attracting the attention of the squadron but, as Phil wrote in his diary, "I guess not one of the 170 men up there was looking down."

CHAPTER ELEVEN

The Navy Crashes In

John Nelson and Franny Harrington were the first of the Coberly crew to hear the news. A Lun Dayeh hunting party came back to Long Nuat with word that yet another planeload of Americans had landed—near Limbang, a bit inland from Brunei Bay in northern Sarawak. By the time the news of these other downed airmen reached John and Franny, this second group of Americans had been in Borneo for more than a month. A lot had happened during that time.

Shortly before noon on Saturday, January 13, 1945, a U.S. Navy Liberator (called a PB4Y) was eight thousand feet above Brunei Bay between two layers of clouds, flying as part of Squadron VPB-101. This flight was scheduled to be the last for the Liberator's ten-man crew before a long-awaited forty-five days of home leave. Starting out that morning from their air base on Morotai, the navy men had had the unglamorous task of dropping "Liberation" leaflets on communities in the oil fields of northwest Borneo just south of Brunei Bay. Three months had passed since the Battle of Leyte Gulf, and things were quiet in this corner of the war. In fact, this crew had not fired a shot in anger during its entire eighteen-month tour of duty with the 101st. When the last of the pamphlets had slipped out of the bomb bay, a cheer went up as the copilot,

Lt. (j.g.) Robert J. Graham, turned the plane northeast, back toward Morotai. Having completed the mission, they were now due for a rest.

Bob Graham had been married only a few weeks when he had shipped out for this tour of duty, and seeing his wife again was uppermost in his thoughts—when he could stay awake. The sun was streaming in, it had been a long day already and he was a bit sleepy. He needed a sandwich, a smoke and a stretch. He asked the pilot, Lt. Cdr. Marvin "Smitty" Smith, to take the controls for a bit and accepted one of the sandwiches that the nose gunner, young Sheridan Poston, was handing out.

Smitty was not only the pilot of this plane but also the executive officer for the whole squadron. He was glad to have a turn flying the Liberator. But he had barely taken over the controls when two pairs of Japanese fighter planes suddenly emerged from the clouds. A shout came through the intercom from waist gunner William John Fischer: "Bandits, bandits at twelve o'clock." Within seconds, enemy aircraft knocked out two of the Liberator's four engines and hit nose gunner Poston in the legs. The plane's artificial horizon was also destroyed. With the plane rapidly losing altitude, Smitty steered away from the populous towns along Brunei Bay, where the Japanese were known to be in force. He looked for somewhere soft and flat to crash-land the plane. While he peered downward, two of the enemy fighter planes reappeared above. The top turret gunner Reuben Lloyd Robbins and waist gunner Bill Fischer got solid hits on one of them. Avoiding a mountain in his path, Smitty found a flat, wet rice paddy. The PB4Y skidded 150 yards in the mud and came to a complete stop—a perfect belly landing.

But Smitty was painfully aware that they were not as far away from the Japanese-held coast as he had hoped to be. On the plus side, except for Poston, who was hemorrhaging from the bullet wounds in his legs, they all seemed to have come through without injury.

As soon as the plane shuddered to a halt, some of the crew moved quickly to destroy all documents that might be of use to the enemy while others broke out a one-man rubber raft to lower Poston down from the wrecked plane. Grabbing a silk map of Borneo, a Malay/English word list, two first-aid kits and a radio set, they headed for the shade of some trees that lined the rice paddy. Just before they reached the trees, Poston died in the rubber raft.

The crew was down to nine: In addition to Smitty and Bob Graham, Fischer and Robbins, there were aviation chief machinist's mate Talmadge Cyrus Thurmond; 2nd radio Kenneth R. Platte; sea gunner Melvin Joseph Roth; navigator Alvin Marvin Harms and 2nd mechanic James Ronald Shepherd.

Smitty was tall, well built and red haired. Another pilot described him as the "kindest man I met in the service. He wasn't flamboyant ... I never saw him drunk or loud." His men had always felt ready to follow him anywhere, and now they were about to do so.

As they sat under the trees—out of the midday sun but still in the sultry heat—Smitty explained what he had in mind. Like Phil Corrin, he knew he and his men must try to put as much distance as possible between themselves and the northwest coast where, thanks to the oil fields, the Japanese were present in fairly large numbers. He had heard that the occupiers had the more-or-less willing cooperation of the Malays and of some of the natives near the coast, and the reluctant support of the terrified Chinese. He guessed this was true all along the Borneo coast. He had no idea what the people of the interior were like, except that he had heard that they all were—or had been—headhunters. Still, the interior natives were less likely to turn the airmen in, because, it was thought, there were fewer Japanese in the interior.

On the other hand, Smitty thought their best plan would be to get off this island and back to their base as soon as possible. The briefers had told him that there was usually an Allied submarine waiting off the north coast of Borneo near Kudat, ready to pick up stranded airmen. But it would take weeks to walk northeast through the mountains to reach that part of the coast and, once on the north coast, they would have to dodge the Japanese. But he saw no other valid option than to head inland and then north to Kudat while trying to avoid running into the enemy. The others agreed.

They were wearily gathering up some tools to dig a hole to bury Poston when they noticed that they were being observed. A pair of natives had appeared. They wore loincloths, carried blowpipes with spearheads, and each had a knife belt holding a machetelike knife. The natives called out in Malay to the airmen, stuck their blowpipes in the mud and approached with offerings of sticky rice.

The flyers, with the help of the Malay/English word list they had rescued from the plane, managed to convey their wish that their dead comrade be buried. The natives agreed but seemed anxious not to stay too long with the airmen. They urged the Yanks to move on quickly away from the coast, away from the Japanese.

Using the silk map of Borneo he had been issued, Smitty showed the crew that the simplest way to Kudat seemed to be to follow the Temburong-Trusan river system southeast across eastern Brunei and northern Sarawak up into the Crocker Range, which was just inside the British-protected state of North Borneo. Their guides indicated the best crossing place would bring them into North Borneo just south of the village of Pa' Matang. From there, they could follow the Matang and

Tomani rivers due north to the Padas River, continuing north past Kemabong and Tenom to the coast and Kudat.

The airmen set off without guides. Except for worries about being seen by the Japanese or their collaborators, the trip looked relatively straightforward, judging from the silk map. But the path turned out to be not nearly so smooth.

To avoid getting lost, they stayed close to the rivers. Smitty sent Bob Graham ahead to see if he could locate a village where a guide might be found. At the first village, Graham, word list in hand, was kindly received by the village chief, but the chief said that the Japanese were certain to make reprisals if they learned that he or his villagers had helped the airmen. He let Graham bring the others to spend the night on the dirt floor of his hut and made sure they were given rice to eat, but he was clearly anxious for them to move on. The airmen were loaned a guide to take them to the next village, but no farther. This pattern continued at each place the navy men stopped.

Smitty had been right to worry about landing so near the coast. Not only were he and his men much nearer to the Japanese than Coberly's crew had been, but the terrain they passed through, well into the rainy season, was full of malarial mosquitoes, and dysentery was widespread among the villages where they paused for the night.

For thirteen days, they walked twelve hours a day with only rice to eat. Some of the men got dysentery, and most of them had attacks of malaria after the Atabrine wore off. After crossing the steep and slippery Crocker Range and arriving inside North Borneo, the nine utterly exhausted navy men reached the village of Long Pa' Sia on the Matang River. Here, the people lived in longhouses and the Malay word list was useless.

Smitty and his party stopped at the first longhouse they came to. Bob Graham went in ahead, as usual. Inside the dark and smoky longhouse, Graham saw a picture on the wall of

Jesus having his feet bathed. The lieutenant drew out the G.I. New Testament that he carried in his shirt pocket and showed the natives the identical picture. Immediately, the Tagal tribesmen warmed to him. They seemed to be asking if he was a missionary. Graham tried to indicate that there were no missionaries in his party but that they were surely in need of help. The Tagal longhouse chief seemed to understand and took pity on them. He agreed that they could stay in his village until they were strong enough to travel.

The navy men were lucky to have come into North Borneo so far inland from the north coast. The airmen did not know it but, unlike the Lun Dayeh whom the army aviators had met, the Tagal tribes of the Padas River system were divided in their thinking as to how best to deal with the Japanese occupation. The upriver Tagal were mostly Christians and were generally pro-Western. But the downriver Tagal, who lived near the coast, where the Japanese were in control, were anxious to get along with the occupation authorities. Some of the northern Tagal were actively collaborating with the Japanese against the Allies.

To avoid discovery and to reduce the burden on their hosts in an area of food scarcity, Smitty split his crew up into three groups of three. He had lost his .45 in the plane crash and so Graham lent him his nickel-plated .32 revolver. Graham, who still had his G.I.-issue .38, took Harms and Robbins, the two sickest of the crew, south so that they could recover a bit farther from the coast before rejoining Smitty's group to make the trek north. With guides to help them, Graham's party got across the border to Long Tefadong, a Lun Dayeh village in Dutch Borneo.

Smitty and the other five remained at Long Pa' Sia. During this pause to rest up for the journey north, Smitty's group got sicker from malaria and dysentery. The Dayaks offered the

Yanks hot water with wood ash in it for the malaria, but this cure did not work.

On February 12, the Tagal chief at Pa' Sia came to Smitty ashen faced and managed to make him understand that the Japanese had followed the airmen's trail across the Crocker Range. There was now a party of thirty Japanese in Pa' Matang, just an hour's walk north. Smitty, with no time to contact Graham in the south, rounded up the other five airmen in Pa' Sia and prepared to leave immediately. The Pa' Sia chief gave them guides to take them north as far as Kemabong.

Smitty figured it might take his group as much as a month's hard walking to reach Kudat. He looked his crew over; the men were in dreadful shape, especially Jim Shepherd, the assistant crew chief, who was too weak from malaria to walk at all.

The Tagal chief arranged for Shepherd to be brought to one of the huts in the rice field and promised to see that he was fed and cared for until he was well enough to join Smitty or Graham's group in the south. With that, Smitty and his remaining four men and their guides began the trek north along the Padas River. By dint of sheer will and their guides' help, they got halfway to Tenom in twelve hours without being detected by the Japanese. As night fell, their Pa' Sia guides handed them over to the care of other Tagal tribesmen.

Smitty and his men had left Pa' Sia just in time. That afternoon, a seven-man Japanese patrol arrived from Pa' Matang and occupied the same quarters that Smitty had slept in the night before. Jim Shepherd, lying in his hut in the rice field racked by malaria, could hear the Japanese soldiers. One party passed within three hundred yards of where he lay. He ignored the sand fly bites as he willed his body to be utterly still.

Six days later the Japanese left. The villagers carried Shepherd back to the longhouse. For the next week, a Tagal husband

and wife took turns watching over him, putting rice in his mouth whenever he seemed able to eat. Finally, on February 26, Shepherd could stand up for the first time in nearly a month. He asked his hosts to take him south by dugout canoe to where Graham, Harms and Robbins were hiding.

Though a Japanese patrol was heading in roughly the same direction, Shepherd and his Tagal oarsmen successfully reached Long Tefadong, the little Lun Dayeh border village where the Graham group had gone. But once there, Shepherd found only Alvin Harms and Robby Robbins. They told him that Lieutenant Graham had heard that there were other downed American airmen in Dutch Borneo a few days' walk farther south, and he had gone to try to find them before going on to Kudat. Graham had left behind a .38 pistol (the only gun they had) and seventeen rounds of ammunition. They were waiting for his return.

Jim Shepherd looked at his two crewmates; they were in worse shape than he was. In Graham's absence their health had deteriorated. Harms was dehydrated from dysentery. The intestinal cramps were excruciating and made it impossible for him to sleep for any length of time. Robbins was in even worse shape, with a tropical ulcer on the base of his spine that was some four inches in diameter and exposed the bone underneath. He was exhausted by the pain and delirium, and he could not retain food.

Shepherd had no choice but to wait with them for Graham's return. As the days passed with no news from the lieutenant, morale among the three airmen fell. At one point, Robbins became so lifeless that Shepherd started to dig a grave for him.

The Lun Dayeh villagers did everything they could to help the sick airmen. One of the women tried different foods for Robbins, to no avail, until she gave him rice fried in wild boar fat. He managed to keep that down. The grease slid the rice through his damaged lower intestinal system without causing any harm. From then on Robbins stopped losing weight and even regained some, though the pain from the ulcer persisted.

Other people gradually learned of the navy men's presence, including a Chinese Christian named Thomas Koh. Koh, who was working in Lawas, Sarawak, as a rice-purchasing clerk for the Japanese, whom he had come to loathe, was on a trip up-river into Lun Dayeh and Tagal areas to buy rice when he heard of the airmen, who were now walking north in North Borneo.

Koh, because he traveled so widely, knew that the Japanese were building a headquarters at Tenom, directly in the airmen's reported path. He sent a message via his most trusted Dayak to the airmen telling them to turn around and head back into Sarawak to Long Lopeng, where they would be safe. But when Koh's messenger reached Pa' Sia, the Japanese patrol was in residence and Smitty and his four airmen had already left.

Smitty and the others got about halfway to Tenom and had been handed over by their southern Tagal guides to two northern Tagal guides, who took them as far as Tomani, four hours' walk south of Tenom. The navy men were by then so ill, so tired and their leech-infected feet in such bad shape, that they agreed to the suggestion of Tomani's two Tagal longhouse chiefs to stay in Tomani, after which the chiefs promised to provide guides to Kemabong, just south of Tenom.

Unaware of the new Japanese headquarters at Tenom and also not knowing that the northern Tagals did not share the anti-Japanese views of their fellow tribespeople to the south, the five navy men gladly accepted the offer of a few days' respite in Tomani.

They had been there just two days when a native porter for the Japanese came to the village and spoke quietly to the chief of the Tomani longhouse where the airmen were staying. Within minutes, all the Dayaks dashed outside. Within seconds, the airmen heard a fusillade of bullets hitting their longhouse.

The Japanese, firing blindly into the bamboo walls, did not hit any of the airmen. Then a mixed patrol of two Japanese, six Malays and eight Chinese rushed the longhouse. One of the navy men ran out, heading for the jungle, and was killed by a Tagal spearhead. Two other airmen tried to make a dash for it. One (probably Smitty) reached the jungle and disappeared into the brush, but the other one was shot dead as he climbed down the log ladder through the longhouse veranda floor. The remaining two unarmed navy men surrendered.

The patrol stayed in Tomani with the two prisoners for the next week while the American in the jungle continued to elude his would-be captors—though he was no more able than Tom Capin had been to find food in the wild. Eventually, a Tagal working for the Japanese army tracked the man down and guided the Japanese patrol to where he was hiding. The patrol fired away from a distance without hitting the target, until all the ammunition was spent. The patrol leader then returned to the longhouse compound and convinced one of the two captive airmen to persuade his friend in the jungle to give himself up. The Japanese said that if the airman succeeded in bringing his friend back, all three of them would be well treated.

The man in hiding then gave himself up, undoubtedly in the hope of saving his two crewmates. But when the two airmen returned to the longhouse, they found the bodies of their two dead crewmates dismembered and burning in a fire, and the remaining prisoner being whipped with rawhide. Too angry to care anymore about their safety, the two returning navy men fought the Japanese patrol hand to hand. A red-haired man (Smitty) was seen picking up a Japanese by the leg and swinging him against a tree, killing him in the process. After that—one version of the story has it—all three surviving airmen were trussed up and marched off to Beaufort, North Borneo, where they spent a month as prisoners before being marched to Jesselton, where the trail ends. Another version—one more likely to be true—says the men were murdered on the spot and buried at Tomani on or about February 20.

Bob Graham, having left his two sick companions in Long Tefadong, had gone to find the other downed American airmen who, he had been told, were being hidden farther to the south, at Long Nuat. He and his Lun Dayeh guides traveled at a terrific pace farther into Dutch Borneo through the mountainous area along the Kemalu River. They reached Long Nuat in late February.

There to meet Graham were the astonishingly fit and well-rested Franny Harrington and John Nelson. While he waited to be presented to William Mongan, his wife Maria and their three wide-eyed children, Graham glanced around at the civilized little village with its church and a few Dutch colonial houses and gardens, and was thoroughly taken aback. So, too, were John and Franny. This ragged, desperate navy lieutenant was a reminder that the war that had receded somewhat from their consciousness was still very present in northern Borneo.

Perhaps because he now felt safe, Graham collapsed from exhaustion, hunger and malaria. While his Long Tefadong guides returned home, the Mongans and the army airmen worked hard to help Graham get well, though they were in no hurry to have him go back to the other navy men. Their wish to keep the lieutenant with them was strengthened when

Mongan learned through the native grapevine that three of the village chiefs who had hosted the navy airmen up north had been taken away, tortured and then killed by the Japanese.

Bob Graham slowly recovered and resumed eating proper food, cooked by Maria Mongan. When he wasn't sleeping or playing cards with John and Franny, Bob would read from the 1933 edition of the *Literary Digest,* the only English reading material available, except for his G.I. New Testament. But once he started to get well, he grew more insistent about getting back to the two men he had left over the border. As the ranking airman, he obtained Franny's and John's grudging consent to their catching up with Harms and Robbins and then joining Smitty and the others on the road to Kudat.

Early one morning during the second week of March, Bob, John and Franny bade an emotional farewell to the Mongans and the villagers of Long Nuat. It felt like leaving home.

They had been on their way less than a day and a half when their Lun Dayeh guides suddenly began talking to one another in an agitated manner. The guides told the airmen that there was a Japanese patrol just minutes away, but the airmen saw no sign of such a patrol. Without trying to explain themselves further, the Dayaks urged the Americans to turn around and go back to Long Nuat. When the three airmen protested, the Dayaks ran away, toward Long Nuat.

Graham and the others did not know what to think. Why had their guides abandoned them? Were the natives going to kill them after all? Or turn them over to the Japanese? Eventually, Bob decided that John and Franny should go back to Long Nuat while he went to Long Tefadong alone. If there really were Japanese patrols in the area, he argued, one man made less of a trail than three.

Graham made his way to the border village and found not only the ill men he had left behind but also a third sick airman, Jim Shepherd. Worse still was the news about Smitty and the four men who had gone north with him—news that Robbins, Shepherd and Harms had recently been told by their frightened Long Tefadong hosts. This terrible news was what had so agitated Graham's Long Nuat guides and made them abandon the plan to continue north.

Graham now set about trying to lead the three very ill airmen back to Long Nuat without attracting more enemy attention. He had no guides this time but, having done the trip both ways now, he felt sure he could manage it. But as much as he had benefited from the two weeks of rest with the Mongans, he could not carry all the food and equipment himself. The people at Long Tefadong had given the airmen sacks of uncooked rice and a valuable but heavy large iron cooking pot. Graham decided that he and Shepherd would go first and take turns carrying the iron pot while Harms and Robbins followed with the sacks of rice.

It had taken Graham two days to reach his men at Long Tefadong but he now had to slow his pace to match that of the slowest man, the assistant crew chief, Jim Shepherd. Shepherd had very painful hemorrhoids. Between that and the residual effects of malaria, Shepherd no longer had the stamina to complete the journey. On the second day, they were only halfway to Long Nuat and Shepherd was swaying as he walked. He told Graham that they should just leave him and go on while they could. Twenty-two-year-old Graham knew that this was not an option for either Shepherd or for the safety of the rest of the navy airmen.

Graham and Shepherd had little in common. Graham was from suburban Pennsylvania and a smart city boy. Shepherd had been raised on a potato farm and, in Graham's view, "was not too brainy or too worldly." Graham, searching his mind for some way to inspire or goad his crewmate to make the last necessary effort, remembered a short story he had once read. It told of a doctor and a diabetic patient being stranded in the Nevada desert after their car broke down miles from the nearest house. As they walked along toward town, the diabetic became weak and desperate for his daily dose of insulin. The doctor had nothing to give him, but he knew the man's body would produce its own insulin temporarily if whipped into a sufficiently excited condition. The doctor, who also had the diabetic's wife as his patient, invented a story that he was having an affair with the wife and told the diabetic the car breakdown had been their way to get rid of him so that the two lovers could marry. As the doctor had hoped, the diabetic's fury kept his insulin level up until the two men reached town.

Adapting the technique to the current circumstance, Graham said he had always known Shepherd was a coward, a weakling, a quitter and utterly unreliable. As the lieutenant had hoped, his taunts filled the crewman with a murderous rage, giving him the adrenaline to keep going.

By the next day, though Graham and Shepherd were keeping pace, the other two were falling behind. It was mid-March, the season of some of the longest, heaviest rains, and the hikers grew not only soaking wet but cold. Harms and Robbins had recurring attacks of malaria so extreme that they had to stop and find rest and shelter. The four men were taken in for the night in a little Lun Dayeh hamlet. Robbins's malarial chills were so bad that Harms and a Dayak boy had to lie on top of him to try to keep him warm. A few hours later, it was Harms's turn to start shivering and Robbins and the Dayak boy now lay on top of *him*. The airmen nonetheless got up early the next morning and walked a nightmarish thirteen hours.

Late in the afternoon of the fourth day, they reached the little village of Long Nuat, in its picturesque setting ringed by mountains. No place had ever looked so good.

By way of greeting, Franny Harrington said jokingly to Graham, "What have you done to us? Go away!" Graham knew his bringing the new men there had increased the risk of discovery, but he also knew that "these very sick men [had] to be cared for." To add to the burden of their Long Nuat hosts, the Kemalu River chose this time to overflow its banks and destroyed the Mongans' vegetable gardens. For the first time since the army airmen had arrived there, food was scarce.

The downed American airmen in Borneo were now clustered in two groups, the four navy men—Bob Graham, Jim Shepherd, Al Harms and Robby Robbins—and two army men, John Nelson and Franny Harrington, with the Mongans, and the remaining five army airmen—Phil Corrin, Dan Illerich, Jim Knoch, Eddy Haviland and Tom Capin—with Makahanap four or five days' walk farther southeast. When it was just a question of hosting John Nelson and Franny Harrington, the Mongans had wanted them to stay with them indefinitely. But now, with food so short and the number of fugitives in their care tripled, the Mongans were not opposed to some of the four navy men making the trip south; they also resigned themselves to losing John and Franny. Leaving the two sickest navy men (Harms and Robbins) behind, John, Franny, Jim Shepherd and Bob Graham set off to join the group with Makahanap around March 19.

More than a month earlier, Makahanap had become increasingly anxious about the safety of the five downed airmen with him. His campaign of encouraging the natives to oppose the occupiers had predictably led the Japanese to send another patrol upriver from Malinau. And though Pangeran Lagan and his men had eliminated the patrol with their usual dispatch,

Makahanap had come to feel that his American charges were in too much danger if they stayed in Long Berang. Not only was Long Berang now a Japanese target, but there were far too many people in town who knew the airmen were there. The district officer wearily concluded it was time for the Yanks to move again. Where should they go next? He decided on a Christian longhouse upriver at Bang Biau that was headed by his friend Sudai Agung. He knew he could count on Sudai and his people to take good care of the airmen.

Phil and the four other crewmen, accompanied by Makahanap, Yakal, Binum and two of her friends, left Long Berang early on February 10.

After Makahanap settled the airmen in a nearby longhouse for the night, he said he was leaving for other parts of the Krayan to organize the natives into a guerrilla force similar to what he had in Mentarang District. Phil, who hoped that at least some of the rumors he had heard about U.S. forces being in Borneo were true, gave William a note to pass along to any Allied forces he might meet.

The next morning, Yakal led Phil and his party on foot in the rain. On the third day, they arrived at Bang Biau. It was Valentine's Day. Yakal hunted and killed a wild boar, which made a welcome addition to everybody's dinner at the longhouse.

Phil, Dan, Jim, Eddy and Tom settled easily into life at Bang Biau, though Phil kept hoping that Franny and John would join them soon. By now, Phil and his men felt comfortable with the Lun Dayeh way of life. They had reached the point of enjoying tree mushrooms, and Phil even confessed to liking roasted grasshopper, which he said tasted like lobster or crabmeat. There were still things that annoyed the airmen, such as the roosters that woke them before dawn, and the fleas and lice that found their way into the seams of the Yanks' clothing. But the longhouse people were almost embarrassingly generous and considerate hosts. When they realized that the Yanks had run out of cigarettes, tobacco packets started arriving in such quantities that the Yanks could have opened their own smoke shop.

The Kemah Injil church and its activities played a big role in Bang Biau. Little cards with colored illustrations of Bible stories that the airmen remembered from their Sunday school days were prominently displayed, and Sunday services were the main event of the week. The first Sunday after the Yanks' arrival, the Bang Biau worshippers offered several prayers for the airmen's benefit, including one that asked God to cure Phil's occasional bouts of diarrhea. The Lun Dayeh also asked God to forgive them for killing the Japanese. These Christians told the airmen that they worried that killing even such bad people as the Japanese might keep them from getting to heaven. The airmen were touched by the degree of the community's commitment to its church nearly three years after the last foreign missionary had been taken away.

During the week, the Yanks would joke with the villagers within the limits of their shared vocabulary, and the villagers would retaliate in kind. Often the Dayaks would point to one of the older girls or young women of the longhouse and tell one of the soldiers, "That's your girl." The one they paired off with Jim Knoch was, in Phil's view, "the ugliest woman I've ever seen." Her name was Iwak, and she was Binum's friend from Long Berang, who had carried little Victor Makahanap on her back to Punan Silau when Mama and the children fled to safety. Phil and the others did not know that, and they began calling her "Jackass," as they might have done as boys together back in California. The villagers, not understanding what the word meant, called her "Jackyass" from then on.

When the Yanks got better at understanding the Dayaks, the Dayaks asked them the question all Dayaks liked to ask strangers: How many children do you have? Phil, for the fun of it, said he had five. Eddy, getting into the spirit of it, said he had eight and Jim claimed to have ten. Dan, who had not been paying attention, answered truthfully that he had none. Minutes of silence followed. The Dayaks clearly were torn between being scandalized by Dan's inadequacy and feeling pity that he should lack the chief treasure that life could bring. The Yanks had already noticed that Dayak children were never hit or punished. They seemed to grow up on love and laughter and were given a great deal of freedom to play where they wanted and say what they thought.

In early March, Makahanap returned to Bang Biau with four Eurasian N.E.I. soldiers who had escaped from a Japanese prison camp. The Yanks were thrilled to meet them. Except for Safri, these were the first even half-Westerners they had seen since leaving the air base in Morotai in November. Furthermore, these soldiers spoke quite good English. The stories of their time in the prison camp near Kuching, Sarawak, horrified their listeners. They said that not only military prisoners but also civilians had been tortured and then killed. They described the Japanese prison guards placing lighted cigarettes in prisoners' eyes, ears and noses. Other prisoners had their arms and legs chopped off before being given the final blow. And this in a camp run by a Japanese Christian, Colonel Tsuga!

Despite their experiences at the camp, these N.E.I. soldiers were remarkably lighthearted. They liked to sing, and knew some American songs. In all, they were a welcome addition to longhouse social life, and the airmen and the Dayaks hated to see them pack up and leave two days later.

The N.E.I. soldiers were determined to make their way

northwest over the mountains to Sarawak where, they had heard, the Allies had landed. Phil gave these cheerful young men a note for the Allies, describing their whereabouts.

Makahanap, who did not share the N.E.I. soldiers' confidence in the reports of an Allied landing, left Bang Biau the same day but went in a different direction. He headed due north to Long Nuat in hopes of convincing John and Franny to return with him to Bang Biau, because Phil and the others wished it. On the road north, however, he heard from Dayaks that Japanese patrols were looking for nine survivors of a U.S. bomber's crash-landing at Telehak, near Limbang Town. This was the first time the D.O. had heard about the downed navy airmen. As he traveled farther north, he learned that the Japanese had already found five of these airmen. Next, he heard that the Japanese were sending patrols down from the north and northwest to look for the remaining four.

Makahanap turned back toward Mentarang District to avoid running into the Japanese. He came across one of his best Lun Dayeh informants, who warned him that the Japanese were planning to send a patrol to Long Berang as soon as the water level on the Mentarang fell. Makahanap had long expected this, but he now focused his attention on the logistics of the problem. Bang Biau was too near the Japanese route, he realized. He decided once again that he must move his Yanks. This time, he would send them to where Mama and the children had been staying since mid-January, the animist longhouse in the hidden valley of Punan Silau, and he would get word to the Mongans that they should send their Yanks there as well.

Phil and his four crewmen arrived on March 23, Phil's birthday. Reaching Punan Silau the same day were John and Franny, looking fit. The seven Coberly crewmates had not been together since just before dropping into Borneo on

November 16. Nobody had word of photographer Philipps, but the rest of the crew was now reunited. Also present were Bob Graham and Jim Shepherd. With this crowd of Americans and with the special cakes and puddings prepared by Mama Makahanap, it seemed like a real birthday party, though Phil confessed to his diary that he had hoped and expected they would be out of Borneo by now.

Wonderful as Mama's cooking was, Punan Silau was not Long Berang. The animist longhouse was in the least accessible area of north central Borneo. Punan Silau was not on any map, even those that were more complete than Phil's silk rectangle. It had had almost no contact with Westerners, and food was scarce there. For the most part, the airmen had to return to living the way the longhouse people lived. The airmen, who slept on the outer veranda, kept a stick at their side to discourage the flea-ridden dogs from climbing up to chew on whatever they could find.

The Dayaks provided meat for their foreign guests as well as sugarcane, coconuts, papayas and bananas that were collected from farther down the mountainsides. Sometimes they would catch fish in big traps for their guests. They would bring back edible wild plants: fern tops, which could be boiled and added to a mound of rice, and tiny tomatolike fruits, so acidic that their juice would take the skin off one's lips. The Lun Dayeh here also ate mashed hot chili peppers as a relish. The Dayaks could take half a gourdful to spice up their rice but the Americans could not tolerate such fiery food. Since chilis were both rare and precious, the Dayaks were no doubt pleased that the Americans refused them after the first try.

Salt, though rare and valuable, was necessary to them all and caused one of the few near-fights between two of the airmen. It was triggered by Franny, who still had trouble walking because of hard-to-heal blisters on one of his feet. On top of this irritation, Franny would sometimes get so annoyed at being constantly surrounded by such young companions that he would have to get out and walk by the river until he cooled down. His entire manner was different from that of the other airmen. Not only was he a decade older, with a generally more profane and skeptical attitude, but he was also a Roman Catholic and pulled out his rosary to pray five times a day, until he lost it in the river.

Franny disliked officers more than Jim Knoch did, and one evening he told Lt. Bob Graham that he would "beat the shit out of him" if Bob ever again took so much salt with his rice. Franny saw himself as protecting one of the natives' most precious commodities. Graham was moved to respond in kind, denying he had taken too much. But after a short exchange of threats and obscenities, they both settled back down.

Such outbursts were rare, though the different approach to life among the Dayaks between Phil and his group and Tom Capin, who had come to think of himself as an honorary Lun Dayeh, had already introduced some tension among the airmen. Tom saw the others as ignorant and they saw him as a show-off. But all the Yanks by now had learned more or less how to behave in a longhouse. They knew to urinate and defecate discreetly in the woods or, if need be, at the edge of the longhouse veranda. Lacking toilet paper, they imitated what they saw the Dayak men do—go down to the river and quietly slip off their loincloths, lower their buttocks into the river, and let the water clean them.

Punan Silau, in the trough of a valley, saw the sun only four hours a day. During the few hours of daylight, when it wasn't raining, the airmen taught the Dayaks jiu-jitsu. The Lun Dayeh had a sport much like it, and both sides enjoyed throwing one another off their feet onto the soft mud of the riverbank. Still, the time passed slowly. The Dayaks were full of hopeful rumors about Allied landings, but the airmen saw nothing that convinced them that anyone was coming to liberate Borneo. Using the deck made at Polecat Gulch from the jungle-survival pamphlet, they played cards for hours.

Bob Graham, who had been checkers champion at his high school in Rosemont, Pennsylvania, got one of the Dayaks to make a checkerboard and a set of checkers, using charred wood for the black pieces and wood stained with vegetable dye for the red. There was one longhouse man who knew how to play, and Bob would challenge him. The other Dayaks lined up alongside to cheer them both on, and Bob would play in such a way as to ensure that half the games were won by his opponent. Later, Phil and Dan Illerich made drawings to show a Dayak woodworker how to make chess pieces. The woodworker followed the drawings all too literally: The pieces lay on their side rather than standing up on the board. The airmen did not have the heart to correct their kindly artist and passed many hours with their special chess set. The longhouse onlookers thought that the winner was the player who captured the most pieces, and they sometimes congratulated the loser.

In the evening, Mama would make the airmen coffee and encourage them to sing while she presided over them as if she were their loving parent. She worried especially about Eddy Haviland, nearly as young as John Nelson, because his chest still hurt, but she loved them all, especially her original four. In addition to Eddy, there were Phil, whom she thought of as so calm, gentle and thoughtful; Jim, who managed to seem carefree; and Dan, who could always find a reason to smile. It had cheered her up when Dan and Jim had learned how to say in Lun Dayeh: *Mama sleg matot inan God idita*—Don't be afraid, Mama, there is a God above.

Despite their hosts' efforts, the airmen were hungry most of the time. They longed for more and better-tasting food, especially fruit. When the Dayaks would bring back unripe bananas, pineapples and papayas, Mama would leave the fruit to ripen in a small storeroom she had made inside the longhouse. One evening, when everybody was sitting on the longhouse veranda after dinner, Mama noticed that Jim was not there. She went back inside to look for him and found him alone in the storeroom, eating an almost ripe banana. She did not protest or blame him, but he never did it again. When the Yanks quarreled, Mama would be visibly upset; Phil would get them to calm down again and apologize to her.

On April 1, Easter Sunday, the airmen's former host Sudai Agung, from Bang Biau, appeared at Punan Silau with a few others from his longhouse to bring the magazines that the Yanks had taken from the Presswood house, along with the rest of their clothes. Sudai also brought word that all the Japanese had left Malinau and Tarakan. If this was true, there would finally be a clear path by river for the Yanks to leave Borneo. If only it was not a rumor. Makahanap said he would ask Pangeran Lagan to check it out. Meanwhile the Yanks' impatience was palpable. It had been four and a half months since they had dropped into Borneo. As Phil wrote in his diary, "It seems as if the days are getting longer and longer. If only help will come soon."

CHAPTER TWELVE

Help from on High

The nine Yanks with Mama Makahanap suffered the frustration at not being able to do anything—not only did they lack training in jungle warfare but they had little knowledge of the terrain or even the local languages. But Makahanap was busy. Late in March, he had news of a new eight-man Japanese patrol on its way to Long Sempayang, disturbingly close to Punan Silau. With Mama, the children and the airmen all in one place, Makahanap felt that he had to find out for himself what the Japanese plans were.

He got word to Ah Tin, who came over to Punan Silau from Long Berang. The Chinese dressed himself and Makahanap in Lun Dayeh fashion and the two of them went to Long Sempayang. Upon arrival, the D.O. found the Japanese were already staying at the longhouse, so Ah Tin slipped away. Makahanap, regardless of the danger, could not fail to enjoy this moment of pure theater, as he gestured to the first Lun Dayeh he met not to call the Japanese soldiers' attention to him. When he could speak to the elders, he told them he had come to arrange to kill the men of the patrol. The villagers agreed to pretend that Makahanap was Lun Dayeh.

As Makahanap had feared, the Japanese patrol had come to the longhouse to find out what the Dayaks knew about the American airmen in the area, and if they knew where the traitor Makahanap was. Sitting with the elders in the long-house, the patrol leader saw Makahanap off on the side and seemed curious about this strange-looking Dayak.

Walking over to look hard at Makahanap, the patrol leader asked him some questions directly in Malay. Makahanap, in his loincloth and with another cloth twisted round the crown of his head the way Ah Tin had showed him, looked blank, as if he did not understand. The patrol leader turned to Buing Udan, a Lun Dayeh assistant pastor of the Long Sempayang Kemah Injil, who spoke Malay. Serving as interpreter between the longhouse people and the Japanese, the young pastor was spared having to answer falsely on his own behalf. Going along with Makahanap's pretense of not speaking Malay, Buing Udan translated the patrol leader's question into Lun Dayeh.

The time for translation gave Makahanap a chance to get his thoughts in order before answering. Then, in fluent Lun Dayeh, he told Buing Udan to tell their honored visitor that there were no strangers at Long Sempayang and that if the Japanese were looking for the airmen or for Makahanap they should go to the Mentarang.

The Japanese questioner nodded; the traitor Makahanap had, indeed, been reported in the Mentarang. Still, it was clear from the way the patrol leader looked at Makahanap that he found something odd about him. Suddenly, he ordered Buing Udan to ask the man why he had facial hair. Makahanap had anticipated this question and answered through the interpreter that it was because he came from upriver, where the people look somewhat different. For the moment at least, the questioner seemed satisfied and walked away.

But it was clear from the way the Japanese soldiers held on to their weapons at all times—in bed, when bathing—that they were on their guard. The patrol leader must have known that other patrols had come inland and simply disappeared, but neither he nor his superiors back in Brunei knew where to begin retaliating. The Japanese did not have the forces to police all of inland Borneo.

The next day, the patrol leader ordered his soldiers to split up. Four of the Japanese headed west and the other four went east toward Long Berang, perhaps to find the criminal Makahanap.

For the Japanese to divide their patrol in half would prove to be a mistake on their part. The attacks were brief and bloody, and none of the eight Japanese soldiers reached the far bank of the river alive. For the moment, Makahanap could feel confident that his family and the airmen in Punan Silau were safe. But for how long?

Two days later, Punan Silau had a visitor whose news seemed like an answer to a prayer. William Mongan had come south from Long Nuat, where he was still caring for Alvin Harms and Robby Robbins. The quiet little man was visibly excited by his news. With a stick he drew an odd, mushroom-like image in the dirt below the longhouse: a parachute. As Makahanap explained to Phil and the others, Mongan said (Phil wrote in his diary) that the previous week "seven white men and one interpreter . . . either landed or bailed out four days from here for the purpose of organizing the natives into guerrilla bands to fight the Japs. They say planes are dropping them supplies and that they have a radio!" This specific news was in another class entirely from the rumors they were used to hearing. Pastor Aris Dumat in Belawit sent Makahanap a note giving much the same news and noting that the new arrivals were Australians and their leader was a British major. Bob Graham scribbled in his diary: "Australian guerrillas landed in Borneo . . . March 25."

Phil, daring to hope this time that the story was true, took a few sheets of paper from one of William's lined school exercise books and wrote out a letter in his best Palmer Method penmanship:

April 3, 1945
Dear Sir:
    We just received word that there are seven of you
who have landed in Borneo for the purpose of
organizing the natives in warfare against the Japs.
There are seven of us from a U.S. Army B-24 which was
shot down November 16 and two from a Navy B-24 shot
down January 13. We are staying with William
Makahanap—a man from the Celebes who is District
official for the Dutch in this area. Under his supervision
the natives here have killed all Japs that have come into
this area. They are anxious to carry their warfare down
the river to Malinau and Tarakan and want you to
come to Long Berang to help them. They need the help
that modern warfare weapons can give them. And of
course we Americans would like very much to see you.
Several of us are in need of medical aid and naturally
we would like to get out of here as soon as possible. If
there is any way that you could send word out so that
we might receive some supplies or possibly be picked up
someplace, we would appreciate it very much. We hope
to see or hear from you soon.
        Sincerely yours,
        Philip R. Corrin, 2nd Lt. AC AUS 0-776633

The other eight airmen signed it in roughly the order of their coming under Makahanap's protection and included their ranks and serial numbers.

This time, it was not a rumor.

A week earlier, on the Plain of Bah, Kelabit elders at the Bario longhouse were surprised to see their men return early from the fields and forests. The men said they had seen what appeared to be two bunches of men coming down through the clouds to the earth, hanging from strings below big white tents. The longhouse headman and the Penghulu (the Sarawak equivalent of a *pangeran*) Lawai Bisara rounded up the other aristocratic elders and held a hasty conference in the middle of the longhouse.

Who were these creatures? Someone suggested that they might be the angels that visiting missionaries in the old days had spoken of, but this idea was roundly dismissed. If they were men, were they friends or foes? Were they soldiers? Were they Japanese? If not, would they attract the notice of the Japanese who they had heard were down on the coast? Up to now, the Japanese had seemed ignorant of the Plain of Bah and its paddy fields of surplus rice. The Kelabit hoped they would stay that way.

Excitable and anxious, several of the elders urged the quick killing of these creatures coming down from the sky, whoever or whatever they were. The Plain of Bah did not need this trouble. But Penghulu Lawai Bisara disagreed.

Lawai, mild mannered though he usually was, was not only the government-appointed leader of the people of the Plain of Bah, but was also the most knowledgeable man about the outside world in upriver British Borneo. Decades earlier, he had killed a man in Dutch Borneo. To avoid a long international headhunting war of vengeance, the Sarawak authorities had sent Lawai to be jailed downriver at the *kubu* (administrative fort), where he had done his time as a gardener for the Englishman who was the district officer. Oddly enough, he had emerged from this experience feeling more favorable toward white men than did his less sophisticated neighbors.

Suddenly, there was a great explosion of howling and yapping from the dogs on the outer veranda. At the top of the notched log appeared a small, slender man in a slouch hat who had skin and features not unlike their own but who acted and dressed like a white man. The newcomer spoke Malay. A brief exchange of questions and answers between him and Lawai, who also spoke some Malay, quickly revealed that the man was one of the eight soldiers who had dropped from the sky and that they were not Japanese.

When Lawai passed this news to the Bario elders, the question remained whether to befriend this Malay-speaking foreigner and the other foreign soldiers, or to kill them all and avoid future problems with the Japanese. As usual among the Kelabit, the argument grew heated and occasionally raucous. But, also as usual, Penghulu Lawai's views prevailed. The stranger, Sgt. Fred "Sandy" Sanderson, of the Australian Imperial Forces (AIF), was an Australian-Thai veteran of jungle fighting on the Southeast Asian mainland. He explained that he was with Major Harrisson's party as Malay interpreter and contact man. Sandy was given a rolled-leaf cigar and made welcome.

From Lawai's time in detention downriver, he knew some odd facts about white men. He knew, for example, that a white flag was a sign of nonaggression, and so he promptly had one of the longhouse's precious pieces of white cloth rigged to a length of bamboo. He told three young Kelabits to go out and wave the flag in view of the three strangers they could see standing in the muddy rice field below the longhouse. Lawai also instructed them to see if the newcomers had written material on them and if it had thin writing or thick-and-thin jabs. Meanwhile, Sandy let off a flare from his Verey pistol to alert his crew that it was safe here.

Soon, the Kelabit envoys were back on the veranda with the three white strangers and the white flag. It was clear that the eldest one knew his way around a longhouse, even if his Malay was not as good as the tan-skinned stranger's. Though tall, the older white man kept his torso low when he reached out to shake hands. His pale eyes seemed to take in everything—from the skeletal heads hanging above, to the large dark jars by the walls—and gave every indication that he liked what he saw. He offered cigarettes to the longhouse people, using the Malay word for "please accept this," *Silakan*.

British army Maj. Tom Harrisson, a thirty-three-year-old Englishman, did indeed like what he saw. He had spent his twenty-first birthday not far from where he now stood. He had been the student leader of an Oxford University expedition of undergraduates invited by the Sarawak government to record the fauna and flora of upland Borneo. Harrisson had spent months with the upriver longhouse people, with whom he had learned to communicate in basic Malay.

It was because of that youthful experience that Harrisson, a graduate of wartime officer-candidate training at Sandhurst, had been inducted into the British Special Operations Executive (an organization created by Churchill to encourage resistance activities behind enemy lines) and sent on loan to Australia to help its equivalent organization, Z Special, insert a clandestine unit into Borneo. The unit Major Harrisson commanded was called SEMUT 1 (from the word *semut* which means "ant" in Malay). SEMUT 1 was supposed to go into Borneo ahead of a planned June 1945 Australian-led Allied invasion to retake the oil-rich Borneo northwest coast around Brunei Bay. Dropped from two Australian Liberators onto the Plain of Bah, SEMUT 1 was meant to gather intelligence from the natives that would facilitate the invasion.

The other seven members of SEMUT 1, six Australians and one New Zealander, were much younger than their British major, but they had years' more combat experience—in the jungles of New Guinea and mainland Southeast Asia and the sands of North Africa. But only Major Harrisson had been to Borneo before, and he had his own ideas about how to soldier there. He had his own ideas about a lot of things. Physically tough and intellectually inventive, he had an ego as big as his accomplishments.

The major, with Sandy translating, was soon deep in discussion with Penghulu Lawai and the other elders. The *penghulu*, having learned that there were still four soldiers out on the plain somewhere, as well as packages of parachuted supplies (called "storepedos"), sent the young men of the longhouse out to round them up. Nothing this exciting had ever happened on the Plain of Bah before. David Labang, a five-year-old Kelabit visiting Bario with his father from a nearby longhouse, had been out with the Bario men when they saw the strangers dropping from the sky. He was hoisted up on his father's shoulders to get a better look. He then ran home to get his older brother Lian.

By the time David brought eighteen-year-old Lian back to Bario, the four soldiers from the second plane had reached the longhouse, which was now in the center of a hive of activity. Kelabit youths were all over the plain helping gather up the tons of stores that had been dropped by parachute. On a hill behind the longhouse, two SEMUT 1 radio operators were wrestling with their Boston wireless transmitter-receiver, which had been damaged in the drop. At the major's request, Penghulu Lawai sent out runners for twenty miles around, and by nightfall there were some five hundred people squeezed into the longhouse eyeing the newcomers.

Unlike the Yank airmen, Harrisson and his party had

known where they were going when they dropped out of their planes. Lian later told an interviewer:

When Tom Harrisson arrived in Bario, he had with him pictures that he must have gotten from the Sarawak Museum of people and houses from the old days in the Kelabit country. He showed these pictures of Kelabit *penghulus* and heads of longhouses from olden times and other pictures of Kelabit. And the Kelabit quickly decided, "This is a good man, who already knows so much about the Kelabit." And he showed them pictures from New Guinea and explained that not everybody lives in this one country, that the place the Kelabit live is Borneo and that these other people [Papuans] lived halfway to Australia and nobody of our people knew about these other places, such as Australia, at that time. They found what Harrisson said very interesting.

That first evening, March 25, Penghulu Lawai Bisara and the people of Bario and nearby longhouses of Pa' Trap and Pa' Umor welcomed the strangers with singing, dancing and copious amounts of *borak*, which helped the visitors wash down the Dayak food.

The next day, still more visitors appeared. The chief of the southern Kelabit, Penghulu Miri, arrived from his longhouse at Pa' Dali, bringing with him special treats for the foreigners. He brewed coffee sweetened with honey and he fried cassava-flour pancakes. More importantly, he produced a torrent of good advice in fluent Malay on how to win over the people of the inland highlands. He suggested sending someone through the upland who knew how to treat yaws, diarrhea and other common illnesses, to gain local goodwill and collect information.

Harrisson quickly sensed the quality of the leadership he was dealing with and realized that, although his assignment was merely to build an intelligence network ahead of the Australian Ninth Division's invasion of Brunei Bay planned for early June, these inland people were capable of much more than merely providing information. So, exceeding his instructions (as was his wont), he became determined to create a behind-the-lines guerrilla army. He told his Bario hosts that he was ready to accept volunteers and that headhunting would be permitted, provided the heads were Japanese.

The Kelabit, ex-headhunters like their Lun Dayeh cousins across the border, were eager to accept the major's invitation. Like the Lun Dayeh, the Kelabit were delighted to be able to return to the sacred raids of their songs and stories, even if only against Japanese.

By the second evening, the makings of an even greater feast were assembled in the Bario longhouse. After dark, the Dayaks began dispensing more food, music and dance, and much more *borak* than the night before. By now Harrisson could see that it was SEMUT 1's turn to entertain their hosts. When the *borak* had conquered his men's inhibitions, he led them in a sort of line dance the length of the longhouse interior while they sang the only songs all eight of them knew: "Three Blind Mice," "Silent Night," "She'll be Coming 'Round the Mountain" and, as an encore after still more *borak*, an army song best known for its chorus, "Fuck 'em all, fuck 'em all, the long and the short and the tall."

The SEMUT 1 men, having been through months of preparation and having spent five days trying to find a hole in the clouds, were swept up in a flood of relief and *borak*. Ric Edmeades remarked to another of the SEMUT team, "What a wonderful way to go to war!"

The next day, thanks to Penghulu Miri's suggestion, Australian Sgt. Jack Tredrea, a tough, handsome towhead who had been a tailor in civilian life, left Bario, to quickly become one of the most popular people in north central Sarawak. Over the next three months, he would give injections for yaws, lance boils and treat dysentery while collecting intelligence about Japanese movements. He also recruited and trained a force of thirty Iban tribesmen from the subcoastal area farther downstream, drilling them in the use of his Bren machine gun, Owen and Austin submachine guns and .303 rifles. The Iban, the notorious "wild men of Borneo," had been the most feared of Borneo's headhunters in the old days and, as Sgt. Tredrea observed their quick mastery of these new weapons of war, he could easily see why.

A few days later, Harrisson's deputy, Capt. Ric Edmeades, an exceptionally fit and experienced young New Zealander, was sent out as well. His assignment: To walk the length and breadth of northern Borneo, obtaining intelligence and recruiting guerrillas. As the word spread, SEMUT 1's guerrilla ranks quickly swelled to several hundred, with Edmeades recruiting warriors from all over upland Sarawak.

Harrisson sent other SEMUT 1 operatives off in ones and twos with groups of Dayaks. They were ordered to stay barefoot whenever they were in or near a Dayak village so that their footprints would not be noticed. And they were given no food to take with them. "Eat what the natives do," Harrisson told his men. He established these rules for one simple reason (which he never told his men): that they would not succeed in their mission unless they had the wholehearted cooperation of the local people. So his men would have to learn to blend in and not seem like foreign occupiers. If the SEMUT operatives could not make the Dayaks like them enough to feed them, they were as good as dead. The major was making an asset of the situation that the downed Yank airmen had confronted—being dependent on their native hosts for everything.

The SEMUT 1 operatives quickly learned how to eat, bathe, walk, track and hunt the way the Dayaks did. They communicated in the local language (having no English-speaking pals to talk to) and generally learned how to behave courteously and competently in inland Borneo. Harrisson's style of guerrilla warfare was invented by him on the spot in order to maximize the benefit of his Aussies' physical toughness while avoiding potential problems from the then prevailing Australian prejudice against nonwhites. He knew that if the Aussies under his command ever showed the contempt for nonwhites that those back home often displayed, they would be quickly turned over to the Japanese.

Another Harrisson rule was to keep his men constantly on the move. When they finished one task and came back to report to him, he would promptly send them somewhere else. As a consequence, Harrisson knew what was going on all across northern and central Borneo. It also made it harder for the enemy headquarters on the coast to learn about—much less locate—these Allied guerrilla leaders.

Harrisson's rule about going barefoot won him special notoriety. This was what Kibung had taught Tom Capin but it horrified the Australians' senior medical officer Capt. "Doc" Ian McCallum. McCallum arrived in mid-April with the second group of eight SEMUT operatives. Citing the risks of parasites and snakebite, Doc McCallum protested to no avail, and soon left Bario in order to get out of shouting distance from the man he and others called "the mad major."

Within days of his arrival in Bario, Harrisson—walking barefoot—traveled around the Plain of Bah and met the longhouse leaders in their own homes. During these visits he heard from Kelabit in touch with their Lun Dayeh cousins that there were American fugitives being hidden over the border to the east. The major had arrived in Borneo with instructions from his Australian bosses to locate and help repatriate the downed American airmen rumored to be in northern Borneo and now he knew where they were. He set off to find them.

On April 5, he walked across the border mountains to Pa' Kabak, and the next day he walked along the rich, irrigated rice fields of the Bawang Plain to Belawit.

When he got to Belawit, the longhouse village chief, Pangeran Lasong Piri, was away. But there to meet him were other elders of the Belawit longhouses and the head for all Dutch Borneo of the Kemah Injil Church, the plump and genial Pastor Aris Dumat. Major Harrisson was also introduced to Bolong, Maulker, Kusoy and Sualang, the Eurasian N.E.I. soldiers whom Makahanap and the Yanks had entertained earlier. The four soldiers told him they had been looking for a rumored force of Allied troops near Brunei Bay. Instead, Maulker had been recaptured by the Japanese and had been used as a servant and interpreter for a Japanese officer. Then he had run into one of Harrisson's Australian operatives, Jack Tredrea, and had immediately changed sides. Now safe in Belawit, he and the other three were ready to join the SEMUT 1 guerrilla forces. They had more precise information about the American airmen than the major had received from the Kelabit. They could tell him that they were mostly now under the protection of the Mentarang district officer, William Makahanap.

Major Harrisson listened carefully to what these Dutch East Indies soldiers had to say, absorbing it and quickly working out how to use this information. Harrisson was accustomed to dealing with strange people and strange places. Born into an upper-class English family building railroads in the Argentine, he had taken up bird-watching during a lonely childhood. He had been sent "home" to England to boarding school and had become a pioneer in ornithology while still a teenager at Harrow. He had dropped out of Cambridge University after little more than a year, leaving behind a reputation for being drunk and disorderly. By then, he had already been the ornithologist on Oxford expeditions to Arctic Lapland, upland Borneo and the cannibal islands of Melanesia.

Even without a diploma, Harrisson came to prominence in Britain in the late 1930s by helping to found a social-survey organization called Mass-Observation that drew on his bird- and cannibal-watching techniques to discreetly observe and make notes about Britain's working class. When World War II began, he adapted these techniques to help Whitehall gauge the morale of the man on the street in 1940 to 1941 as Hitler's bombs blitzed Britain. Hard drinking, fast moving, articulate, original, outrageous and a charismatic leader, Harrisson had managed to use his prewar Borneo experience to get himself an assignment to Australia's special operations organization. He spent months in England learning how to kill silently and unarmed, how to use invisible ink and how to parachute out of bombers. A year in Australia followed, where he learned how to avoid being tailed in a Melbourne street and how to walk barefoot carrying a heavy pack over snow-topped mountains.

Makahanap left Punan Silau with Phil's letter on April 3 and headed west for Belawit. Taking three days instead of the usual five, he reached Belawit and met up with Maj. Tom Harrisson and his New Zealander second in command, Capt. Ric Edmeades. Harrisson, wearing an American visored cap with a major's star on it, was now being addressed as Tuan Mayor. (*Tuan*, literally "lord," was the polite Malay title for any white man and *mayor*, pronounced my-or, was the Kelabit for "major.")

Makahanap had met Englishmen before, but this one had a vibrancy of voice, a brusqueness of manner and an intensity of gaze in his pale eyes that were almost frightening. The major was not fully at ease, either. In the mission house in Belawit, he was no doubt missing the soothing effects of the *borak* that his Plain of Bah hosts had served him.

Harrisson was to discover that meetings with leaders from the Dutch part of Borneo would not be as easy or relaxed as were those with their counterparts in Sarawak. Harrisson had immediately felt at home among the noisy, rough and ready, less Christianized native inland people of Sarawak, people who had experienced only the lightest touch of a colonial British presence and who tended to regard white people as their equals, though higher in rank. In contrast, the Dutch East Indians had been accustomed to the formality and deliberation of the Dutch and found this English major unpolished and abrupt, even rude.

But both sides, Harrisson and the local leaders in Dutch Borneo, realized they had no choice but to work together. During that evening with Makahanap and Aris Dumat, Harrisson and the others pooled their intelligence to figure out how to protect the downed airmen and fight the Japanese.

Harrisson took a few minutes to write a letter in reply to Phil's. He gave it to Makahanap to bring back to Punan Silau, along with various "comforts" and weapons for the airmen. Makahanap left early the next day with a group of porters to help him. He flew downhill a day faster than he had climbed up.

CHAPTER THIRTEEN

SEMUT Finds Work for the Yanks

Phil opened the letter from Harrisson three days after it was written.

> *April 6, 1945*
> *My dear fellow,*
>   *(As an Englishman I had better start like this.)*
> *Your note is greatly welcome. I have brought in a party*
> *of eight (Australians, New Zealanders and a Siamese)*
> *not only to bugger up the Japs but also, and specifically,*
> *to look for lost whites and help them to get out in any*
> *way we can. I am sending you what stores I can by*
> *bearer. We can, and of course will, supply you with*
> *everything you need that we have. We are also in a*
> *position to supply arms etc. to natives and can bring*
> *planes over to drop us stuff.*
>
> *There are two immediate difficulties for you:*
>   *1. Your area is virtually unmapped and I don't think*
> *a plane could find you. It was hard enough to find our*
> *very obvious plain we dropped in. (It took four attempts*
> *from Mindoro.)*
>   *2. I am at present responsible for all guerilla*
> *activities in this area, and I am sure you will agree that*
> *they should be coordinated. I know the military plans*

for landings and we want to synchronize our efforts
with these, in one well-organized blitz.*

*For these two reasons, I think it most necessary that
you come and meet me at Belawit in the upper Bawang.
It is an ideal dropping place, known to our planes, and
at the same time I can discuss with you:*

a. a guerilla plan for the area.

*b. how to get you blokes out as quickly as possible. I
will readily, after seeing you, allocate some blokes and
arms to Long Berang. I am 100% for this. I know you
will realize it has to be done carefully though. I have
had some experience with guerilla work elsewhere, and
it can easily develop into large scale shambles.*

*I would also like your radio man to come over. He
could be invaluable to us, on loan, till we could get you
out. Anyone else who cares to join my circus is more
than welcome. Our base is safe, comfortable, etc.*

*I will signal your names and numbers the day after
tomorrow, so your relatives will know you are O.K. I
will also signal your position as far as it is known, in
case a plane can find you.*

*Believe me, I want to help you all I can. I wish to
God I had more stuff with me to send you. I'll bring
over my bottle of Scotch to celebrate our meeting. If you
simply can't make it, send someone else (or bring all).*

*By a strange coincidence on January 16 I was on a
recce over here, with Navy search, and we were looking
all around Brunei Bay for the lost Navy B-24 of
January 13th.*

*You know, maybe, you Yanks have taken Iwo Jima
and landed on another island 300 miles from Japan.*

---

*This is a reference to the then secret plans for Allied landings in Brunei
Bay on June 9–10.

Colossal raids on Tokyo. Negros taken. B-24 ships on
Palawan. Jolo taken. In Europe, Montgomery and
Patton over Rhine, Russians near Berlin. Roosevelt,
Winchell, Dorothy Parker and Eisenhower all alive.
> *Yours sincerely,*
> *Tom Harrisson (Major)*
> *Reconnaissance Corps*

As Makahanap watched, the Yanks hugged one another
and laughed out loud while tears rolled down their cheeks.
Phil noted in his reply that "our friend Makahanap returned
to us this morning with your note and the news of your party
and, of course, all hell broke loose immediately and lasted for
quite some time." With the letter had also come porters laden
with several Austin 9-millimeter submachine guns, some pistols and the comforts the major had mentioned in the letter.
From the major's comforts, Bob Graham had his first cigarette
in three months. Makahanap killed a goat, which was roasted
for dinner, and Mama made fried bananas with chocolate
sauce for dessert.

Meanwhile, in Long Nuat, the two navy men who remained
with the Mongans had begun recovering from their most recent
attack of malaria when Harms had a setback. Leech bites in
his left foot became infected, and his foot swelled to twice its
normal size. The Mongans and Robbins had no way to help
Harms. The Lun Dayeh villagers treated his foot by piercing it
in numerous places with sharp skewers of bamboo to drain the
pus. At the same time, Harms's right foot developed a purple
knot, which also exuded pus. Between the two infections,
Harms was unable to walk for the next nine weeks. Then, on
April 9, Long Nuat had a visit from Sgt. Fred Sanderson, who
had been sent by Harrisson to bring medical supplies.

Sandy, the part-Thai sergeant, had set off on April 7 from Bario with two Kelabit porters carrying medicine and silver coins for the two Yanks, and sarongs and gold coins for the Mongans. He and his party had spent five days on the road to Long Nuat, slowed down because of a painful tropical ulcer on Sandy's ankle. After stopping at various longhouse villages overnight, the party reached the top of the huge rise above Long Nuat the morning of the fifth day, and Sandy saw "there, way below, a stream running through the native settlement. It looked like paradise and it took us all day to reach it."

Sandy found Robby Robbins and Alvin Harms bathing in the stream with the villagers. When he introduced himself, one of the Yanks said, "We were told in America that if we were ever lost and there were any Australians in the area we could count on being rescued." Sandy felt suddenly very proud of his slouch hat and his country.

After giving the Americans Aspro, Atabrine and sulfanilamide tablets, plus a handful of Dutch silver coins, Sandy stayed up all night exchanging information with the airmen and the Mongans. Thanks to the medicine Sandy had brought, Robbins immediately started to recover and even Harms began to improve.

Following the major's instructions, Sandy and William Mongan headed back to Bario the next day. Walking had become an excruciating ordeal for the SEMUT sergeant, who by now also had a painful lump in his right groin. Nonetheless, they kept a rapid pace and were over the mountains and at SEMUT 1 headquarters in Bario by 2 P.M. on Friday, April 13.

That date did not augur well and, indeed, they found Major Harrisson at his most irritable. Hungover from a *borak*-filled night of consulting with visiting *penghulus* from all over northern Sarawak, the major also was suffering from an ulcer on his leg, which had him horizontal on a hammock in his hut when he most wanted to be up and about. He also was nervous about the forthcoming arrival of another pair of Australian B-24s bringing eight more SEMUT operatives—headed by a New Zealander major who was Harrisson's rival and senior in rank. The planes were expected that day, but Harrisson had had no news from them in some time, a worry that added to his annoyance.

He greeted the limping sergeant by complaining that Sandy was half a day late, and made clear that he now had no interest in talking to William Mongan. To Sandy's enduring chagrin, the major sent this Good Samaritan back to Long Nuat with no thanks or anything to show for his pains. Sandy was ordered, despite his limp, to go up the hill to the wireless and operate the hand generator for the signals man, Sgt. Doug Bower. Knowing better than to argue, Sandy went up the hill.

Judging by what Major Harrisson wrote about Sandy to his superiors, he respected and liked the sergeant enormously, finding him to have "real brains and a perfect absorption of the job in hand . . . a first class man in every respect." But he would never let Sandy know what he thought of him. Harrisson had always claimed that he had kept his Oxford expedition to Sarawak in order when he was its leader twelve years earlier by getting the members of the party to share one strong emotion—hatred of their leader. It had worked well then, and he may have been trying to do the same thing now with his odd assortment of brave but quarrelsome Aussies and Southeast Asians.

The Americans, knowing little about the major except what they had read in his letter, started out from Punan Silau for Wy-Agong on April 10 to meet Harrisson. They were barefoot and dressed in the shorts Mama had made for them out of old sacking. With them were Makahanap, his wife's brother Uncle Louie (from Long Sempayang) and his son Christiaan. The Yank party consisted of Phil Corrin as senior officer and Dan Illerich and Tom Capin as radio operators, who were responding to the major's request for help with SEMUT 1's communications with its overseas headquarters.

Each night was spent in a different longhouse village, the biggest and best one in Long Sempayang, where the schoolchildren sang hymns in four-part harmony and played on instruments made from bamboo that sounded like a cross between a xylophone and a recorder. The airmen and their escort left there regretfully to continue their journey.

On the evening of April 13, after walking up and down steep hills all day in blinding rain, the party reached the meeting place near the border mountains, Wy-Agong, which Phil described as "just one big mud hole." They spent that night in a longhouse. While Phil and Dan were playing chess the next day on their Dayak-made set, a big head in a slouch hat poked up through the ladder hole. It was not Major Harrisson but SEMUT 1 Warrant Officer Rod Cusack, who met them on the major's behalf.

Cusack, a six-foot-six, burly AIF veteran from Brisbane with a cheerful, positive manner, climbed onto the veranda. He seemed bigger than life and drew the admiration of these young airmen, who had never taken part in a land battle, when they had the chance to draw him out on his war experience as they smoked real cigarettes. With his broad Queensland accent and his slouch hat worn at a jaunty angle, Cusack was the Yanks' idea of what an Aussie soldier should be.

The Yanks were pale and painfully thin from their long stay in the jungle. The kindly veteran took into account their obvious poor health and brought them and the weary Makahanap by easy stages to Belawit. By the afternoon of the next day, they were on the southern end of the high Bawang Plain. For the first time since arriving in Borneo, Phil and his men saw wet rice paddies, with their beautiful patchwork made up of bright green, gold and watery silver, each square showing a different stage of maturity of the rice crop. They learned that the Lun Dayeh of the Bawang Plain and their Kelabit cousins of the Plain of Bah across the mountains in Sarawak had the only fields in interior Borneo that could grow rice this way. In addition to being beautiful, the wet rice paddies could produce two or more crops a year, almost always creating a surplus, whereas hill-rice farming as practiced by the other Dayaks produced only one rice crop a year, just enough to feed the community. If that crop failed, the people went hungry. They arrived April 18.

Aris Dumat, the pastor from the Celebes whom the Yanks had met before, made them welcome at his house. The food was good and the school orchestra played "My Country, 'Tis of Thee" on bamboo instruments, though Cusack insisted the song was "God Save the King." Next came three exhausting days of sliding up and down in the wet to cross into Sarawak's Plain of Bah, to Major Harrisson's headquarters in Bario.

Phil was delighted to finally meet the major, whom he described in his diary as "a swell guy." The major gave the Yanks the fullest real news from the outside world that they had received since parachuting into Borneo five months earlier. Phil was shocked to learn that President Roosevelt was dead. But more important to their immediate situation was the news "that the Australians are due to invade Tarakan in a week and the Americans [bringing landing craft in support of the Australian Ninth Division] are going to hit Brunei."

Harrisson gave the Yanks the promised bottle of George V Scotch as well as chocolate, cigarettes, cookies and peanut butter. Better still, he sent Doc McCallum to them with medicine for "the itch." The itch, the medic explained, was from scabies and he dosed it with the new wonder drug, penicillin. Harrisson noted in his diary that he found the Americans "all anemic, the D.O., too," but he was glad to have the Yanks there. He had fulfilled his orders from Z Special to try to find them, and now they might prove useful to his team.

The next day, he divided his rapidly growing native force into five platoons and put Phil in charge of training Platoon No. 4 with eight rifles, five hand grenades and ten blowguns. Phil was happy to be acting like a soldier again.

The same day, Dan Illerich was asked if he could help with sending and receiving messages on SEMUT 1's Boston wireless transmitter-receiver (W/T) radio. The major had learned from the eight new SEMUT arrivals—who had finally dropped into Bario April 16—that his first signals man, Doug Bower, had a very bad "fist" as a transmitter. One of the new arrivals, radioman Warrant Officer Bob Long, told Harrisson that Bower's messages had not been understood and that Z Special advance headquarters in Mindoro wondered if the radio had been taken over by the Japanese. Harrisson's solution was characteristic; he commandeered the services of Long, who had been dropped in to work for Harrisson's rival, Maj. Toby Carter of SEMUT 2, and released Bower for other duties.

Dan, who had maintained the best health of any of the Yanks, made his way up the steep hill to the radio shack to serve as Warrant Officer Long's assistant. He was happy to have a chance to put his skills to use after such a long period of enforced inactivity. He found Bob Long sweating and cursing under his slouch hat as he struggled with the Boston wireless set. Long was being helped by two Kelabit men, who were armed with machetes and blowpipes. These Dayaks spent the day guarding the little W/T lean-to that barely kept out the rain. In the evening, before they went down to the longhouse, these Dayaks helped wind the hand generator.

Long, a sociable creature as well as a conscientious signaler, was glad to have the Yank's company, but his pleasure increased as Dan's competence became evident. The corporal's fluency in Morse code had not suffered during his time in the jungle. After only one day with Dan on the team, SEMUT 1's signals had improved by "at least 90 percent," the major noticed. After that, Harrisson's enthusiasm for Dan's contribution to his operation never flagged.

Dan had been on the hill only a day when a message came from the major ordering Bob to close down the wireless station that night and to tell Z Special's transmitter in Darwin that the set would be on the air two days later at 8 P.M.

The two radiomen spent the night alone on the mountain. They both had hammocks that were hung as high up as possible. But the act of getting themselves into their hammocks was tricky until they got the knack of it. At first, they ended upside down on the rubberized cover meant to protect the sleeper from rain. Spilling out of the hammock onto the jungle floor in the dark, though, would have been worse.

Breakfast came from the longhouse with the men who wound the generators, but the food held little appeal: unsalted boiled rice and very tough half-cooked pig meat that tasted of the human excreta that the animal had fed on. At Dan's suggestion, they sacrificed some of Bob's canned butter to fry a handful of grasshoppers. The two soldiers agreed that the grasshoppers were not bad, "if you didn't think about 'em."

Bob and Dan got on well together from the beginning, and Dan's presence made it possible for the warrant officer to leave Dan at the closed-down W/T site with the two Dayak helpers while he went down the hill the next morning for his first break from his radio duties since landing in Borneo a week earlier.

When Bob Long got to Bario, he found that all seven operatives who had jumped in with him on April 16 except Doc McCallum had been scattered by the major to other parts of northern Borneo. Missing his buddies, Bob was not impressed by Bario but he was entranced when a near-naked young girl "stepped forward, slim and brown, and commenced her dance" to honor his visit. Her movements were sinuous and elegant. "The setting was fantastic; she danced only a few feet away in the gloom and smoke, highlighted only when the flames flared. No modern stage production could have arranged the light and dark to the dancer's movements better."

Bob left the next morning for his new radio transmission site, above the village of Pa' Main. The warrant officer and his party got to the Pa' Main longhouse that afternoon and began the arduous trip uphill to the new W/T hut. Bob's porters from Bario, mostly young women who were dressed in short black woven-bark skirts and little else, had to take the heavy wireless equipment straight up a steep mountainside, assisted only by bamboo treads that were placed on the ground two feet apart and held in place by wooden pegs. Cursing his aching leg muscles, Bob finally reached the hilltop, which had been cleared in preparation for his arrival.

A small hut with three sides and a roof stood under a clump of large trees. It was just big enough for a bamboo bed and the small bamboo table that held his transceiver and signal pad. His Kelabit porters cooked some meat for him on a small, smoky fire, shook his hand repeatedly to say good-bye and left with the erstwhile generator winders. For the moment, Bob Long was alone and wishing he had not left Dan behind. He went to work setting up the Boston so that he could have communications back onstream by 8 P.M. the next evening.

The next morning, Bob Long was awakened by the chattering of monkeys overhead. He drank a mug of black tea made from a tea tablet he had brought with him, ate some of the leftover meat and rice from the night before, checked his carbine and his .32 automatic and looked over his new surroundings. The ground dropped away into dense jungle on three sides. The only possible access was from the fourth side, up the almost vertical path down to Pa' Main. Confident that he was as safe as he could make himself, he spent the day alone, reassembling the hand generator and putting up the aerial in the tall tree that sheltered the hut. Then he plugged into the transceiver a pile of messages that needed to be encrypted. Aside from a short break to eat at midday, he worked steadily on the outgoing messages until dark.

That evening, with their path lighted by flaming damar resin torches, four sturdily built young men appeared, each dressed in a bark-cloth loincloth and carrying a blowpipe, a poison-dart box, a bamboo cigar container and a machete. They climbed up the five-hundred-foot hill to take turns winding the generator, making it possible for Bob to keep his promise to his Z Special audience in Darwin, Australia. While one of these men wound the generator, Bob tuned the set for a tense moment. If the set did not work, Z Special would probably give up on SEMUT 1, assuming the team had been captured—the fate of most of Australia's special operations in the Far East. Long remembers: "Luck was on our side for, at the appointed time, I sent the call sign IRK and Darwin replied with the letter K, which was to go ahead with any traffic I had."

After the first message was sent, another Kelabit took a turn. It was exhausting work. While one Dayak wound the handle, his large brass earrings jangling, the other three were making and smoking local cigars.

Bob began receiving messages after all the outgoing messages had been sent, a welcome change for the Dayaks; receiving took only half the energy that sending did. By the time the last incoming message arrived, the Dayaks had been working hard for four or five hours. At about 11 P.M., they finished. The men shook Long's hand, relit their torches and headed back down the mountainside for Pa' Main. Before they left, they managed to indicate that they would be back every evening as long as they were needed.

In a week or so (presumably after the major had decided the new W/T post was safe), Dan joined Bob above Pa' Main, and another bamboo bunk was built for him in the small hut. Dan, after a week without his usual bath in the river, was missing one of the few pleasures he had enjoyed during his months of waiting to be rescued. The busiest time was in the evening, so he thought, Why not go down to the river and get a proper bath that morning? Bob, who had been making do with occasional showers from water collected by the Dayaks in bamboo tubes, thought about it and decided there was no reason not to.

There seemed to be no one around when they got to the riverbank. They quickly stripped and waded into the water, which felt wonderful against their bare skin despite being very cold. Bob knew that it was unwise to leave their weapons on the shore next to their only set of clothes, but he was growing confident, since there had been no threat of a Japanese visit since they had arrived.

Bob and Dan soon found that they were not alone. They had got only waist-high when a young Kelabit from the nearby longhouse joined them. Undoubtedly sent ahead to make sure that the foreigners were safe, the youth swam the length of the river pool to show Dan and Bob the local swimming stroke, a cross between an overarm and a butterfly. Dan and Bob demonstrated they knew how to swim. But when they wanted to get out of the water—which seemed colder than ever—they looked up and had what Bob called "one hell of a shock."

On top of the rock face overlooking the river pool were eight young Dayak women gazing down at them. The women had noiselessly appeared, each carrying empty bamboo tubes that they used to transport river water back to the longhouse. Bob remarked to Dan that it looked as if the village had run clean out of water at just this time. Still, he conceded later, it could have been worse. It could have been Japanese soldiers looking down on them.

Tom Capin had joined Major Harrisson with Dan, since he also had had some radio training. For the moment, though, the tall redhead's feet were in as bad shape as Harrisson's, and the two men spent the next days talking in side-by-side hammocks. Harrisson no doubt told Capin of his colorful life up to then and the improbable-though-true events of his extraordinary career. Capin was more struck with the major's arrogance than with his accomplishments. Harrisson, however, welcomed Capin's ability to understand Kelabit and Lun Dayeh.

By April 25, both Harrisson's and Capin's feet were better and the major had an assignment ready for the redhead. A bunch of storepedos had arrived packed with English .303 Enfield rifles, and so he asked Capin if he could take some of the Dayak guerrillas out and show them how to sight in, load and shoot these guns. Capin agreed. He had infantry training before he transferred to the air corps and felt entirely comfortable doing this. Harrisson caught up with him several times that day and, clearly liking what he saw, told Capin, "I'm going to send you to a place, Pa' Dali, that will need your language." Capin went eagerly. Finally he was getting into the war.

"It was good traveling," he recalled. "I killed a wild boar that crossed our path with my .38 Police Special belly gun. I was carrying one of the Enfield rifles over my shoulder but I never thought of using it." Upon reaching the longhouse at Pa' Dali, he found two ex-members of SEMUT 1: Doug Bower, who was very capable in the bush though he had proved a poor radioman, and medic Doc McCallum.

Capin, though he—following the advice of his Iban friend Kibung—also insisted on staying barefoot, was soon in his element working for McCallum, who later described the Yank sergeant as having spent months as "second-in-command of all medical services" for much of northern Borneo. Dressed in a pair of Australian shorts and a wool shirt, Tom Capin helped Doc treat all the sick natives in the region who came to Pa' Dali.

He did occasionally wish that he was in a real hospital, with an elevator that went to their sleeping quarters, which were located out of the village and up a cliff on the other side of the river. Going from there to work and back was every day a horrendous trip, but the distance was judged necessary to minimize the danger to the people of Pa' Dali. Still, despite the climb, Tom knew there was nothing on earth he wanted to do more than what he was now doing among the upland people he had come to love during his months at Pa' Ogong.

On April 27, William Makahanap was back at Punan Silau. He passed the word to Mama and the others that the Australians had promised to get the Yanks out of Borneo within six weeks. Meanwhile, he told them, the major was preparing to move his SEMUT 1 headquarters over into Dutch Borneo. Lieutenant Graham wrote in his notebook that this was "the best news we've heard yet."

Soon, at the major's request, Warrant Officer Rod Cusack came down to see the remaining Yanks at Punan Silau. (Navy airman Robbins was there with the others by then, having recovered his health sufficiently to leave Long Nuat on April 22.) Cusack had good news for them. First of all, SEMUT 1 now had a guerrilla force of some five hundred men. Second, Tarakan Island, with its air base, was to be invaded by the Allies that week. And, best of all, the Aussies planned to have the Yanks out of Borneo within a month. Hard as it was to believe, the Yanks knew that, this time, it was almost certain to be true. The main question was: What was the best way out? A Black Cat seaplane had sufficient range to reach them and return to the Allied-held parts of the Philippines, but there was no stretch of water big enough or calm enough for such a craft to land in this part of Borneo.

If the Mentarang-Sesayap river system was free of Japanese and their collaborators, the Yanks could go downriver by *perahu* past Malinau to Tarakan Island and fly out from Tarakan airfield once it was liberated. For now, though, Tarakan was still in Japanese hands, as was the river route to the sea. The Yanks, having waited so long with little hope, were finding it hard to continue waiting, now that hope had been rekindled.

Cusack set out on April 30 to gather more intelligence. By May 7, he had Makahanap's Dayak forces working for him. Thanks to the storepedos dropped to SEMUT 1, Makahanap's men now had uniforms (shorts and shirts), carbines, grenades, food and cigarettes. Cusack and the four Menadonese soldiers—Bolong, Sualang, Kusoy and Maulker—trained these Lun Dayeh in the use of the new weapons. Cusack sent them north to Lumbis, near the border with North Borneo, to check out rumors of Japanese troops at Pensiangan and Sapulut. On May 9, he sent Makahanap's men to Mensalong, due east of Long Berang, to watch for troop movements up or down the Sembakong River. As with all the forces that SEMUT 1 had enlisted, they were not supposed to let the people downriver know that any of the Allies had arrived. They were also supposed to avoid combat if possible until the Allied invasion along Brunei Bay, which was scheduled for June 9 and 10. But meanwhile, this strange coalition of SEMUT 1's Dayaks, Makahanap's Dayaks and downed American airmen seemed to be working well.

With the help they were getting locally, Harrisson's SEMUT 1 team could control the central highlands of upriver Borneo against the Japanese. So the major decided that it was time for the Yank airmen staying with Mama Makahanap in Punan Silau to move back to Long Berang, where they would be more accessible when it came time to move them to the coast on their way back to their home base in the Philippines.

On May 12, Jim Knoch, John Nelson, Franny Harrington, Eddy Haviland, Bob Graham, Jim Shepherd and Robby Robbins accompanied Mama and the children, and various helpers and porters including Binum and Iwak, on an eight-and-a-half-hour walk to Pengutan, where they spent the night. This was the trip that had taken Cusack less than four hours. The next day, they reached Long Berang. This time, the Yanks stayed in the Presswood house, and it really felt like they were returning home.

But it was not a time of peace. Jim Knoch, who was the Coberly crew's hero when he helped keep their Liberator flying over Borneo and away from Brunei Bay, now tried to keep busy drilling the Long Berang Lun Dayeh in the use of what few modern weapons they had. Bob Graham, who had single-handedly brought three of his crewmen to the safety of Long Nuat, wrote in his notebook that he and the other airmen at Long Berang were "waiting for the major to arrive," adding wistfully, "plenty of fighting near here."

On May 15, they looked out the window to see Phil Corrin

limping toward them on the swaying suspension bridge. From the way Phil walked, they could tell that his feet were in bad shape but that the rest of him was somehow more grown-up, more self-assured than when he had left with Makahanap, Dan Illerich and Tom Capin to meet the major a month ago. Over Mama's hot cocoa, he told them what he had been doing since leaving the major's headquarters in Bario.

Phil had spent a week in Bario helping train a Dayak platoon in the use of modern weapons. Next, he was assigned by Harrisson to return to Long Berang with some porters bringing twenty .303 rifles to help strengthen Makahanap's forces. Starting out, Phil was accompanied by Harrisson's second-in-command, the New Zealander Ric Edmeades. On April 30, the night before they left Bario, they drank *borak* with the Kelabit. Phil judged the Bario hooch to be superior to what he had drunk on the Dutch Borneo side and was amused that, instead of being teetotal, the Kelabit invariably prayed before drinking and that the Bario Kelabit women liked to hold your glass and empty the contents down your throat.

The next morning, May 2, Ric had left Phil and headed down the Trusan river system, with orders to collect intelligence and recruit fighters as he went. Phil's travels without Ric were less amusing, and the endless walking in such inhospitable conditions was taking its toll. Phil had the itch quite badly (he had not had time to get enough penicillin to cure it) and leech bites were making his feet sore as he headed to the next longhouse, where he found many of the Dayaks sick with boils, dysentery and fever—as was often the case toward the end of the rainy season. He dispensed some of the medicine he had been given by the major and enjoyed a chance to chat with the people there, though they were no doubt sorry to learn from him that the Japanese occupation money probably would not be honored when the Allies won. One man, shrugging off his disappointment, offered Phil a Japanese occupation guilder to roll his cigarette with.

By May 3, Phil was having trouble finding porters because so many of the people in the longhouses on his route were ill. "The poor carriers I do have are overloaded," he wrote in his diary before he left Pa' Omong the next morning with "women, children, and anybody not sick" helping to carry his load.

A few hours into that day's walk a gratifying event occurred. The porters spotted a great hornbill and asked Phil to shoot it. He had never been a crack shot and so, when he pulled the trigger on his .303, he had few expectations. But he hit the great bird foursquare. "It couldn't have been a better shot if the thing had been sitting on the end of the barrel." All velvet black except for white tail feathers and a yellow throat, the bird was as big as a turkey, with a wingspan of some six feet and a curved beak at least a foot long. The porters cooked it for lunch and Phil discovered that the meat tasted a bit like chicken liver.

Two days later, his feet desperately sore, Phil was at Long Sempayang again. He stayed at a native Christian schoolteacher's house. As instructed, he cached some of the goods the major had given him. He attended services at the church that the Dayaks had built before the war. Although his feet were so swollen he could hardly walk, he could not help laughing inwardly when he recognized that the tune being played by the bamboo band was "Pack Up Your Troubles in Your Old Kit-Bag."

Phil sent the guns ahead to Long Berang with porters the next day and decided to stay another day at Long Sempayang in the hope that he would be able to walk better after a day's rest. A day turned into a week and, on May 13, with one of Long Sempayang's schoolteachers to escort him, he finally left for Long Berang. He arrived there two days later, on the day that (the airmen soon learned) the Japanese had been forced out of Malinau. Three B-25 bombers had been directed there from the ground by SEMUT 1's Sgt. Jack Tredrea, who was hiding nearby with his Iban irregulars. The air attack had killed as many as thirty-five Japanese, and the others had fled into the jungle. One of the Allied bombers, however, was shot down and another flew too low and crashed into a hill, killing everyone aboard.

Now that Malinau was no longer in Japanese control, the airmen began to think it might be safe to follow the river to the coast and across to Tarakan Island. But the airfield there was still in enemy hands. And so they waited.

At the Presswood house, young John Nelson was glad to be back with his favorite buddy, Eddy Haviland. The two of them had blowpipe contests trying to hit objects across the longhouse.

Bob Graham spent a lot of his time playing hearts with the other guys. He now had time to think about his bride, Janet. Bob was so bright that he had finished high school at age sixteen but had hung around the school, learning typing and business skills until he was old enough for college. He had been sitting in a typing class when Janet, a fifteen-year-old high school kid, pointed out "this cute-looking guy over there" to a girlfriend and said, "I'd like to marry him someday." They had dated for the next four years while he became an officer in the navy, marrying only when he knew he was heading overseas. He worried about her and the missing-in-action message she would have received.

Between bouts of malaria, all the airmen spent time swimming in the river, fishing, eating and waiting. The prewar *Reader's Digest*s had lost their charm and were now used to supply cigarette papers. The men played "Stardust" and

"Lullaby of Broadway" over and over on the phonograph that Jim Knoch had repaired months ago. It seemed as if they had spent their whole lives waiting.

Jim, now reduced to wearing a loincloth, seemed to take the waiting hardest. He had always been happiest doing things that were useful, and now he found nothing useful to do. News came from the major that the war in Europe had ended on May 9, and it felt as if the war ought to be over in the Mentarang District, too. Perhaps because he could now think of things other than survival, Jim began to have amorous thoughts about the beautiful Binum. He got in the habit of going up to her when the Yanks and the Dayak girls were in the river together, and pinching her on the buttocks underwater. Binum just laughed. But Jim's crewmates found nothing funny about it. They made it clear that they would restrain Jim physically if he continued to threaten their safety by forcing his attentions on Binum. They had been told that the first Japanese to be beheaded had been those who had approached the young women of Pangeran Lagan's longhouse.

The Dayaks did their best to keep their visitors amused. They noticed that the Americans all wanted to spend as much time in the sun as possible. The Dayaks, especially the women, were puzzled at that. They kept out of the sun whenever possible to avoid darkening their skin, since light skin was regarded as more attractive. Some concluded that the Yanks might be trying to darken their skin so they would not stand out among the natives. Except for swimming, the Yanks in Long Berang had run out of things to do. Time was hanging heavily as they waited for things to happen, things over which they had no control.

CHAPTER FOURTEEN

A Way Out

Eight more Australian special operatives arrived in the Borneo highlands on May 26. Assigned to reinforce SEMUT 1, they were dropped in from the Philippines by two Liberators from Z Special's own "Flight 200." But due to a mix-up, Major Harrisson was waiting with Dan Illerich in Lembudut while the Flight 200 pilots had the men jump into Belawit (where Pastor Aris Dumat entertained them as best he could). After hours at Lembudut looking up and listening for the planes, the major learned from runners sent by Dumat that the men were at home with him. Harrisson stomped back toward the border to Pa' Kabak and sent Dan to fetch the reinforcements from Belawit.

The next day, as they scrambled laboriously up a sixty-degree slippery, wet, leech-filled slope, Dan grinned as the new men complained that their guides deliberately went over the crest of the mountains, rather than going around them. The new men found Major Tom Harrisson waiting for them. One of the Australian reinforcements, driver Philip Henry, remembers his first impression of his new commanding officer at that May 27 meeting. The major was

> barefooted; he wore a sarong round his waist, a shirt and
> an American soldier's work cap with a crown [the symbol

of a British army major] in the centre. The natives called him *Tuan Besar* [the boss]. He was very definite in his instructions, such as: If any of us had anything to do with native women he would personally shoot us!

Harrisson's erratic temper was strongly in evidence that day. He may have been annoyed at the unnecessary walk to Lembudut the day before. He still may have been recovering from a hangover earned two nights earlier, when he had drunk *borak* all night with his Lun Dayeh hosts. At one point that night, he had been offered a native wife, an honor (he wrote in his diary) he had "difficulty in refusing," though refuse he did.

On a more positive note, he had been passed Japanese documents found in the possession of a recently captured native police constable in Sarawak's Trusan valley. These documents showed that the Japanese were still unaware of the presence of SEMUT 1 in Borneo—they were merely issuing vague warnings to Borneans to watch out for "possible dropped spies, black or white."

After a few more remarks to the new arrivals, Harrisson gave the men individual marching orders and sent them on their separate ways. He was, as usual, scattering most of the new arrivals in a wide arc across northern Borneo.

Before they left, however, one of them passed on to Harrisson a crucial bit of news: that the long and hard-fought battle for Tarakan was winding down and that the island's airstrip was now in Allied hands. Harrisson's diary for that day records that he had received "a midnight note from Colin McPherson [one of the reinforcements], re air strip."

It was just a little scribble in the major's diary. But it was shorthand for the single-most important event to affect the future of the eleven stranded American airmen.

———

When Harrisson had first confirmed the Yanks' presence in SEMUT 1 territory, he had sent a signal to Darwin to ask if Z Special could send a small aircraft to collect the airmen—one by one if necessary—provided SEMUT 1 prepared a landing strip for the plane. The answer had been no; the only short-takeoff-and-landing plane available, the Auster (similar to a Piper Cub), had a range of just two hundred miles, whereas the nearest airstrip in Allied hands was perhaps a thousand miles away from SEMUT 1 territory, in Mindoro, the Philippines.

The major wanted a two-way transport link between SEMUT 1 and its headquarters. And Harrisson knew that the best way to sell the idea to his Z Special bosses was to point out that creating such a link would be the fastest and best way to get the stranded Yank airmen out of Borneo. And now, with the news that Tarakan airfield was available for Allied use, Harrisson could get what he wanted.

When the SEMUT 1 reinforcements were accidentally dropped into Belawit, Harrisson realized that the Bawang Plain was the best possible place to build an airstrip for a plane such as the Auster.

The morning after learning that the Tarakan airfield was liberated, Harrisson sent a wireless signal via the Boston radio to ask the Royal Australian Air Force to do an air reconnaissance of the Bawang Plateau to determine the feasibility of building an airstrip there. Not waiting for an answer, he decided to build the strip at Belawit and obtained the permission of the leader of the northern Lun Dayeh, Pangeran Lasong Piri.

The major had met Lasong Piri in early April, but the two men had not become friends the way the major had with Sarawak Dayak leaders such as Penghulu Lawai Bisara and Penghulu Miri. It was not just personal chemistry that was to blame. The Kelabit had long had an informal and friendly relationship with the whites, thanks to the policies of Sarawak's eccentric English "White Rajahs" who had instructed their English administrative officials that the natives were "not inferior, just different." The rajahs had forbidden merchants, missionaries, lawyers and the pushier tribes from farther downriver to interfere with the upriver people and had essentially left the upland people to run their own communities, once they had agreed to cease headhunting. A similar free and easy manner toward Westerners prevailed among the Lun Dayeh in areas where the Dutch colonial administration had barely reached. The Yank airmen could sense that ease in the presence of Pangeran Lagan.

But Pangeran Lasong Piri, although the Dutch administration had granted him the title of paramount chief, felt he had never been respected by the colonial officers. (The Dutch had not been respectful of Lagan either, but they had, at least, let him alone.) The colonial Dutch tended to have little regard for any native no matter what his rank, unless the native was sufficiently "Dutchified." This personal history complicated Lasong Piri's relations with any white person.

As Tom Harrisson remarked:

> [Lasong Piri] could not help calculating who he was, who we were . . . At any moment, Lasong Piri felt that an Englishman or Australian might start behaving like a Dutchman. But in intervals when he forgot about this, he was the bold master of thousands of willing men who obeyed him even though they disliked him.

Harrisson noticed that Lasong Piri, like some of his fellow chiefs from other areas of Dutch Borneo, was clearly "tormented by doubt and latent dislike."

But somehow Harrisson convinced him of the importance of the airstrip. And despite "the hot breath of the Japanese blowing up the wide Trusan and prosperous Bawang straight into his alertly shifting eyes . . . [Lasong Piri] brought in more than 1,000 volunteers to build an airfield on his own land."

The major, with his usual disregard for rank, assigned one of the SEMUT 1 reinforcements, Trooper Bob Griffiths, to be in charge of building the Belawit strip and another of the new arrivals, Lt. Jeff Westley, to be the trooper's adjutant.

Bob Griffiths was a good choice for the job. He was a tough, scrappy veteran of an Australian armored regiment. He had a history as a troublemaker that may have prevented his winning the honors he deserved, but he was not only physically strong, but also stoic when ill and a man of many talents. He had been a cook for his infantry unit before joining special operations. Later, while engaged in upriver North Borneo for SEMUT 1, he was given the local name of Tuan Ubat ("white medicine man") since he was dispensing pills, giving shots and recruiting warriors, the way Jack Tredrea had done in Sarawak and Dutch Borneo.

Like Jim Knoch, Griffiths could make things work. At one point he turned a four-gallon kerosene tin, stones, mud and a bamboo flue into a working stove. He may have been involved in the ingenious conception of the Belawit airstrip; he certainly was the man who turned the concept into a reality.

SEMUT 1's clever construction plan took advantage of the Bawang Plain's wet rice fields. The builders drained an unused portion of a paddy and leveled its bottom, with the outside banks remaining intact. They made a decking of split bamboo thirty feet wide and a hundred yards long (supposedly the length needed for an Auster). The decking was anchored to the ground with sharp pegs. In case of a visit by the enemy, SEMUT's Dayak guerrillas could make a hole in the bank and flood the field so that it looked like an ordinary rice paddy. Griffiths would have preferred to use *atap*, the palm-leaf material used for longhouse roofing, for decking but it was too scarce. It was already a sacrifice on the part of Lasong Piri and his Lun Dayeh to let the airstrip project use so many long strips of bamboo because bamboo of that type was essential for fencing the rice fields against wandering cattle.

At Harrisson's insistence, the airstrip construction work started immediately, though it was the time of year when the dried rice stalks were burned off the paddy fields, raising the local temperature to 110 degrees Fahrenheit.

Griffiths nonetheless took to his task with gusto. With the cooperation of Lasong Piri, he got the local people to start work right away. Soon, word spread of this novel activity and volunteers poured in from other tribes.

In the smothering heat, Griffiths sat in his little lean-to at one end of the construction site with his English/Malay word book and wrote out sentences in fractured Malay such as *Saya mahu bawa tanah dari disana, dan daput disini* (I want earth brought from there and put here). Lasong Piri then corrected the worst of the errors and made Griffiths repeat the phrases until the trooper could pronounce them well enough to be understood.

On May 29, less than twenty-four hours after the work had begun, Harrisson's diary notes "good strip progress." The native workforce had begun clearing the area, burning off what could not be removed with sticks, hands, homemade hoes and their own feet. The men dug and flattened while the women put the excess earth into reed baskets and carried it away. The men cut down the biggest stands of tall bamboo they could find. Bamboo stems fifteen to twenty feet in length and between nine and twelve inches in diameter were sliced into two-inch strips.

The women opened the bamboo strips, flattened them out and laid them on the soft wet ground. "The bamboo was so elastic and strong, that it never really sank into the mud," Phil Corrin wrote. The strips were fastened to the ground by sharp bamboo pegs driven through machete-bored holes.

At 8:30 A.M. on May 30, a Catalina flying boat from Morotai flew over the Belawit strip, and dropped spades and other tools. Harrisson later claimed the idea of asking for these tools had come from the Yank airmen (Capin and Illerich). Harrisson had agreed and Bob Long had wired the request to Z Special, and the RAAF had been prompt to oblige.

Years later, the Dayaks still remembered the day the metal tools rained down from the sky. Many of the tools fell into the muddy paddy fields. They had been dropped from too low a height for their storepedo parachutes to open and a lot of digging out was required. But the tools mystified the Dayak workers. The women politely tried heaping the soil onto the new spades rather than using their reed baskets to carry it.

Trooper Griffiths attempted to show the women how the spades should be used. But then he realized that the sharp edges were unsuitable for anyone with bare feet. He shrugged and let the Dayaks go back to their old methods; it was hard to imagine how anyone could do the job faster than they were doing it.

On May 31, the airstrip was in good enough shape to drain off the water. Seeing that the airfield would soon be ready, Dan Illerich went to Major Harrisson and asked him if he could continue to help Warrant Officer Bob Long send and receive radio signals until the last plane was ready to leave. The major was touched by this request and recorded it in his diary, with the comment, "Fine chap." Three weeks later, Harrisson would report to Z Special headquarters that Illerich was "our pet American. I dread the day he is evacuated. I do not know what we will do without him. I do sincerely hope you will be able to get him some sort of gong [medal] for the way he has so unselfishly and tirelessly helped us."

Now the airstrip—perhaps the first split-bamboo strip anywhere in the world—was nearly ready. It ran a hundred yards, starting at the edge of a thirty-foot ravine and ending just a few yards before the deep mud of a wet rice paddy.

But who would be damn fool enough to try to fly into it? The answer: the 4 Army Co-Op Squadron. The Australian squadron had been formed in Lae, New Guinea, to escort the Allied landings. It was part of an air wing that had been cobbled together the last year of the war to help the Allies retake the South Pacific and Southeast Asia.

The air wing was an uneasy union of the air force and the army. But the squadron's mixed parentage was not without advantages for the pilots. Theoretically, the squadron was under the control of the RAAF, so that when the pilots, who basically ran their own operations, thought they were being given silly or impractical orders by army officers who did not know their way around an airplane, they would bump the problem up to the RAAF, which almost always let the pilots have their way. As for food, the squadron did better than many, because the crews flew to places where they could get fresh tropical fruits, then a rarity for servicemen posted in Australia.

The squadron had been assigned in April to assist in the liberating of Tarakan Island. The squadron's commanding officer, Flight Lt. Frederick Chaney, later recalled:

> The idea of the Tarakan "adventure"—and I call it that—
> was that the troops would capture the island, the air strip
> would be lengthened and repaired and made fit to take op-
> erational squadrons, which would then enable landings to
> be made at Labuan, on the other side of Borneo, and also
> at Balikpapan in the south.

The Borneo operations were meant to cut off the island's oil from the Japanese, who were by then very dependent on it.

Taking back Borneo would also help the Allies get in place for their planned offensive up the Asian mainland, from Singapore to Japan itself (an offensive that only the August atomic bombings of Hiroshima and Nagasaki would make unnecessary).

Tarakan Island is fifteen miles long and eleven miles across at its widest point. When the Australians got there, there were only 2,100 Japanese forces on the island. For more than two weeks, the RAAF had flown some three hundred sorties over this small island, dropping two hundred tons of bombs. Next came a two-day naval bombardment and, finally, the landing of 11,000 Australian troops.

As usual, the Japanese withdrew to the interior, leaving the coastal areas in Australian hands. But, also as usual, the interior had to be fought for inch by inch. It took four days of fighting for an Australian battalion to get two hundred Japanese soldiers to withdraw from a small knoll in central Tarakan. By then, the Australians had fired 7,000 shells and 4,000 mortar bombs, and lost 20 AIF killed, with 46 wounded.

Even at the end of the Tarakan campaign, when the Japanese were fleeing the island by raft, they resisted with rifles and grenades the crews of the Australian landing craft and patrol torpedo (PT) boats sent to rescue them. They accepted stupendous casualty rates, some 75 percent dead. It was this kind of determination by the Japanese that made the Allied forces in Asia realize that, however inevitable their victory over Japan had become, they must expect bitter battles to the end.

Harrisson had convinced his own bosses at Z Special's advance headquarters in Morotai that the Belawit airstrip was the only way to take out the Yank airmen, and that doing this would win Australian Special Operations friends on General MacArthur's staff and in other ways embellish its name among the Allies. In Morotai, Harrisson's arguments had convinced someone that the Army Co-Op Squadron's Auster aircraft had the capacity to take out the stranded Americans, one by one.

But it must have taken some eloquence to convince even such a daredevil Aussie pilot as RAAF Flight Lt. Gordon Reid to back this plan. The Austers would have to fly unarmed to save weight over enemy territory, much of it jungle, where a plane and its crew could be lost forever. As a precaution, the 4 Army Co-Op Squadron decided to send two Austers at a time so that, if one crashed, the surviving plane would be able to tell where the other plane had fallen.

In preparation for the Austers' flights, three Liberators flew from Mindoro to Borneo's central highlands and dropped two storepedos each, full of supplies, at Belawit on June 4. The supplies fell on target at 10:30 A.M., just before the daily cloud cover moved in.

Bob Griffiths had arranged to receive the drop. The major had done his part by sending SEMUT 1 forces with Eureka/Rebecca radar equipment, colored flares and a white calico sign on the airfield in the shape of an H. The H sign meant: "drop here, all is well." Bob Long had come down from the wireless shack with Dan Illerich to watch. He recalls,

> When we were satisfied the planes were in position, about a quarter mile from us, I pressed the Eureka button and we could see that the bomb bay doors were opened and seconds later storepedos burst from the aircraft, store parachutes blossomed and we knew we were watching a perfect stores drop.

Trooper Griffiths had a hundred Dayaks still working on the strip on June 6 when Gordon Reid flew over in a borrowed American Catalina and dropped storepedos containing a hundred gallons of fuel that would be used to refuel the Austers for the return trip. The Auster's fuel capacity was fifty gallons, which, when the plane was stripped down enough, was just sufficient to make one leg of the round-trip.

Squadron Commander Flight Lt. Fred Chaney and Flight Officer Johnny White, the pilots chosen to fly the first two Austers to Belawit, were aboard Reid's borrowed Catalina that day, scouting out Griffiths's airstrip. Reid reminded them that, given the Auster's small fuel-storage capacity and its high consumption, there could be no turning back once they were halfway there. Reid also explained to his passengers that they would have to leave their radios behind, to save weight. That would add to the challenge for the pilots, who would have no margin for navigation errors. (RAAF transport planes, perhaps because of scarcity or tradition, did not carry parachutes.)

A day earlier, Fred Chaney had been sitting in his tent on Tarakan's airbase, relaxing with his boon companion and second-in-command Johnny White, when Reid had turned up. Reid had introduced himself and said, "I'm looking for a couple of volunteers to go into the middle of Borneo and pick up some Americans—and you two are the volunteers."

It was a lucky accident that Chaney was in the right place to be "volunteered" for this mission. Chaney had many hours of experience flying unarmed light aircraft, often flying cross-country at night by dead reckoning, with no light until the flares of the airstrip appeared. Chaney had been flying into battle zones all over the South Pacific for four years. He could land his light aircraft almost anywhere, and had recently collected wounded men from New Guinea in his little Auster.

But the biggest asset to the current operation was Chaney's character, a very Aussie blend of courage, self-discipline and diffidence. With a genuine modesty overlying a strong commitment to justice and fair play, Fred was a natural leader. He had signed up for the RAAF in 1940, having been intrigued by flying ever since he had watched air force planes performing aerobatics over Maylands Aerodrome near his boyhood home in North Perth. One display, in which three planes took off with their wingtips joined by ribbons, had thrilled him.

The RAAF in those days still operated like a gentleman's club. Chaney was both amused and appalled that he had to have references from three reputable citizens included in his request for admission into officer training. He had to wait eighteen months as a reservist before beginning training in August 1941, only months before the Japanese entered the war.

After the war, Fred would become a "reputable citizen" himself: Sir Frederick Chaney, KBE, CBE, AFC (see glossary), a Liberal Member of Australia's Federal Parliament from 1955, holder of various federal offices, including administrator of the Northern Territories from 1970 to 1973 and, from 1978 to 1982, Lord Mayor of Perth. But, during the war, he was a lot like many of the irregulars who made up SEMUT 1, a gallant warrior with a checkered armed services career.

Fred's great abilities would get him promotions, and then his high jinks would lead to his new rank being rescinded. On two memorable occasions, he lost his promotion to squadron leader before he had time to put the ribbons on his uniform. Fred, when accused of being heroic, or even courageous, would simply say that almost anybody would have done the same as he had. He said that during dangerous flying operations he had often been frightened, "but provided you don't panic with fear, it doesn't matter how frightened you get."

On June 6, 1945, the view from Gordon Reid's Catalina down onto the Bawang Plateau was enough to frighten Chaney and White. "It didn't look too promising," Chaney conceded, many years later. Nonetheless, Fred and Johnny (who was equally daring) planned their next day's route when they returned to Tarakan. It was annoying not having a radio, but they were going to have to keep radio silence anyway, when they brought back the American airmen, so they shrugged off the danger. Reid promised to fly alongside them in his Catalina, to show them the way to Belawit.

On June 7, the three planes took off, along with a Liberator whose mission was to drop more fuel and other stores on the Bawang airstrip. Harrisson commented in his diary that four planes overhead in one morning was probably more air traffic than those central highland skies had ever known.

Gordon Reid, when he offered to escort the Austers in, had not taken into account the low speed at which an Auster traveled. Chaney's and White's planes were flying at about seventy knots but Reid's Cat was making over a hundred knots, so Reid had to circle several times trying to keep back with the Austers.

Bob Long was looking up as the Austers approached the field. "It was now late morning and the upper level cloud had already closed in, while the ever-increasing lower clouds billowed at random like giant cotton wool balls." Between the clouds and knowing that they were almost out of fuel, the two Auster pilots confined themselves to a very brief circling of the strip before coming in to land. Johnny White came low from the west and made a perfect landing, to the satisfaction of Trooper Griffiths, the other SEMUT 1 men and the crowds of Lun Dayeh, Kelabit and other Dayaks who had gathered to see their airstrip being used.

Johnny White's Auster had barely come to a halt when Chaney's plane touched down. Chaney judged that at his present rate of ground speed he would crash right into Johnny's plane and so, halfway down the runway, he abruptly turned off the bamboo and into the soft muddy earth. One fact was now evident: The bamboo strip was too short.

Trooper Griffiths got his workforce to begin extending the bamboo decking, while Dan Illerich and Bob Long helped inspect the extension work. Major Harrisson, however, was aware that the Allied invasion of Brunei Bay was due to begin within the next few days. He was desperate to get out to Z Special advance headquarters before the "balloon went up." He cast an eye on the ever-thickening cloud cover and urged Fred Chaney, whom he had just met, to take him out to Tarakan at once.

Chaney conceded that "the only way to see if the strip was long enough was to try it" and agreed to do so as soon as his plane could be pulled out of the mud and refueled. "News traveled fast," Bob Long recalled, "and by takeoff time, villagers for miles around had gathered to witness this exciting event." The assembled throng helped pull Chaney's plane out of the mud. But when the engine roared to life, "most sightseers took a step or two back." This was, after all, the first wheeled vehicle that most of the villagers had ever seen up close. Dan Illerich and Bob Long held on to the tail until Chaney decided he had sufficient revolutions per minute. Bob Long later remarked that it was "surprising, in that almost continuously damp country, how much rubbish can be whipped up by a fast revving propeller," but he and Dan hung on grimly, the wind tearing at their clothes and hair, their eyes full of mud, until Chaney gave the signal to stand back.

The Auster moved off; Fred was obviously coaxing all the power he could out of the engine. Halfway down the strip, the wheels of his plane cleared the last of the bamboo decking. The Auster gained another two or three feet but then it yawed, lost height, and the left wheel struck a small mound. The plane fell over on its nose, then onto its back and the fuselage broke, bringing to a dramatic end the first flight out of Griffiths's field.

Luckily, Fred and the major emerged uninjured. The

lengthening of the strip took on a new urgency, but the cloud cover was too heavy to make possible another flight out that day.

The unexpected presence of the two Auster pilots presented a catering problem for their SEMUT 1 hosts. When Bob Long and Dan Illerich's Dayak "cook boys" brought in the usual full cooking pot from their longhouse, these courageous Aussie pilots found they could not bear to be near the food. Bob Long recalls that "Dan and I were accustomed to native food such as boiled rice, bamboo shoots, wild pig and locally grown *ubi kayu* [cassava root]." Chaney, to the end of his days, insisted it was boiled monkey that he had been served "and it smelt like a dog that had been out in the wet and come in and stood by the fire in your lounge room." He and White finally managed to swallow some of the food, washing it down with *borak* or possibly *arak*. That kept them going until their hosts could find them some bananas and papayas.

That evening Chaney happened to see a little child who was crying hard—a rare event among Dayak children—and he could see that the child was in great pain. It turned out that the infant had been lying too close to a fire and had rolled into it and suffered burns all over his body. Chaney brought out his excellent first-aid kit; he lathered the child with Tannifax, and the child stopped crying. This made a great impression on the longhouse people, and the next morning there was a line of sick Dayaks outside of his hut.

In the morning, the mad major took off with Johnny White in the undamaged Auster. Chaney later described Harrisson as someone "who I don't think knew fear." The major carried instructions to Tarakan for Reid and his Catalina to drop in fabric and the waterproofing varnish known as "dope" so that the stranded Chaney could repair the other Auster.

Though Chaney thought his plane looked to be "a complete write-off," he felt he had to try to fix it so he could fly the sickest Yank out. Chaney found himself trying to repair his plane in a world where everything seemed to be made of bamboo. Things could be worse, he realized. He and White had slept in a bamboo hut the night before and had found it surprisingly comfortable. He was also favorably impressed (aside from the cuisine) by the "Dyaks."

> They were an amazing group of people, these Dyaks. They had irrigation laid on; the showers for their village came down from the mountains in bamboo pipes, and then they had little other bamboos, where you pulled the plug out and you got a shower of water.

Chaney was also struck by the quality of the Dayaks' workmanship:

> Their longhouse, which would have done credit to any sort of building that any person would put up in Australia, was built without a single nail in it, and it was a tremendously big building . . . maybe a hundred feet long, where many whole families used to live, and there was an end for visitors . . . They'd sleep on mats and things which they wove out of the rushes. I don't know how they cut the timber for them, but the beams looked as though they'd been milled in Bunnings Timber Mills.
>
> When they built their houses, they bound thin bamboo strips around wooden beams to join them up, so I, by sign language, got them to mend the fuselage of my aeroplane, to put in new struts of bamboo and bind them up and then I put the fabric that had been dropped from [Gordon Reid's Catalina] and put the dope over it.

All in all, the flight lieutenant found working with the Dayaks to be a "very very wonderful experience." Coming from a family that had coped well with a "mixed" marriage of Catholic and Protestant, Chaney had always believed that social prejudice was wrongheaded. He had been ashamed that "the majority of Australians ... thought that anyone with a dark face was inferior." Later in life, as administrator of the Northern Territories, he would work hard to get justice and respect for Australia's aborigines.

Flight Lieutenant Reid, in addition to the airplane fabric and dope, dropped blankets, pants, shirts and Atabrine (for malaria) for the use of SEMUT 1 and the Yanks in Belawit. The medicines were used to help the local people as well, and proved a great source of goodwill. But the item Chaney remembers best was an object that glittered as it came fluttering down, dangling from its own little parachute.

> When it was brought back to me by the natives, it was a silver flask full of whisky, with a note attached to it from a fellow called Jim McGeoch, second in command of one of the Army battalions on Tarakan. The note read: "This flask was a present from my mother on my twenty-first birthday. It's my prized possession. If I didn't believe you were going to get out of that place, I wouldn't have dropped it to you."

By June 10, Trooper Griffiths's airstrip workers had extended the decking to a good 250 yards. It was now time for Chaney to try out his bamboo-repaired Auster, this time with Seaman First Class Alvin M. Harms, USN, aboard.

Harms, who had been the navigator on the navy Liberator, had been badly affected by malaria in his early days in Borneo. After that, he had begun suffering from badly swollen feet, the result of infected leech bites. Some improvement had resulted from the supplemental food provided by SEMUT 1 in April, but Harms still could not walk. He had been carried to Belawit on June 4, looking "bootless and vague" (according to Harrisson's diary). It was now six days later.

Chaney helped Harms aboard in a litter and the plane started down the lengthened runway. Chaney remembers:

> We staggered off the ground, and then I found the aeroplane was slightly bent in the middle, but it didn't worry me much. But when I got over the mountains—which were very, very high—all of a sudden the aeroplane started to shudder tremendously and I just thought it was going to fall to bits. But what had happened was one of the screws hadn't been done up properly, and the wind was rattling it, and when I throttled back a little, the noise ceased. Then, as I opened the throttle, the noise went up again, so I thought: Well, it isn't the engine that's causing the trouble.

After several hours of going as slow as he could to avoid shaking to pieces, Chaney could see the outline of Tarakan Island ahead. The plane, however, was not yet out of danger.

> They picked up this aeroplane of mine on the radar and they did not know I was in there. It was a very hush, hush operation. The Army air raid siren went and Johnny White, who had got back, suddenly thought [given the direction the plane was coming from] it might possibly be me. He rushed down to the anti-aircraft battery and told them to hold their fire until they recognized the aeroplane.

Cleared for landing, the Auster that had been so painstakingly repaired by the Dayaks touched down on the runway and immediately broke in two. Both Chaney and Harms got out unscathed. If Fred Chaney had not known he was born lucky, he knew it now.

Seaman Harms was brought to the U.S. Navy hospital on Morotai the same day, on his way home to Holly, Colorado. The first of the eleven downed Yank airmen to leave Borneo, Harms had been there for six months.

CHAPTER FIFTEEN

The Allies Arrive

On June 10, while Fred Chaney was flying Alvin Harms to Tarakan, the mad major was at Z Special advance headquarters in Morotai, dictating a forty-page intelligence report for the Allied forces that had established a beachhead that day on the northeast coast of Brunei Bay.

The Japanese along the coast were avoiding combat and retiring to the interior, regrouping behind defensible hills or fortifications. From such redoubts, they normally would fight to the end, causing as much damage to the enemy as possible. But this time they could not.

SEMUT 1, with help from Makahanap's Dayak forces, was already established in a wide arc inland, ready and waiting for the Japanese. SEMUT 2 and SEMUT 3 and their respective Dayak forces were doing the same on the river systems farther south.

Though all the SEMUT 1 operatives complained about the mad major, some of the old-timers were beginning to notice that there were no casualties among the Z Special operatives and very few among their Dayak forces. Some Z Special veterans would later acknowledge that the major's insistence that the men try to live in the same tough way as the native people may have been crucial to helping them survive, which every single one of his forty-odd SEMUT 1 operatives did. (SEMUT

1 also accomplished much more, in terms of intelligence gathering and killing the enemy, than all the rest of the Australian WWII special operations put together managed to achieve, even those operations with high casualty figures.)

One of the rare battles in SEMUT 1 territory in which the natives suffered losses had occurred just one week before the Allied invasion, and had been led by Warrant Officer Rod Cusack. By the time of the battle, Cusack, N.E.I. Cpl. Bolong, acting as Cusack's adjutant, and the Dayak force raised by Makahanap had grown impatient to get into real action. Since May 20, Bolong and his "Guerrilla Troop No. 1" had been at Long Buluh on the Sembakong River, with one Bren gun, two Owen submachine guns, eight rifles, four hand grenades and three hundred rounds of ammunition. Their orders were to report all Japanese movements and kill any Japanese using the river, provided the enemy numbers were not too great. But if they were not certain to win easily, Bolong's men were merely supposed to report to SEMUT 1 headquarters everything of interest occurring downriver as far as Mensalong and upriver as far as Semelumung.

For two weeks, Cusack and Bolong waited. Finally, with Bolong to guard his back door at Long Buluh, Cusack moved with forty armed Dayaks of Makahanap's forces up the Sembakong to attack the Japanese at Long Simelumung, but there were more Japanese than expected. Cusack reported "fifteen Japanese were killed for sure, possibly more died of wounds in the surrounding jungle." That was a high total of enemy killed for a single SEMUT engagement, but it was accompanied by SEMUT 1's highest total of nonenemy casualties in a single incident: four Dayak civilians from the Sembakong River area killed in cross fire and one of Cusack's own Dayak troops was killed or captured. A more typical SEMUT 1 engagement was one that Ric Edmeades led along the Trusan River on June 11, when his forces killed five Japanese, captured twenty-five enemy auxiliaries along with documents and weapons and suffered no losses, civilian or guerrilla.

By June 13, Tom Capin was in Belawit, having walked there from his medical facility at Pa' Dali. He had been ordered to come to the airstrip so he could leave on the next Auster. Daylong rains had stopped flights after Chaney's takeoff with Harms, but Capin didn't care. He now could be confident that his departure from Borneo would be in a matter of days. The tall redhead filled this time by helping a newly arrived SEMUT 1 medic, Reuben Hirst, establish what the major would call an "excellent medical post" next to the airstrip. The improved medical facility added to the high morale already prevalent on the Bawang Plain as the foreign soldiers and the Dayaks saw their joint labors start to bear fruit. The Dayaks had adopted the airstrip as their own and brought fresh heads, as they would to their longhouses, to add to the place's spiritual power. The heads were put on poles along the airstrip's edge. The decaying flesh and its attendant odor bothered the *tuans* but not the Dayak warriors.

Mustapa al-Bakri, the Malay administrative aide in Malinau who had been collaborating with the Japanese, was now a prisoner at SEMUT 1 headquarters in Belawit. The major recorded in his diary that the Malay was "tearful, begging on his knees for his life and to be allowed to return to Malinau." The major sent a message to Makahanap asking if he thought the Malay's death sentence by firing squad should be carried out. Makahanap, perhaps remembering how the Malay had urged the Japanese authorities to release the Dayak schoolchildren being held in prison as hostages over the missing

Pangeran Lagan, sent a long letter to the major saying that he could not bring himself to ask for the death penalty for this man he had known and worked with so long. Instead, the district officer promised Harrisson he would take responsibility for the Malay and his colleagues and make sure that they stayed in his strict custody. Meanwhile, Pastor Aris Dumat went over the documents that had been found on the Malay official, looking for anything that could be useful to the major's forces or the Allied cause.

The same day that Harrisson wrote to Makahanap, the major received a visit from the village headman from Pa' Tengoa who came with Ric Edmeades. The headman had brought with him the severed head of the chief police officer of Brunei as a present for the major. The senior Japanese official's head had been taken by Iban guerrillas during the Ninth Division's fight for Brunei Town the previous day when the attacking forces had discovered the rotting bodies of eight natives chained to stakes.

Harrisson, wishing to honor the Pa' Tengoa headman's gift appropriately, had it put on a flagpole alongside the airstrip next to poles bearing the flags of the United States, the Netherlands, Japan(!) and Sarawak and the other heads. This haphazard, impromptu line of flagpoles with their mixed collection of symbols fit in with the atmosphere perfectly. Somehow, a wildly disparate collection of people—Dayaks, N.E.I. veterans, Australians and other Commonwealth soldiers, Celebes-born missionaries and even a few downed U.S. airmen—had configured themselves into a strong but flexible fighting unit.

But now it was time for the Yank airmen to leave. Rod Cusack had appeared in Long Berang on June 7 and told Phil Corrin, Jim Knoch and the navy airman Robby Robbins that the major wanted them to leave for Belawit right away. Phil noted in his diary, "We don't know for sure but think the major is having a plane land there somehow and perhaps we'll get out. Six more days of walking. May it be the last!"

Makahanap was away in Malinau, so the airmen could not say good-bye to him. But trying to say an adequate thank-you to Mama Makahanap consumed the departing Yanks' thoughts that night, especially those of Phil and Jim. Facing Mama the next morning, Phil and Jim pledged their undying love and gratitude and told her that they hoped somehow to get the whole Makahanap family to come to the States. When Phil, Jim and Robby left the next morning, they were laden with gifts—machetes, blowpipes, loincloths, reed baskets and woven bark jackets. "Almost everyone was in tears," Phil recorded.

That left five airmen in Long Berang. (Harrisson was staggering the airmen's departures, presumably to reduce the risk of discovery by the Japanese, who were now moving inland, and to limit the catering problems for the various longhouses that would be hosting the Yanks on their way to Belawit.) The villagers of Long Berang, aware that all the Yanks would soon be gone, held a party at one of their longhouses for the five remaining airmen. "They sacrificed a water buffalo," Bob Graham recalls,

> and caught its blood in a bowl, and they all took a lick from the bowl. We didn't. They brought borak and we had to sip it through bamboo straws. A couple of times was more than enough for me, but Franny went overboard and got drunk and sick. He could not cross the swaying bridge over the river and had to be brought back to the Presswood house by canoe. The natives laughed and laughed, and they came round the next day and laughed some more.

Meanwhile, Phil, Jim and Robby made good time their first day and were in Pa' Silau that night. Two days later they were in a village where they found that the Thirteenth U.S. Air Force, alerted by Major Harrisson, had dropped them a few boxes of K rations, six packs of cigarettes and seven pairs of shoes in a size that fit none of them. They merely laughed. Good ol' Uncle Sam.

A greater morale booster was the news that Seaman Harms had already been flown out from Belawit. The three airmen were told that the rest of the Yanks from Long Berang also were now on their way to the airstrip.

On June 15, the sun shone on the Bawang Plain and Chaney's little Auster landed on Griffiths's field at 10 A.M. At 10:30, Chaney took off for Tarakan with Tom Capin as his passenger, after refueling in record time to avoid the oncoming cloud cover. Chaney's last words to Major Harrisson before leaving were that the Auster service would be shut down for the next few days (presumably collecting the wounded from the Ninth Division's invasion). That was the bad news. The good news was that the Austers soon would be flying in and out from the Allies' newly won airstrip on Labuan Island, in Brunei Bay. The major had to be pleased. This would be a better location for Auster flights in every way. The distance from Belawit to Labuan was well within the Austers' range and Z Special now had an advance headquarters on Labuan, next door to the Ninth Division field headquarters. Harrisson's dream of having a good, direct air connection to Z Special soon would be realized. (The major was expecting to be in Borneo a while longer; he was focusing on the thousands of Japanese troops moving inland from the coast. It did not occur to him that the Allied objective of cutting off the oil to the Japanese had now been met and that the Ninth Division was planning to leave soon and close down SEMUT and repatriate its operatives.)

The Yanks kept straggling into Belawit on their bare,

leech-swollen feet. On June 15, Corrin, Knoch and Robbins arrived, having spent seven days getting there, delayed partly due to Jim Knoch's being in the throes of his worst bout of malaria. Jim had become so weak that, one night, a Dayak woman chewed up his food for him and put it in his mouth, knowing that he was not strong enough to chew it himself. The last two navy men, Graham and Shepherd, also arrived later that same day. Because only two passengers per day could be brought out by the Austers, the major found various chores for the waiting airmen who were fit enough.

Robby Robbins was sent to help Dan Illerich, who was still assisting Bob Long. Between them, Bob and Dan had transmitted two hundred messages since they started to work together back in April.

Because Jim Knoch was so ill, he was chosen as the next man to be sent out, on June 17. When he got to Tarakan, he was flown to Morotai and spent three days waiting to reach his old squadron, which was now based on Samar Island in the Philippines. When he reached the squadron, he was still dressed in a loincloth and a bark jacket and carried the blowpipe, machete and knife holder he had been given. He looked and acted oddly enough that he was transferred to the squadron hospital for observation. But he was soon released and was flown to Guam, where his plane refueled for the long flight home.

On June 23, two Austers flew in to Griffiths's field at 11:45 A.M. By 12:45, both planes were airborne with Phil Corrin and Franny Harrington. The airmen would acquire Australian shorts and shirts on Labuan Island. A few days later, they returned to their squadron at Samar.

Eddy Haviland and Robby Robbins left for Labuan the day after Phil and Franny, but not before Eddy had been given a special task to perform. He recalled later that:

Major Harrisson had picked me to head a firing squad. There were some natives there who had sided with the Japanese, and were either Japanese spies or were telling the Japanese what was going on. And they had been captured and the major wanted them killed and so I spent one day clearing the underbrush so that the firing squad would have a shot right at them. Well, I got done and this firing squad was supposed to do its work the next day. But the next day was my turn to leave and the job was given over to one of my buddies. And he told me later the natives, instead of firing just once—they had automatic weapons and bang, bang, bang—they just held the trigger down and cut the natives to ribbons.

The condemned men were each tied to one of the trees that stood at the top of a hill near the village, and ten natives were given automatic rifles. Graham did not fire his gun but stood there, watching the only killing he saw during the war. "Shells from the bullets opened up the belly, and body parts were hanging out. The major went along with a .45 and gave the coup de grace to the back of the head." It is ironic that, by far, the bloodiest incident that the surviving airmen witnessed was this execution. It left a memory of horrifying violence that the airmen would have for the rest of their lives.

Eddy Haviland had escaped being part of the firing squad, but he still had a few anxious moments ahead. The engine of his Auster suddenly cut out while they were still over Japanese-held territory near Borneo's northwest coast. But it came back on again and the plane landed safely on Labuan Island.

Two days after the execution, two Austers appeared again. One plane flew Major Harrisson to Labuan; John Nelson flew there in the other. John had been treated with arsenic for some unspecified tropical illness by one of SEMUT 1's medics, and there had been a time when he wondered if the medicine was going to kill him or cure him. "It came close," he recalled. He was unconscious for a while, but by June 27 he was fit enough to board the Auster. After flying over parts of the rain forest that he knew to be full of Japanese, he touched down on Labuan Island. His buddy Eddy Haviland was there to meet him, and they remained together all the way back to the States. When they landed at Morotai it was the Fourth of July. John did not bother to check to see if his and Jim Knoch's old uniforms were still being washed by the surf.

On June 28, Bob Graham and Jim Shepherd were flown out to Labuan, where they had their first meal without rice since landing in Borneo in January. By July 1, they caught up with their mate Robby Robbins at Clark Field in the Philippines.

On June 29, Dan Illerich, hating to quit while the show was still on, said good-bye to Bob Long and climbed into Fred Chaney's Auster. Dan was the last of the Yanks to leave Borneo. (The missing photographer Elmer Philipps was never found.) To honor the occasion, Dan gave the Australian flight lieutenant one of his few remaining personal possessions— his G.I. Elgin watch, which had stopped working sometime during his seven months in the jungles of Borneo.

A month later, Phil Corrin took off from Honolulu in a C-54 Transport. He recalled,

I was so excited I couldn't sleep a wink the rest of the way, even though we flew in darkness most of the twelve-hour flight. As we approached California the following morning it was so cloudy there wasn't a thing to see. About three miles from the coast, however, the clouds suddenly ended, almost as if it had been planned that way, and there before us on a gorgeous sunshiny morning was San Francisco and

the Golden Gate. I believe it was the most beautiful sight
I shall ever see.

The war in Borneo was still far from over, however. There
were thousands of Japanese troops and auxiliaries who had
moved into the jungles of the interior. And it was Z Special
units with native troops such as those Makahanap had orga-
nized that were keeping the enemy from establishing fortifications inside British or Dutch Borneo.

Even after the atomic bombs were dropped on Hiroshima
and Nagasaki and the Japanese emperor had surrendered,
some Japanese forces in Borneo did not cease hostilities. In
the British state of North Borneo, Japanese soldiers were
marching a column of British and Australian prisoners of war
from the Sandakan prison camp on the island's northeast
coast to a Japanese stronghold at Ranau. The column started
off from Sandakan with twenty-five hundred POWs, but by
mid-August only twenty-eight were left. (A dozen had escaped
along the way, of which only a half dozen Aussies survived.)
The twenty-eight still in Japanese hands were killed at Ranau
more than a week after the war had officially ended.

Farther south, a renegade column of Japanese known as
the Fujino Tai (Tai's company) continued to push its way inland, trying to reach the fertile rice fields of the central highlands, where SEMUT 1 had its headquarters. Major Harrisson
was unable to convince the AIF Ninth Division to let him
keep his operatives in place to deal with this column and protect the inland Dayak villages. The desperate, die-hard Japanese column was taking all the food and food animals in every
settlement in its path and leaving famine in its wake.

Harrisson persisted in demanding a chance to rid Borneo
of the Fujino Tai, and eventually was able to convince the

Ninth Division's new commander to let him keep a couple of Z Special men to join with a few dozen native fighters to surround the column and get it to surrender. The column was one or two days' walk from the Plains of Bah and Bawang when Major Harrisson caught up with it. He accepted Captain Tai's samurai sword on October 28, 1945, and took 340 Japanese soldiers prisoner.

The war in Borneo was finally over. A handful of stranded American airmen, a few local missionaries, a few dozen local guerrilla leaders, a thousand or more local headhunters, a few dozen Australian special operatives, several daredevil Aussie pilots and an eccentric British army major had helped bring to a successful conclusion one of the most extraordinary campaigns of World War II.

Phil Corrin returned home to Los Angeles, went back to college and was soon in the hotel management business, but his memories of the world he had left behind in Borneo kept resurfacing as he faced the "civilized" world and remembered how much there was to admire in people some considered "savages." He researched and wrote a seventy-plus-page manuscript, "In Darkest Borneo." Completed in 1963, it was dedicated to his parents, who had spent long months suffering while he was missing in action; to those of the original crew who didn't return, Tom Coberly, Fred Brennan and Jerry Rosenthal; to the professor at Occidental College who had encouraged him in his research; and finally, "to my friends the Dayaks, may they know peace and happiness forever."

Phil, who died relatively young of lung disease, was not the only survivor who felt compelled to write out a fairly detailed report of his experiences. John Nelson, who had kept in touch with Phil, was instrumental in piecing together Phil's diary, which had been written on scraps of paper while they were in Borneo, turning it into something that could be handed to the squadron's archivist. John went into the construction business in Boise, where he married and had children and stayed involved with veterans' groups. In January 2000, he finished his own manuscript, "World War II: Wildman in Borneo." When he heard that I was planning to write this book, he provided me with every bit of help he could. He died before he could see the fruits of his generosity.

Jim Knoch hitchhiked back to Sacramento after landing at Travis Air Force Base and found strangers living in his family's home. His parents had moved away, too sad to stay in the house that they feared their son would never return to.

Late that night, Jim's girlfriend, Maggie, was lying on a cot on the roof of her family's garage, trying to get some cool air on one of the hottest nights of August. At two in the morning, she decided to go back inside the house to her bedroom and heard a knock at the front door. Her mother, assuming it was her daughter, too sleepy to realize that the front door was unlocked, went to the door, opened it and stepped back, amazed. She shouted out to Maggie, "It's Jimmy Knoch! It's Jimmy!" Maggie shouted out to her mother, "Ma, what are you saying!" But she got up and there he was, so thin—he had lost more than eighty pounds. "It was pitiful to see him like that. We went downstairs to the kitchen and started to make breakfast for him after phoning his parents to say where they could come and get him. He looked like he needed to eat. And he smelled so bad. His sweat smelled of mold, like a steamer trunk that had been left too long in the attic," remembers Maggie. She nonetheless agreed to marry him and share with him his dream of owning a ranch, where he could raise cows and chickens and be his own boss. He was a terrific farmer, inventing new brooding methods for chickens that have now become standard practice, and making everything on his farm work by use of his own two hands and his natural talent. Still a bit misanthropic, he was adored by his wife and kids, and he worked happily on his ranch until the day of his death from cancer in 2003.

Jim avoided reunions of the airmen and never spoke publicly about his adventures, after a local audience didn't believe his story. But he told many stories about the Dayaks of Borneo to his family. He told Maggie, "We're supposed to be civilized and they're savages but they don't beat their wives or rape women or even correct their children under the age of five. There are no orphans or old people left on their own. Everybody takes care of everybody." He mentioned Binum, the "very beautiful woman" who had scrubbed their clothes for them by beating them against a rock in the river. He and Maggie kept up with the Makahanap family, especially the daughter Thea, who visited them often in recent decades before her death in Jakarta of heart disease in 2006.

Dan Illerich was asked to speak to the Presbyterian church of Sacramento, which had sponsored the Boy Scout activities he had taken part in as a child. "They wanted to know if my Eagle Scout training had helped, and I said we hadn't known what to do. The food wasn't easy to find and it was not what we knew to eat. Finally, I said that if it had not been for the Dayaks we would not have survived. I think they were disappointed to hear that, but it's true." Dan, like Jim and all the others I spoke to, had come home with an enormous respect and liking for the Dayaks and a more questioning approach to Americans' implicit assumptions that everything we did was best.

Dan went back to school, enrolling at the University of Nevada, where many of the students were combat veterans and enjoyed swapping stories with him. They had no trouble believing his tales of Borneo. Dan reenlisted in the Air Force

Reserve and was given a reserve commission as a second lieutenant in June 1946. Then he went into the active service and retired as a lieutenant colonel; he is still active in veterans' groups. He stayed close to Jim Knoch and maintains close ties to a number of the SEMUT 1 men, especially his fellow radioman Bob Long. Major Harrisson made good on his private vow to get recognition for his favorite Yank: Dan was awarded the British Empire Medal for his service to SEMUT 1.

Eddy Haviland, after a postwar baccalaureate from the Georgetown School of Foreign Service and a law degree from the University of Baltimore, became a lawyer and eventually made a career with the Social Security Administration in Baltimore. Thus, he fulfilled his dream of having a desk job and only going out of doors to play golf. He married and had five children. He had never spoken much of his time in Borneo until he recorded his recollections on tape shortly before he died of cancer in 1994, so that his grandchildren might someday know his story. After he came back from the war, he visited his friend John Nelson for a couple of weeks in Boise. He later said, "I always regret that we didn't stay close together and I haven't talked to him since."

Before he left for the Pacific, Tom Capin had told his wife, Betty, "No matter what they tell you, don't believe them. I'll be back." She had held on to that thought until the telegram that announced that Tom was alive and would be coming home soon. A month later, Betty and her mother-in-law went out to the chicken coop behind their Fort Wayne, Indiana, house to collect some eggs. When she walked back with the eggs, Betty could not understand why her father-in-law insisted on taking the eggs from her—until she saw Tom sitting on the sofa, a good sixty pounds thinner than when he had left, but still Tom. She was glad not to be holding those eggs.

After returning from the war, Tom Capin's great desire,

Betty explained, "was to get back to Borneo as a missionary to repay the Dayaks the debt he owed them, but he had so many tropical diseases that his doctor said it would be suicide to go back." He began instead to study to be a minister of the Methodist church but had to give that up when Betty became ill with asthma and couldn't work. In July 1947, he, like Dan Illerich, was informed by the War Department that he would be permitted to accept the British Empire Medal, an honor for which the mad major had nominated him in recognition of Capin's work as a medic all those months with the Harrisson-hating Doc McCallum.

His hopes of returning to Borneo quashed, Capin went to work on big construction projects, becoming an estimator. He was forty-five years old when one of his sons died of illness, an experience that brought him back to wanting to serve God. He eventually became an ordained minister of the United Methodist Church in Nebraska, and he also became a licensed psychotherapist. He enjoyed his work as a counselor and continued at it until succumbing to a fatal illness a few years ago. His love for the Dayaks and for what they had taught him shone through every conversation I had with him.

Bob Graham's wife, Janet, though long his girlfriend, had been his bride for a mere two weeks before he had shipped out to the Pacific in 1944. Her hopes for his safe return were strengthened by a photograph the navy had sent of her husband's plane sitting in a rice paddy in northwest Borneo. Around July 4, 1945, she heard from the Red Cross that "Johnny" (as she had always known him) was coming home. Although she rarely touched alcohol, her father insisted that she swallow some rum to fortify her for what she might see before he drove her to the small airfield near Philadelphia where Graham's plane would land. The rum worked almost too well. When Janet saw her husband—bloated and yellow with

Atabrine but otherwise the man she knew—coming down the plane's steps, she ignored the KEEP OUT sign, found a gap in the perimeter fence and ran to embrace him.

Though he suffered from malaria for years thereafter, Graham made a smooth recovery and was pleased and surprised when he was awarded the Distinguished Flying Cross for having saved the lives of his crewmates. He finally got to go to college, and he was within months of completing a bachelor's degree in mechanical engineering when he was offered a job as a sales representative for a big machine manufacturing company. He and Janet had three children, a boy and two girls. Physically fit until a massive heart attack in 2002, he played a lot of tennis and golf.

Graham had been especially struck by the high incidence of disease among the Dayaks—malaria, tuberculosis and dysentery—for which they had no remedy. He was equally struck by how well the Dayaks treated their children. He kept all of his notebooks, including his charts of the heavens and his diaries from his time in Borneo, and he let me borrow them. He never wrote up his experiences, though he told Janet and the children all about his life in Borneo. By the time I tracked him down, he had had a bad experience with a journalist turning his account into an overwritten adventure story for a men's magazine, and he cooperated with me because he wanted the real story told.

More than fifty years after the events described in here, I caught up with the Makahanap family and some of the people in Borneo who took part in this story (though, unfortunately, not the Mongans). By then, William and Theresia Makahanap were long dead and Christiaan had just died, although his widow, Kafit, was still able to remember events from those days. Makahanap and Mama's third daughter, Thea, gave me a copy of her father's unpublished memoir.

Like so much about him, Makahanap's memoir was a fascinating moral mixture of honest recollection and self-serving partial truths. He omitted, for example, all mention of the Mongans and claimed that he and Mama had cared from the beginning for all eleven Yank airmen.

His memoir does, however, tell what happened to him after the war. In November 1945, after the Fujino Tai surrendered to Harrisson, the major arranged for the Makahanaps to move to Malinau permanently and for William to be appointed administrator, replacing the dead, letter-writing *ken kanrikan*, R. Iwasaki. He stayed in that job until April 1946, when the Dutch came back and sent him to Tarakan to be assistant resident under a Dutch officer. He showed his blood chit with the picture of Queen Wilhelmina and her promise that her government would reward those who helped the Allied forces, but no one in Tarakan seemed to take this promise seriously.

In his new job, he had to share an office with a Dutchman who said, "It is not right that a colored man be on the same level with a white man." He left that job soon afterward and spent the next years trying to earn a decent living, generally not succeeding very well. He would get a job as a teacher and then would leave it when it appeared that his credentials were not good enough to get him a raise.

He was given 29,000 rupiahs by the U.S. Embassy in Jakarta in 1950, as a reward for his helping the airmen, but he was told that this was the first and last payment he would receive from the U.S. government. It was enough to buy a small house in a provincial town in Java, but he found no decent-paying work there.

Finding his status as an outer islander and a Christian in the Republic of Indonesia uncertain, Makahanap began to pursue obsessively the idea of getting to the United States. With the help of American missionaries and the U.S. Consul in Surabaya, who knew the Illerich family, he got permission for visas for himself and his family, but the visas had to be issued at the embassy in Jakarta, three hundred miles away. In Jakarta, the American Embassy consular officer told him he must show he had enough money so the immigration authorities could be sure that he and his family members would not work or become public charges. The sum needed was 150,000 rupiahs, an amount that was totally out of the question.

By July 1959, he was back in Tarakan, trying to track down Tom Harrisson (who by then was the curator of the Sarawak Museum and a brilliant, irreverent contributor to fields as various as anthropology, animal conservation and art history). Makahanap planned to go along by *perahu* to Long Berang and north overland to Lumbis, in hopes of finding a way to Kuching, where Harrisson was based. But there was a civil war going on in Indonesian Borneo by then, and Makahanap was captured by the police and brought back to Tarakan under arrest. By the time his credentials were established, he had run out of time and money and had given up hope of meeting Harrisson.

Makahanap eventually returned to Java, defeated and ill. In 1981, he dictated his memoir, "A Hero in the Jungle of Kalimantan (Borneo)" to a family member who was also a notary public. By then, his beloved Mama was in bad health. She died the next year, and his death followed in early 1984 at the age of seventy-five.

In contrast to Makahanap's own full, but not always truthful recollections, the Dayaks whom Thea Makahanap and I interviewed were scrupulous in telling only the facts as they knew them, regardless of how fragmentary those facts were. The Lun Dayeh did not yield to the Western temptation of filling in gaps in their knowledge or memory with what logically should have happened.

They had become Kemah Injil pastors, low-level government servants and office clerks, for the most part making ends meet with some subsistence farming. There were no foreign missionaries living among them, but the Lun Dayeh of that part of Indonesian Borneo were all devout Kemah Injil churchgoers by the time I met them, including Pangeran Lagan's sons, two of whom showed me the wings Phil had pinned onto the *pangeran*'s hat before Lagan went off to kill the Japanese. Most of the family treasures and mementos had disappeared over the years—chiefly as a result of the floods that regularly ravage their homeland now that so much commercial timbering is being done. But Phil's bombardier wings had survived because they had been buried with the *pangeran* and then dug up by his sons when his services to the Allies were about to be honored in a ceremony in Jakarta.

Nobody lives in Long Berang anymore, and the Lun Dayeh of East Borneo no longer live in longhouses. Indonesian government policy is for them all to live in single-family dwellings; fear of fire is the usual reason given. The people I met all now live in or near the small town of Malinau or in Tarakan Town. Instead of loincloths and sarongs, the Dayaks wear simple Western-style cotton clothes and usually wear rubber flip-flops when out of doors.

The whole area of north central Borneo is almost as cut off from the world today as it was during World War II. In 2003, to get from Washington, D.C., to Malinau, it took two and a half days and seven airplanes, each one smaller than the previous one. Slathered with deet against mosquitoes, I avoided contact with leeches but came close, twice, to meeting up with cobras. There was no town telephone switchboard in Malinau, no way of exchanging currency, postal service was very unreliable and none of the maps for the area between it and the Malaysian border agreed. For example, the courses of the rivers were different on every published map I saw.

Church services I attended one Sunday in May 2003 seemed to have brought out most of the Lun Dayeh of the Malinau area—a hundred or more adults, plus children. The service was led by a Lun Dayeh pastor and lasted for hours, with much singing and sharing of news. At the end, everybody shook hands repeatedly with everybody else, causing an intricate crisscrossing of lines of people that would have done Busby Berkeley proud.

During the ten days I was in Malinau and Tarakan, I found more than a dozen Lun Dayeh who had personal recollections of the events described in this book. Yakal was long dead but I learned that he had fulfilled his ambition to be the first Lun Dayeh to become a Kemah Injil pastor. His widow, the once tall Binum, now shrunk by age and illness but with her enormous eyes still bright and beautiful, sat surrounded in her little wooden shack by young people who, though not her children or grandchildren, clearly regarded themselves as such. She told me the story of her naked dance on the flat rock in the river in front of the Presswood house.

"Now I have told you," she said, "I can go in peace to join my beloved Yakal."

ACKNOWLEDGMENTS

Anybody who thinks writing is a lonely task has never tried to research a historical event. Dozens of people took part in all stages of putting this book together, providing vital information, advice and moral support. Aside from those people not mentioned below because they appear in A Note on Sources, the following people and organizations helped me in various ways to find out what happened in Borneo in 1944 to 1945.

The help of the family of William Makahanap was crucial, especially that of the late Thea Makahanap Lasut, who did research in Borneo on my behalf and helped translate her and my interviews of Borneans. Thanks are also due to Thea's son Stefan Lasut, who took me to meet the Borneans involved in the story, and Thea's daughter Tasya Lasut, who obtained the releases for me to use Makahanap material.

Thanks also belong to: the United States–Indonesia Society (USINDO) and its then president, Paul Cleveland, for giving me a travel grant to Indonesian Borneo in 2003 to interview the Lun Dayeh; Ambassador Robert Pringle (who suggested I ask USINDO for a grant and gave me other good advice); the Mission Aviation Fellowship and especially Tim Chase and the MAF staff in East Kalimantan, who got me into and out of Malinau—not an easy task.

Pastor Wesley Arun, chief pastor of the Gereja Kemah Injil (Christian and Missionary Alliance—CMA) in Malinau and his wife deserve special mention for their advice, help and generous hospitality. It was typical of Wesley's efficiency and kindness that, with almost no notice, he borrowed for me, a total stranger, the substantial sum needed to pay my and Stefan's hotel bills in rupiahs when the hotel in Malinau would not accept a credit card, traveler's checks or U.S. dollars.

I was led in the right direction on people, things and events Bornean by: Frank and Marie Peters of the CMA office in Samarinda, Kalimantan; Lelia Lewis (widow of Rodger Lewis of the CMA); Dr. Martin Baier; Dr. Barbara Harrisson; James Ritchie; Lucy and David Labang; Jayl Langub; Prof. Jay B. Crain; Poline and Esther Bala; Sidi and Heidi Munan; Jacob and Garnette Ridu; the Borneo Research Council; Prof. Michael Leigh; the Australian War Memorial Library and the Australian National Library.

Thanks also are due to Andang Poeraatmadja, who helped get my Indonesian back up to speed for the interviews; to Bob Long (who was wonderfully generous with his maps, photos and recollections); and to Harry Marshall (who helped me get back to Borneo in 2005 and found me a great mapmaker, Helen Phillips).

Other resources include: Special Operations Executive; Public Records Office, Kew; the American Bible Society; the USAF Museum at Wright-Patterson Air Force Base and its brilliant researcher Brett Stolle; the Library of Congress; VB 101 *Vagabond News* (which helped me track down Bob Graham) and Mary Jane Garner (who helped in contacting American WWII veterans' associations).

To get the book written and published, I had essential help from the following: my most indefatigable reader-editor and friend, Don Ediger; my friends and readers-editors Linda

Robinson, Edward Shufro, Sir David and Lady Goodall, Harry Inman, Brian Wickland, Betsy Schell and my "sister sister," Soeur Miriam du Christ-Jesus; my book developer Paul De Angelis; colleagues at the Political-Military Action Team (PMAT) in the State Department who gave me moral and material support; my always encouraging and astute agent at Janklow and Nesbit, Eric Simonoff; Jane Turner Rylands (who generously introduced me to my agent) and Doug McElhaney and Giovanni Cavicchi (who introduced me to the Rylandses one rainy afternoon in Venice); and—probably most valuable of all—my Harcourt acquiring editor Andrea Schulz, managing editor David Hough and Marian Ryan, copy editor, who, in the great Maxwell Perkins tradition, all *really* edit.

No doubt I have mislaid the names of others who aided me during the course of the book's long gestation, and to them I apologize.

The three maps were created to my specifications with infinite patience and skill by Helen Phillips of Bristol, England.

GLOSSARY

AFC—Australian Flying Corps.

arak—(Malay) Homemade brandy, often distilled from rice beer or palm wine.

atap—(Malay) Palm leaf used in thatching for a longhouse roof.

Batavia—Capital of the Netherlands East Indies, former name for Jakarta, the present capital of the Republic of Indonesia.

borak—(Lun Dayeh/Kelabit) Homemade rice beer brewed by the Lun Dayeh, Kelabit and other Southern Muruts of north-central Borneo.

British Empire Medal (BEM)—A medal awarded for meritorious service to noncommissioned officers and men and to persons who are not members of the British Commonwealth.

British North Borneo—Post–WWII name for the British-protected state of North Borneo, which, in 1963, became the East Malaysian state of Sabah.

Brunei Town—Former name of Bandar Seri Begawan, the capital of the Sultanate of Brunei.

CBE—Commander of the Order of the British Empire, the third-highest rank in that prestigious order of chivalry, usually awarded to recognize merit in persons not residing in the United Kingdom but who are connected with the Commonwealth.

the Celebes—Big island and associated smaller islands, now called Sulawesi, due east of Borneo. As compared with other big Indonesian islands, it has a high proportion of native islanders who have long been Christian.

Dayak (also **Dyak**)—Derived from a Malay word meaning "upland," **Dayak** is the ethnic label given in Dutch Borneo to all indigenous Borneo tribespeople of Malay or proto-Malay stock, although the term was usually reserved for those who were animist or Christian, not Muslim. (In Sarawak, the term Dayak was and remains more restrictive. It denotes only those indigenous non-Muslim tribespeople who traditionally lived midriver, between the coastal plains and the upriver areas: e.g., Iban, including Sea Dayak and Bedayuh [formerly called Land Dayak]. The people living farther upriver, above the rapids, such as the Lun Dayeh, Lun Bawang, Kelabit, Murut, Kayan, Kenyah, Penan and Punan, were and are referred to in Sarawak as *orang ulu* [Malay for "upriver people"].)

Dutch New Guinea—Also Netherlands New Guinea, former name for the Indonesian province of Irian Jaya.

godown—(Southeast Asian pidgin) Storeroom or warehouse.

heitai—Japanese soldier. (Transliteration from Japanese.)

Indochina—Former name for the region that includes the countries of Vietnam, Laos and Cambodia.

Jesselton—Capital of British North Borneo; now, as Kota Kinabalu, the capital of the East Malaysian state of Sabah.

kain—(Malay) Cloth; also cotton sarong that women wear wrapped tight from waist to ankle, usually worn below a *kebayak*.

kawang—Kelabit equivalent of Lun Dayeh *tafa*.

KBE—Knight Commander of the Order of the British Empire (see CBE). As a knight, he is addressed as Sir plus his given name: Sir Frederick.

kebayak—(Malay) Long-sleeved blouse with a tight, front-opening bodice, worn above a *kain*. The *kain-kebayak* had long been standard dress for Javanese women, but beginning mid twentieth century it became common urban female attire throughout the Indonesian archipelago.

Kemah Injil—(Malay) Literally, Gospel Tent; the name used in the Malay-speaking world for the Christian and Missionary Alliance (CMA), a Protestant evangelical church from North America, headquartered in the United States, that proselytized in Dutch Borneo and the Celebes beginning in the 1930s.

ken kanrikan—(Japanese) Japanese civil administrator for a prefecture.

Long (also *lung*)—(Lun Dayeh/Kelabit) The meeting place of two or more rivers or streams, or where a river meets a stream. As with bus stops at various streets along an avenue, the word **Long** is followed by the name of the smaller stream that meets the bigger one. Often, a longhouse village grows up at such a riverine crossroad and so the word **Long,** followed by the name of the smaller stream, has become a shorthand way of denoting the village or longhouse: e.g., Long Nuat, Long Berang and so on.

Lun Dayeh (also **Lundayeh** or **Lun Daya;** also formerly known as **Southern Murut**)—Collection of tribes (or a member thereof) that live in the upper reaches of what in 1944 was Dutch Borneo and is now the eastern district of Indonesian Kalimantan, and in neighboring upland areas of British North Borneo (now the Malaysian state of Sabah) and Sarawak (also now part of Malaysia, where the Lun Dayeh people are now usually called **Lun Bawang** and used to be called **Murut**). The Lun Dayeh, like the other upriver people of inland Borneo, were headhunters, as part of their animistic religion, until around 1930 when the various foreign governments enforced a ban on the practice. In 1944, those Lun Dayeh who were not still animist were almost all Christian evangelical. They retained their traditional social structure, which had a strong leadership role for an inherited aristocracy, presided over by the longhouse headman. Most Lun Dayeh lived in mountainous areas, where swidden ("slash-and-burn") hill-rice cultivation was the rule. Rice was the staple crop, supplemented by some fruit and some vegetable farming, some domestic food animals (pigs, chickens, goats, water buffalo), river fish (caught in fish traps or by tuba-root poison), and the hunting and gathering of game (wild boar, deer and birds, chiefly) and wild fruits and vegetables. Subgroups of the Lun Dayeh included, *inter alia*, the **Kelabit** people of Sarawak, the **Lun Bawang** of Sarawak and, more distantly related, the **Tagal** of British North Borneo.

lun do'—Kelabit equivalent of the Lun Dayeh term *lun mebala*.

lun mebala—(Lun Dayeh) Literally, "good people," but commonly used to denote the highest class in Lun Dayeh society, those born into the aristocracy.

Malay—When referring to a person, in a Borneo context, it usually means a coastal native Bornean who identifies himself as Muslim and who follows more or less the same traditions as do Malays of the Malay peninsula. It also means a Muslim Malay speaker from anywhere in the Malayo-Indonesian archipelago. When referring to the language, **Malay** is the Malayo-Polynesian lingua franca of Malaysia and Indonesia, where it has been spoken and has a written literature going back to the fourteenth century, if not earlier. **Malay** forms the basis of the official national language of Malaysia, *bahasa Malayu*, or *bahasa Malaysia*, and of Indonesia, *bahasa Indonesia*, and is also the official language of the Sultanate of Brunei and is one of the official languages of Singapore.

Malaya—Former name for West Malaysia (i.e., the Malay peninsula).

Malaysia—Present name for a country consisting of Malaya (the Malay peninsula) and the East Malaysian states of Sarawak and Sabah.

mandau—(Lun Dayeh) Machetelike sword used for everything from hacking away foliage to lopping off heads. The Malay word is *parang*.

mandi—Malay word for a bath in which unheated water is kept in a tank (sometimes with a faucet to refill it), from which the bather scoops water to pour over the body; the poured water drains out through a hole in the floor. The word is also used to denote the room where such a bath is located. When used as a verb, it means "to bathe," including in the river, and sometimes means to swim.

Menado—Also Manado; a city on the northern tip of the Celebes main island, with a big Christian population. William and Maria Mongan and the four Eurasian Netherland East Indies soldiers came from there.

Mentarang—District in northeast Borneo named for the river that is the main artery connecting Long Berang to Malinau, the capital of the prefecture that included the Mentarang and Krayan districts. From Malinau eastward toward the sea, the river's name changes to the Sesayap.

the Moluccas—Former name of the province of Maluku, the Indonesian island group east of the former Celebes.

North Borneo—The British-protected state in northeast Borneo that is now the East Malaysian state of Sabah. It was known from 1946 to 1963 as British North Borneo.

oe—The Dutch spelling for the diphthong written in English or Malay as "u" (e.g., the Dutch spelling of Lembudut is Lemboedoet).

Pa'—(Lun Dayeh/Kelabit) Stream or secondary river; thus, the Pa' Paru is the Paru tributary of the Mentarang River. Also sometimes used to denote a village along that stream: e.g., Pa' Trap. (The apostrophe stands for the sound of a glottal stop.)

pangeran—(Lun Dayeh) Chief, appointed by the Dutch government as head of an ethnic group for a certain area. The word is derived from a Brunei noble title, *pangiran*. In Sarawak the word used for this position, as conferred by the Sarawak government, is ***penghulu***. (Major Harrisson insisted on addressing Dutch-appointed Lun Dayeh chiefs by the Sarawak title.)

parang—(Malay) Machetelike sword the Lun Dayeh call a ***mandau***.

penghulu—(Malay) Sarawak term for a chief responsible to the government for a non-Malay indigenous ethnic group or groups of a specific area or groups of longhouses. See ***pangeran***.

perahu—(Malay) Also *prau*. Canoelike longboat, made from a dugout tree trunk with additional sideboards lashed to the hull to keep water from swamping it. A *perahu* would sometimes have ten or more paddlers and was light enough to be portaged past rapids.

Portuguese Timor—Eastern half of the island of Timor, now called East Timor.

Sabah—A state of East Malaysia; current name for the former (British) North Borneo.

Sangir—Main island of the Sangir group in the northern part of the Celebes. With a predominantly Christian population, it was the birthplace of William and Theresia Makahanap and of Aris Dumat.

SEMUT 1—Name of the first of four Australian Z Special Operations units that carried out intelligence operations and guerrilla warfare in Borneo, beginning in March 1945. The name comes from the Malay word *semut*, meaning "ant." The correct pronunciation is "smoot," to rhyme with "soot," though many of the foreign operatives pronounced it "see-moot."

Siam—Former name of the Kingdom of Thailand.

sulap—(Malay) Shed, hut or lean-to.

tafa—(Lun Dayeh; the Kelabit term is *kawang*) A swathe cut through the brush on a mountaintop, to make an open, squared-off space, usually done as part of the funerary rites in honor of a nobleman.

taicho—(Japanese) Chief military officer.

towkay—(Southeast Asian pidgin) Chinese trader, businessman or shopkeeper.

Tuan—(Malay) Literally means "Lord," but was commonly used as the title to address a white man in the Dutch East Indies, Malaya, Singapore and Borneo.

Warrant Officer (W.O.)—a rank below commissioned—but above noncommissioned—officer, used in the armed forces of the British Commonwealth.

W/T—Wireless long-distance transmitter and receiver used by the Australian military during World War II.

A NOTE ON SOURCES

Interviews

The Airmen and the Headhunters is based primarily on taped interviews with the survivors. Five of the eleven airmen were alive when I began my research: Tom Capin, Dan Illerich, James Knoch and John Nelson (all USAAF) and Robert John Graham, USNR. (As I write this, only Dan survives.) I interviewed them all, some of them several times, over a ten-year period, and they generously provided photos, letters, newspaper clippings and memorabilia. I also was given the transcripts of interviews conducted by others of Tom Capin, Phil Corrin, Eddy Haviland, Jim Knoch and Dan Illerich. I interviewed Betty Capin as a wife and widow, and she and widows Jean Corrin Morris, Maggie Knoch, Janet Graham and Ann Haviland were all enormously responsive to my questions, and gave me new facts, insights and materials.

To get the Borneans' viewpoint, I asked William Makahanap's daughter, Dorothea "Thea" Lasut, to go to Indonesian Borneo (Kalimantan) from Jakarta in 2000, at my expense. She interviewed many of the Lun Dayeh participants in the story and their next of kin, and former students of Makahanap as well as the Makanahaps' adopted son Christiaan (also known as Mugi) and his family. I was in Indonesian Borneo in 2003 and interviewed mostly the same people.

The Borneans Thea and/or I interviewed include:

Binum Bayo (widow of Pastor Yakal Bangau). Binum danced on the rock in front of the Presswood house; she now lives in Tanjung Lapang.

Yohan Pangeran (son of Pangeran Lagan), who lives in Malinau. He had the bombardier wings that Phil had given his father.

Christiaan Makahanap and his wife/widow Kafit (he is now dead but she resides in Tanjung Lapang).

Yesley Makahanap, son of Kafit and Christiaan (Mugi), now living in Tanjung Lapang.

Buing Udan (who lives in Pulau Sapi). Buing Udan is the son of Asing (or Yasin) Buing, who followed the Yanks when they fled from the Malay messengers who brought the letter. Buing Udan, himself, was a young assistant pastor in Long Sempayang in 1945; when the time came to attack the Japanese on the Krayan River, he could not bear to kill them, because he had heard that one of them was a Christian.

Pastor Soleman Tebari, retired Kemah Injil pastor, now in Tanjung Lapang. He fought alongside the N.E.I. soldiers Sualang, Kusoy, Bolong and Maulker and knew Rev. John Willfinger.

Pastor Samuel Basar (son-in-law of Soleman Tebari), now living in Pulau Sapi.

Bapak Barnabas Baru, retired Kemah Injil pastor, now living in Tarakan, and his wife.

Ganit Sakay (Pangeran Lagan's widow).

Litun Pangeran (Pangeran Lagan's eldest son), now living in Pelita Kanaan.

Daniel Lagan Lalung, Makahanap's best student and one of the children jailed by the Japanese in Malinau, now residing in Pelita Kanaan.

Salama Lalung, one of Makahanap's girl students, now living in Tanjung Lapang.

Yari Murang, a boy student of Makahanap's, now living in Tanjung Lapang.

Malai, a student of Makahanap's, who sent his daughter to meet me, living in Tanjung Lapang.

Yudan Ngelo, a student of Makahanap's, living in Tanjung Lapang.

Mrs. Semong Soma, now living in Tarakan. She is of the Kenyah tribe and is the wife of knowledgeable Kemah Injil pastor Semong Soma, but she did not know Makahanap personally.

These interviews in 2000 and 2003 were conducted in Indonesian, and most were taped, transcribed and translated into English by Thea and me, though parts of some interviews did not get onto the tapes and appear only in my notes or my recollection. I also, of course, interviewed Thea and her sister Emma Makahanap when they stayed with me in Washington in 2000, and Thea's son Stefan Lasut when he traveled with me in Malinau and Tarakan in 2003.

For information on the missionaries, I located and interviewed Ruth Presswood Hutchins, the widow of the Reverend Ernest Presswood, whose house in Long Berang figures prominently in the story. Ruth had been in Malinau and Long Berang with her husband shortly after the war, and told me about the Lun Dayeh as they were in those days. She, with the help of her daughter, Mrs. Moore, also provided me photos from that time and clippings from missionary publications, including articles by or about missionaries working in the Mentarang and Krayan districts in the 1930s and 1940s.

For the Auster story, I was able to locate in Perth Sir Frederick Chaney's widow, Mavis, and son Fred, both of whom I consulted several times by phone.

Archives, Private Memoirs and Diaries

The Chaneys kindly allowed me to draw from the archives of the oral history program of the Australian National Library. This archive provided me with Sir Frederick's recollections—many years after the events, but in his own words—of the exploits described in this book, exploits that helped him earn the rank of Knight Commander of the Order of the British Empire. The Australian National Library also provided photocopies of the pages of Chaney's pilot log on the Auster, clearing up some questions about when the American airmen were flown out of Belawit. The U.S. National Archives and Records Administration in College Park, Maryland, provided the best official information about the Navy Liberator and its crew (reference NWCTM-0505404-TKN) and also provided me the Missing Air Crew Reports (MACRs) for Lieutenant Coberly's, Major Saalfield's and Lieutenant Norris's Liberators.

Unpublished memoirs and diaries proved crucial to establishing various facts. For the Bornean view, I have relied most heavily on William Makahanap's account as told to a notary public: "A Hero in the Jungle of Kalimantan (Borneo)" (Jakarta, Indonesia, June 1981), a copy of which was given me by his daughter Thea.

Chief among the unpublished writings by the airmen are Phil Corrin's "Borneo Log," kept during the time he was stranded in Borneo, and a fuller account, "In Darkest Borneo." Copies of these were given me by Phil's widow, Jean Morris, and by John Nelson. I also made much use of brief memoirs by Dan Illerich and fuller ones by John Nelson given to me by the authors. In December 2005, James Ritchie of Kuching, Sarawak, East Malaysia, gave me a diskette with text from his draft book about Limbang that provided useful information about Lun Dayeh and Lun Bawang customs and history and also gave some new-to-me local accounts of what happened to the crew of the U.S. Navy Liberator that crash-landed near Brunei Bay in January 1945 and the consequences to Borneans of the navy men being there. For the massacre of the five navy airmen who went north toward Kudat, I relied heavily on an unsigned note to Maj. Tom Harrisson by one of his Australian Z Special operatives (in the Australian War Memorial Library in Canberra), written within a few months of the events. To check on facts and dates, I made frequent use of Tom Harrisson's 1945 manuscript diaries, also located at the Australian War Memorial Library.

Reconciling Differences

Learning the sequence of events and their exact dates proved complicated. Although I felt fairly safe relying on William Makahanap's writings to explain his actions and motives, his accounts of the dates and the sequence of events were not very reliable, having been recorded many years later. Surprisingly, his daughter's and my interviews of Borneans in 2000 and 2003, respectively, were often able to clarify the order in which things occurred. The Borneans seemed to remember a great deal, perhaps because they have a strong oral tradition, and undoubtedly because the events were so unusual in their lives. I found that, if a Lun Dayeh knew only a piece of the story, he would tell that part, and he would usually give the provenance of his assertions—himself, his father, village gossip or other sources. When sources disagreed on details, I have tended to give more weight to the Borneans' accounts and, for the airmen's side of the story, to Phil Corrin's "Borneo Log," to Tom Harrisson's manuscript diaries for 1945 and to the letters between Harrisson and Corrin because, in all these written documents, events were recorded at—or close to—the time they took place.

Published Sources

Published material is understandably scarce. The most useful to me was my own book, *The Most Offending Soul Alive: Tom Harrisson and His Remarkable Life* (Honolulu: University of Hawai'i Press, 1999; London: Aurum Press, 2002, 2nd ed. 2003; and, in French, *Le Dernier des Derniers:* Toulouse: Octarès, 2005), because, having originally planned for the airmen's story to be included in that book, I did much of the research on it then—the interviews of Kelabit, for example. Other useful published sources (in alphabetical order) were:

Bala, Poline. *Changing Borders and Identities in the Kelabit Highlands.* Dayak Studies Contemporary Society, no. 1. Kuching, Malaysia: University of Malaysia Sarawak, Institute of East Asia Studies, 2002.

Baldwin, R. E., and T. W. McGarry. *Last Hope: The Blood Chit Story.* Atglen, PA: Schiffer Military History, 1997.

Courtney, G. B. *Silent Feet: The History of "Z" Special Operations 1942–1945.* Melbourne, Australia: McPherson's Printing Group, 1993.

Crain, Jay B. "The Lun Dayeh." In *World Within: The Ethnic Groups of Borneo,* edited by Victor T. King, 160–184. Kuala Lumpur, Malaysia: S. Abdul Majeed & Co., 1993.

Dynes, Phil. *Leyburn's Liberators and Those Lonely Special Duties Air Operations.* Sandgate NSW, Australia: Hinchcliffe Printing Services, 1999.

Gerry, Allen [pseud. of a Navy Liberator pilot, USNR (ret.), from VPB 101]. *Who's a Hero?* Port Townsend, WA, privately printed, 1992.

Hall, Maxwell. *Kinabalu Guerrillas.* Jesselton: Borneo Literature Bureau, 1962.

Hamilton, Bob. *Pacific Warbird: Coming of Age in World War II.* Philadelphia: Xlibris, 1999. http://www.xlibris.com/bookstore/bookdisplay.asp?bookid=213 (accessed April 6, 2007).

Harrisson, Tom. *World Within.* London: Cresset Press, 1959.

Hoare, Alison. "Food Resources and Changing Patterns of Resource Use among the Lundayeh of the Ulu Padas, Sabah." *Borneo Research Bulletin* 34: 94–119, 2002.

Horton, Dick. *Ring of Fire.* London: Leo Cooper/Secker and Warburg, 1983.

Janowski, Monica. "The Forest, Source of Life: The Kelabit of Sarawak." BM Occasional Paper 143. London/Kuching: British Museum/Sarawak Museum, 2003.

Klokke, A. H., ed. and trans. *Fishing, Hunting and Headhunting in the Former Culture of the Ngaju Dayak in Central Kalimantan.* Borneo Research Council Monograph Series, no. 8. Borneo Research Council, 2005.

Long, Bob, ed. *"Z" Special Unit's Secret War: Operation SEMUT 1: Soldiering with the Headhunters of Borneo.* Hornsby, New South Wales: Australian Print Group, Maryborough, Vic./Transpareon Press, 1989.

Long, Gavin. *The Final Campaigns.* Australia in the War of 1939–1945, Series One: Army VII. Canberra: Australian War Memorial, 1963.

Morrison, Hedda. *Sarawak.* 2nd ed. Singapore: Donald Moore Gallery, 1965.

Piazzini, Guy. *The Children of Lilith: A French Exploration into the Up-river Country of Borneo.* Translated by Peter Green. New York: E. P. Dutton, 1960.

Presswood Hutchins, Ruth. *No Sacrifice Too Great: The Story of Ernest and Ruth Presswood.* Camp Hill, PA: Christian Publications, 1993.

Reece, Bob. *Masa Jepun: Sarawak Under the Japanese, 1941–1945.* Kuala Lumpur: Sarawak Literary Society [1998?].

"Survival in Borneo." *Naval Aviation News,* February 1960, 29–31.

Ugaki, Matome. *Fading Victory: The Diary of Admiral Matome Ugaki, 1941–1945.* Edited by Donald Goldstein and Katherine V. Dillon. Pittsburgh: University of Pittsburgh Press, 1991. (See 517–519 for entry for November 16, 1944, in Brunei Bay.)

United States Army Air Forces/Office of Flying Safety, Safety Education Division. *Survival: Jungle-Desert-Arctic-Ocean Emergencies* [1942?].

For a more general sense of what American flyers in Liberators did and felt in late 1944 and early 1945, I drew on—and recommend—the following books (especially those by Hynes and Fussell):

Ambrose, Stephen A. *The Wild Blue.* London: Simon & Schuster, 2001.

Bradley, James. *Flyboys.* New York: Little, Brown, 2003.

Fussell, Paul. *Doing Battle: The Making of a Skeptic.* Boston: Little, Brown, 1996.

Hynes, Samuel. *The Soldiers' Tale: Bearing Witness to Modern War.* New York: Penguin, 1997.

Terkel, Studs. *The Good War: An Oral History of World War II.* New York: Pantheon, 1984.

I came across several 1945 U.S. newspaper and magazine accounts that drew on journalists' interviews of some of the airmen, but they tended to have fictional elements that the journalists or their editors had added, perhaps seeking to add luster to the airmen's unvarnished accounts. Looked at today, most of these articles seem terribly dated because of the false additions, which call to mind old hand-colored photographs of people with improbably pink skin and golden hair.

INDEX

9 780156 033251